CRITICAL INSIGHTS

The Pearl

CRITICAL
INSIGHTS

The Pearl

Editors

Laura Nicosia & James F. Nicosia

Montclair State University, New Jersey

SALEM PRESS
A Division of EBSCO Information Services, Inc.
Ipswich, Massachusetts

GREY HOUSE PUBLISHING

Cover photo: 3dsguru, istock.

Copyright © 2019 by Grey House Publishing, Inc.

Critical Insights: The Pearl, published by Grey House Publishing, Inc., Amenia, NY, under exclusive license from EBSCO Information Services, Inc.

∞ The paper used in these volumes conforms to the American National Standard for Permanence of Paper for Printed Library Materials, Z39.48 1992 (R2009).

Publisher's Cataloging-In-Publication Data
(Prepared by The Donohue Group, Inc.)

Names: Nicosia, Laura M., editor. | Nicosia, James F., editor.
Title: The pearl / editors, Laura Nicosia and James F. Nicosia, Montclair State
          University, New Jersey.
Other Titles: Critical insights.
Description: [First edition]. | Ipswich, Massachusetts : Salem Press, a division
          of EBSCO Information Services, Inc. ; Amenia, NY : Grey House
          Publishing, [2019] | insights | Includes bibliographical references and
          index.
Identifiers: ISBN 9781642653113 (hardcover)
Subjects: LCSH: Steinbeck, John, 1902-1968. Pearl. | Steinbeck, John,
          1902-1968--Criticism and interpretation. | Human ecology in literature.
Classification: LCC PS3537.T3234 P435 2019 | DDC 813/.52--dc23

First Printing

PRINTED IN THE UNITED STATES OF AMERICA

Contents _____

About This Volume: Steinbeck, Capitalism, Economics, and Nature at Odds_____

Laura Nicosia and James F. Nicosia

Although *The Pearl* may have begun its life as a brief parable, an allegorical novella about a poor fisherman finding a pearl, becoming greedy, and subsequently suffering a Job-like loss, it has remained in the literary conversation for nearly three-quarters of a century for reasons that seem to exceed its original goals. Begun as a retelling of a myth Steinbeck heard during a six-week, 4,000-mile Pacific Ocean expedition he and longtime friend Edward F. Ricketts undertook in 1940, Steinbeck penned "The Pearl of the World" for the 1945 issue of *Woman's Home Companion.* In the folktale, an Indian boy from La Paz, Mexico, dreams of discovering an extraordinary pearl that attracted all sorts of greedy characters from the four corners of the globe. The town is besieged by wealth seekers, who transform the town from sleepy village to travel destination, and the result strips the town of its beauty, goodness, and natural resources. Still, the Indian boy believes that if he were to find the pearl, it would transform his life; he would be free to do as he chooses, no longer a victim of his poverty. Of course, he finds the pearl, but, economics being what they are, he is offered a mere pittance for his treasure; those in power still recognize their advantage, for they want the pearl while the boy needs it. Now in possession of something priceless that he cannot sell, his life is in danger from those who would steal it from him. Ultimately, he must return the pearl to the ocean in order to free himself from the burden the pearl has become. In 1947, Steinbeck releases his own story with the simplified title, *The Pearl,* setting the narrative on a three-quarter-century expedition of its own. The novella continues to be taught in schools, even when his more critically acclaimed works like *The Grapes of Wrath, East of Eden,* and *Of Mice and Men,* are not. Brevity alone cannot account for its longevity, but its universality, its nod to the uncanny, and its timelessness in an era where socioeconomics and ecological concerns have caught up to Steinbeck's sensibilities, can.

The critics who respond to *The Pearl* in this collection bring a breadth of insight into this seemingly simple story. While many readers still see the novella as a parable rife with religious symbolism, new generations of readers have plumbed its depths and found other, often competing, readings. Though Steinbeck himself had socialist statements to make in this, and many other, narratives, prevailing responses to the novel said this was an allegory about greed and what happens to a man when he finds riches and trades his soul for wealth. Subsequent readings suggested that greed was not at the heart of protagonist Kino's tragic downfall at all. In fact, they said, this is a story that reveals how the capitalist system that fed so many mouths in the twentieth century did so by taking food out of the mouths of the downtrodden. Furthermore, *The Pearl* revealed, the socioeconomic system functioned at its fullest when it kept down those who were already down. Kino, in other words, was never meant to partake in his share of the wealth. He and those like him were destined to be victimized by the system so fully that, even if suddenly brought into wealth by, say, finding a pearl, he would not gain enough economic power to withstand being exploited by the system. His only possible destinies: to be defeated by the system or to refuse to continue to take part in it (by, say, throwing the pearl back into the sea).

Most recent readings, then, have taken another tack entirely. They recognize Steinbeck's lifelong ecological tendencies and read *The Pearl* as a revelation of his green-friendly statements and warnings. Ecocriticism's interdisciplinary approach considers literature from a variety of perspectives, each of which considers the way texts and/or authors reveal their own environmental concerns, or the way texts reveal the attitudes shared by people at a certain time period. In the case of Steinbeck in general, and *The Pearl* in particular, ecocritics agree that Steinbeck was a strong proponent of nature who saw man as a threat to the environment. The scope of ecocriticism is broad enough, however, to include a number of different approaches that may or may not coincide with each other.

Steinbeck's Life and Work Inform Each Other

Melinda Knight establishes the historical context for this novella in her essay, "Steinbeck's Vision of Mexico," and reveals an innate understanding of Steinbeck in doing so. She takes readers on a quick, lucid trip through a complex Mexican history that is possibly more edifying than most American readers were likely to have received. "John Steinbeck was fascinated by all things Mexican," she begins. "He traveled frequently to Mexico, lived for three and a half months in Mexico City in 1935, and roughly a third of his works have Mexican settings or characters or both." By the conclusion of her essay, readers seem to know everything Steinbeck seems to have known.

Knight identifies several historical factors that influenced Steinbeck: political and social developments in Mexico between its Independence from Spain in 1821 to the beginning of the Mexican Revolution in 1911; the concomitant extreme income inequality; severe poverty and harsh living standards for its indigenous people; Steinbeck's creative and scientific relationship with Ricketts; and the legend on which Steinbeck based the novella.

Knight takes us on a roller-coaster ride through the region we now know as Mexico from the arrival of Spaniards in 1519 to the 1940s, when Steinbeck penned *The Pearl*. She does so with touches of vibrant details that inform without overwhelming. She segues flawlessly into Steinbeck's friendship with marine biologist Ricketts, beginning in 1930. Ricketts and Steinbeck chartered *The Western Flyer* and collected specimens in a two-month, 4,000-mile trek of the Pacific. They released their results in a travelogue/marine-life catalog/philosophical treatise, *Sea of Cortez,* in 1941. "In many respects," Knight says, "Steinbeck was following the grand tradition of Spanish expeditions to the American Southwest and northern Mexico." The narrative in *Sea of Cortez* also contained the germ of the story that became "The Pearl of the World." "The book appears to be as much about Mexico as it is about a study of marine biology," Knight notes, "for every chapter describes the location and the people who inhabited it, very much in the spirit of the grand narratives of an earlier time." In her brief but telling discussion of the original story that Steinbeck uncovered at this time, Knight reveals how the legend influenced Steinbeck greatly, touching on terminology that resonates in both stories, and how Steinbeck's education, experiences, and philosophy helped mold *The Pearl* into the story it would become.

Knight then goes on, in her essay "How a Neglected Novella Became a Classic," to comprehensively chart the history of Steinbeck criticism during the past three-quarters of a century. She traces his reputation as a controversial figure in his own lifetime, someone whose every release was received with fanfare, both positive and negative. One thing is certain during his lifetime, Knight recognizes: "Steinbeck was enormously popular and successful," if critically overlooked. Even his winning of the Pulitzer Prize, the creation of film versions for his works, failed to win him literary respect. Resultant criticism, she says, varied between those who saw his work as "sensational propaganda" and those who recognized the literary merit of his social criticism. Though his work before World War II is generally considered superior to that which comes after, *The Pearl* is one clear exception to that rule, and it remains his most frequently discussed work in American public schools.

Ecocriticism and Steinbeck: A Perfect Pairing for the Twenty-First Century?

Steinbeck's own life experiences and voyages (before, during, and after World War II) clearly influenced his writing, and made him a voice for the people. Several critics have traced the influences of nature on Steinbeck's writing, and have revitalized his corpus in light of ecocritical concerns. Indeed, though ecocriticism was not a term during Steinbeck's career, the writers in this volume make strong cases for him as a proponent of *ecological concerns*. Steinbeck, in fact, undertook a journey in 1940 to the Sea of Cortez, Mexico, where he first encountered the story of a poor fisherman who discovered a pearl that would have changed his life but didn't (as least in the ways one would think). In exploring the intertidal zones of the Pacific coast with Ricketts, Steinbeck undertook his own

Darwinesque adventure, and he became facile with the principles of ecology as a result.

In "'So That One Beautified the Other,' An Ecocritical Perspective on Character and Place in John Steinbeck's *The Pearl*," Kyler Campbell challenges *The Pearl's* relegation to mere parable and makes a strong case for ecocriticism as the strongest, most insightful approach to the novella. Campbell suggests that *The Pearl* functions on a much deeper literary level than parable, with the author's juxtaposition of character and setting as wholly reliant on each other for moral development. Campbell lends insight into Steinbeck's mastery of craft and his ability to weave complex critical perspectives by merging character and setting into one inseparable whole. He suggests that Steinbeck's three distinct settings within the novella serve as indications and projections of Kino's crumbling mental and moral state, starting with the pastoral ideal of his beachfront home, leading into the shifting streets and suspicious motivations of the town, and eventually ending in the mountain ranges where Kino loses both his literal path and his moral fortitude. Campbell also suggests that these environmental elements allow the novella to demonstrate Kino's descent within the natural order of being, and traces Kino's devolution from a pillar of his community and devoted family man to something much more primal.

One of the ways in which a story like *The Pearl* gains an extended life span is when readers recognize other narratives that inform it or are influenced by it. As a result, students and scholars begin to see a work as instrumental to the development of a literary time period, or artistic eras that follow it. Jim Plath's "Pearls, Marlin, and Small Tragedies: Steinbeck's *The Pearl* and Hemingway's *The Old Man and the Sea*" does much to assert the timeliness of Steinbeck's novella in the twenty-first century. Linking the two narratives through robust historical and biographical research, Plath finds commonalities in the two writers' texts that go beyond the obvious and indeed make it hard to see them as anything but inextricable. In discussing the stories' shared symbolism; struggles for survival; similar structures of "loss followed by triumph followed by loss again"; and professions of universal truths, Plath not only brings the two stories to life, but the modernist literary era in which they were produced. He goes so far as to even suggest that Hemingway may have been influenced by Steinbeck's success to reclaim his own struggling career. Ultimately, Plath asserts both works continued relevance today, and his succinct and readable prose does much to revitalize consideration of the two writers.

Lowell Wyse's "Of Mollusks and Men: An Ecocritical Approach to *The Pearl*" frames *The Pearl* cogently in terms of this twenty-first-century critical lens. Wyse states that the novella need not simply be seen as a cautionary tale against greed and individualism, but "of human attitudes toward the natural world." He aptly notes how the narrative opens with "a threat from nature—the scorpion that stings the baby Coyotito," and identifies it as "an accident that leaves Kino and Juana essentially defenseless." As Wyse proceeds, he identifies Kino's distancing himself from the "essential ethic of his community, which we might now call environmental sustainability." He also perceives the pearl buyers as apt symbols of capitalist greed, as contrasted with the oyster divers, who are symbols of responsible, sustainable fishermen.

Wyse asserts that Kino's pearl, while a symbol of the protagonist's desire to ensure the very existence of his family, influences the attitude and behavior of the entire village, "disrupting the natural order and causing them to focus on the instant wealth that comes from the irresponsible extraction of natural resources." Ultimately, Kino's returning of the pearl to the sea is "an activist stance that mirrors contemporary protests against fossil fuel companies and other unsustainable extractive industries that undermine communal values," Wyse says. Using thoughtful historical research, Wyse reads passages of Steinbeck's texts closely to model one way in which ecocriticism can be applied in order to lend new insight into a text. At its heart, his essay is an exposé of the greed that is contained in Steinbeck's text, and a revelation of the tools that critics can use to reveal the greed that exploits the natural landscape (as seen in the text). Ultimately, Wyse says, greed that exploits the environment destroys the earth "we call home."

Chris Bowman's "'This Is the *Whole*': Ecological Thinking in John Steinbeck's *The Pearl*" gives *The Pearl* its allegorical due, while also suggesting that the story's longevity is due to "a pervasive sense of ecological awareness in the narrative." Bowman is careful to note how Kino's discovered pearl "highlights the risks of an industry that inherently causes ecological disruptions," and throughout his analysis, focuses on the reading more as a discussion of humankind's effect on nature as represented in the rich symbols of *The Pearl*. "As we grapple with issues such as sustainable land use, environmental justice, and the consequences of extractive economies," he notes, *The Pearl* is a great narrative to return to, for it contains a wealth of statements about the interconnectedness between humankind and nature.

Steinbeck recognized that interconnectedness, Bowman suggests, and called attention to the tenuous interplay between humans and their environment in this novella. When one element (usually humanity) throws off the balance, he states, the very equipoise of existence is undermined. The taking of the pearl from the ocean, for example, is the greatest destabilizing act, and the novella's entire ecosystem does not get righted until Kino returns it to the sea in a passage of "serene, descriptive nature writing. . . . [T]his environmental parable argues for a rejection of extractive industries by those who are typically exploited by them. For although Kino imagines that this pearl will open up better futures for his family, the reality of this system is that this is never truly accessible to them."

Michael Zeitler's "Steps to a Littoral Ecology: Community and Nature in John Steinbeck's *The Pearl*" traces the influences of society and ecology on the novella, citing Steinbeck's forward to Rickett's second edition of *Between Pacific Tides:* "[T]here are answers to the world questions in the little animals of tide pools, in their relations one to another." Steinbeck continually frames the issues of tradition, fate, ambition and community, Zeitler says, within a Darwinian natural world where what is death to one is life to another. He notes that although Steinbeck-as-writer might focus on human conflicts, Steinbeck-as-naturalist recognizes that one cannot merely study individual organisms, but must study entire interdependent biological and social ecosystems.

Kino's discovery of the pearl ignites his personal ambition to transcend the limits placed on him by class, race, and education and thus threatens to disrupt the intricate interdependencies that make up the human community. As Kino's brother warns him: "You have defied not only the pearl buyers, but the whole structure, the whole way of life, and I am afraid for you." Stripped of his human culture, at the end symbolically and literally naked, Kino's flight from his unknown assailants reduces him to the level of biology, hiding like an animal being pursued by a predator.

In light of humanity's newfound understanding of ecology and interconnectedness, then, *The Pearl* is equally relevant today as it was in 1947, for now the language of ecocriticism has caught up to the ecological empathies Steinbeck had imbued in it. The novella's continued interest, these ecocritics recognize, comes from a recognition of the injustices of economics and ecology that we are only in the last few decades recognizing and resisting. As such, attention to the literary ecological history will help us to inform our responses to the environmental challenges that we will face going forward.

The Economic Implications of *The Pearl*

Jericho Williams' "The Song of Inequality: Sickness and Wealth in Steinbeck's *The Pearl*" resists the positioning of *The Pearl* as a parable. Instead, Williams calls the book "a deceptively complex novella that confronts inequality partially from an angle of health and social wellness." Instead of reading the novella as a parable in the Romantic tradition, Williams asserts *The Pearl*'s realism, and in particular the elements of poison, sickness, and medicine as they relate to the dualistic concepts of wealth and poverty. It centers its attention on the conflict between the doctor and Kino in highlighting "the inequity that prevents a father from gaining immediate care for his son in an emergency situation, and then speculates how this trauma and the father's subsequent interactions with a corrupt doctor impact his reckless plight that comprises the remainder of *The Pearl*."

In light of twenty-first-century concerns about expanding globalization, the unchecked engorgement of multinational corporations, income inequality, climate change, drug epidemics, and general concerns of human health and wellness, Williams asserts that texts like *The Pearl,* and reading them with an eye toward their foresight into contemporary culture, are more vital than ever. But instead of rejecting previous interpretations as some contemporary criticism may seek to do, Williams "calls attention to key details that also ground the novella's sense of realism. It pays closer attention to the function of poison, sickness, and medical treatment as they relate to poverty and wealth." In doing so, Williams centers his attention on the conflict established between Kino and the doctor rather than the trials Kino endures after coming into possession of the pearl.

Williams' focus is on the economic inequity that is prevalent in the novella between the haves and the have-nots, and he pays particular attention to the concepts of health, wellness, sickness, and poison as they reveal themselves in the scenes concerning the doctor. He asserts that the scene outside the doctor's house is one of the novella's more pivotal moments—one in which readers place themselves among a community waiting outside a powerful doctor's door. Williams thus asserts that *The Pearl* illustrates the detrimental impacts of the inaccessibility to health care based on race, social status, and class. *The Pearl,* Williams reveals, is as much a twenty-first-century cautionary tale against the inextricability of for-profit health-care industries, wealth, degradation, and greed.

Steinbeck and God, Sometimes at Odds
Historically, readers and critics have identified *The Pearl* as a parable, and, like most parables, it continues to be vibrant and reveal lessons with subsequent readings. Kelly MacPhail reveals his own take on the spiritual implications that Steinbeck imbued in the novella in his essay, "'The Detachment of God': A Theopoetic Reading of Steinbeck's *The Pearl*." In his study, he questions religion's accounts for why bad things happen in the world. MacPhail reads the novella

as a theodicy—a theological justification for the problem of evil and concludes that "*The Pearl* offers only pessimistic answers," and even "complicates common assumptions about theological responses to the human situation." He interrogates *The Pearl*'s general reception as a simplistic narrative, but does not resist the word *parable*.

For MacPhail, the parable is a complex form with "several layers of application to the complex ultimate questions of human life." Steinbeck's novella, however, does not merely contain a warning against greed, but in fact reveals the myriad evils that Steinbeck saw in the world—evils that might hide any sense of God's goodness. Steinbeck links his rendering of this Mexican folktale to Christ's parable of "The Pearl of Great Price" as well as the pious late fourteenth-century poem, "The Pearl." MacPhail identifies metaphors of light, dark, mountains, sea, the destroyed ancestral boat, and Kino's perspective of the ants that mirrors "the detachment of God," given God's transcendent perspective of suffering human beings. He also unveils in Kino and Juana, a Latin American religious hybrid that blends Catholicism with traditional Indian beliefs that are revealed in the ritual songs that enshrine the goodness of family against the evils of the forest and of men who seek to do the family harm. Ultimately, MacPhail concludes, the greatest evils come from other men and not from what Kino sees as divine fate. As good and evil play out in *The Pearl*, it is human greed—as they are not only cheated by the doctor, priest, and salesmen, but also tracked and assailed by the armed hunter—that leads to the ultimate downfall of Kino and his family. They find loyalty only with family as the plot moves from the luck/blessing that fates Kino to find the pearl toward the greatest terror, the death of Coyotito, that parallels the sacrificial death of Christ.

Just as God's detachment may still reveal much about the nature of good and evil, criticism does not need to merely champion a work in order to lend insight into it. In fact, those who challenge the success of a work can bring light to its meanings, as well. John J. Han's "Surrendering: Steinbeck's *The Pearl* as an Artistic Failure" reveals much about the novella by challenging prevalent beliefs and readings. He disputes the discussion of *The Pearl* as a morality tale about greed, and as a religious parable in which Kino saves his soul by rejecting the pearl at the end. *The Pearl,* Han goes so far as saying, reveals Steinbeck's "moral confusion" at the time. Though Steinbeck had championed working-class people and warned against corporate and individualistic ideological and capitalist greed, in *The Pearl* he asserts that Kino has every right to pursue well-being for his family and achieves his goal of finding the pearl through hard work. However, Han asserts, the second half of the novel fails to adequately champion Kino as a victim of society, and thus fails as a work of art. He cites Erich Fromm's *Escape from Freedom* as a critical framework to exhibit how *The Pearl* "unwittingly extols a medieval way of life for poor people like Kino," wherein their sacrifices to social stratification lead to a sense of security. There is no "moral victory" for Kino as he sheds himself of the pearl in the end. Han questions how Steinbeck can show sympathy for the downtrodden in this novel, yet prevent them from escaping the evil cycle of poverty and despair. In earlier works he "empowered the powerless" but grants Kino and his family no such empowerment.

In his essay, "Who Stole Kino's Cheese? Socioeconomic Determinism in *The Pearl,*" Arun Khevariya also recognizes a fatalistic pessimism akin to Han's critique, as he examines determinism in Steinbeck's novella. Khevariya takes a look at Steinbeck's assertion that the common citizen became dependent upon the whims and fancies of the greedy industrialists during the twentieth century. Socioeconomic forces thus act as a villain in *The Pearl,* and instead of extending help to those who need it, deprive people of their individualistic freedom. Khevariya states that *The Pearl* exhibits internal and external economic and social deterministic factors and distort the actions and achievements of Kino, who, even as possibilities seem to be revealed with the discovery of the pearl, has extremely limited freedom of choice. Socioeconomic forces always determine humankind's actions, and Steinbeck reveals that there is little anyone can do to escape one's fate.

Comparing *The Pearl* Keeps the Discussion Fresh

The continued discussion of *The Pearl* in classrooms across North America exhibits its timelessness, even though the novella met with lukewarm responses upon release and continued to be considered second-tier to his magnum opuses, *The Grapes of Wrath, Of Mice and Men, East of Eden,* and even *Cannery Row, Travels with Charley,* and *Tortilla Flat.* Perhaps because it evokes so many universal concerns, it is often studied in context with other works and stands up to such comparative scrutiny. In this collection, along with Jim Plath, Emily Hamburger, Elisabeth Bayley, and Tammie Jenkins each place *The Pearl* next to other works to show how they inform each other.

Hamburger's "The Portrayal of 'Poverty People' in John Steinbeck's *The Pearl* and *Tortilla Flat*" studies Steinbeck's attitude toward, and championing of, the poor in their attitude toward families and, in particular, infants. Indeed, if infants are the most helpless of all humans, how society treats its most helpless members reveals a lot about the nature of the socioeconomic systems it establishes. "Students of literature should consider, when encountering the death of a young child or children in fiction, what those figures may represent beyond the confines of the story they inhabit," Hamburger states. Examining the stories with an eye toward the children in each, Hamburger asserts that their respective infants become symbols for personal dreams, socioeconomic hopes, generational aspirations, and communal resilience. "Finally," she says, "the death of a young child, and how that death is experienced by other characters in a story, could be representative of the precariousness of a desired future for a particular demographic group." Her study identifies how the two infants in *The Pearl* and *Tortilla Flat* represent the whole of the underprivileged class, for they are victims of forces entirely beyond their sphere of influence.

In "A Comparative Exploration of Devaluation of Women, Ownership, and Violence in John Steinbeck's 'The Chrysanthemums' and *The Pearl*," Bayley notes a parallel exploration of Steinbeck's texts, noting what Wendell Berry calls in the "Violence of Commerce" the devaluation of life. In both stories, characters are excited with the potential of liberation from a certain position in life. However, through these positions, different characters find themselves victims to a devaluation of their lives and are denied access to liberation, especially when it has to do with financial advocacy, participation, and ownership. Bayley explores the notions or acts of violence that occur through devaluation, the desire to take part in the story of violence, and the disposability of persons who are deemed of lesser value (because it is understood that they have limited or no rights to alter the economic framework of their lives).

Tammie Jenkins exhibits how *The Pearl* does not merely inform and respond to works of Steinbeck and/or his own time period, but how it ties into contemporary literature, as well. In her "Culture, Identity, and Otherness: An Analysis of Kino's Songs in John Steinbeck's *The Pearl* and Pilate's Melody in Toni Morrison's *Song of Solomon*," Jenkins uses exhaustive research to bring the music of these two seemingly disparate works to light. She recognizes how Steinbeck and Morrison integrate songs into their works as part of their character's internal and external discourses and as "an element accentuating their story's action." Her narratological close readings of *The Pearl* and *Song of Solomon* identify areas of similarity and disparity in Steinbeck and Morrison. Each, she says, uses music "to represent the culture, identity, and otherness of their characters," and explores how Kino's and Pilate's lyrics "give readers insight into their personal, spiritual, and social lives in these texts." Both texts, she asserts, "blend narrative with musicality in ways that connect the culture, identity, and otherness of these characters with their songs." In her work, as in most of the new approaches to *The Pearl*, Jenkins reveals how Steinbeck's novella is refreshed by a contemporary reconsideration.

Steinbeck may not have intended for *The Pearl* to provoke such a wealth and breadth of readings and responses, but he certainly imbued it with multiple levels of possible interpretations. His attitudes and convictions toward the underprivileged, as well as toward a natural world that was beginning to be exploited by an increasingly industrial world, found their voice in Kino's quest and his family's tragedy. Its presentation of Mother Earth, economics, and family in an inextricably interconnected, interwoven whole has prompted strong responses from its new generation of readers, scholars, and critics, who, even and especially when at odds, reveal the vibrancy of the still seemingly simple, short narrative.

On *The Pearl:* Defying Some Critics, Satisfying Many Readers_____

Laura Nicosia and James F. Nicosia

Even as a child, John Ernst Steinbeck was fond of science. His mother, a schoolteacher, had instilled in John and his three sisters a sense of culture and a love of learning. Now, at age 38, the writer, fresh off of publishing his finest work yet, *The Grapes of Wrath,* was about to embark on a new adventure. He and best friend Ed Ricketts, a renowned marine biologist, had planned a 4,000-mile, two-month journey in spring 1940 around the Pacific Ocean off the California/Mexican coast. They chartered a boat, took notes, recorded observations, collected specimens and, during the mission, were introduced to a myth centered on the Mexican city of La Paz. In that story, a poor Indian boy dreams of finding a legendary pearl that would free him from his poverty but led to only more suffering. The story stayed with Steinbeck enough to prompt his retelling of the myth in "The Pearl of the World," a short story published in *Woman's Home Companion* in 1945. It would not be his finest, longest, or best received story, but it was the birth of one of his most enduring works of fiction.

Since its publication, to coincide with its concomitant movie release in 1947, *The Pearl* has been continuously in print and has consistently been included in secondary school curricular lists and on college literature syllabi. Its current publisher, Penguin Random House, reissued the novella as recently as 2002, to coincide with the centennial of Steinbeck's birth, with French flaps and deckle-edged pages. Clearly, though the novella never achieved world-class status, it has received world-class respect, and treatment.

As of this writing, the Barnes & Noble sales ranking for *The Pearl* is #897, overall. Amazon's site lists *The Pearl* as: #904 in books, overall; #18 in Teen & Young Adult Classic Literature; #11 in Literary Criticism & Theory; and #26 in Classic American Literature. These are impressive numbers for a small, seventy-year-old text. Certainly, despite any mixed critical reception, *The Pearl* is a popular and successful book. As Michael Meyer asserts, while:

> Steinbeck's *The Pearl* is considered one of the staples of America's high school curriculum . . . the novella is usually relegated to a discussion in the freshman year of high school or even earlier, not only because of its brevity (87 pages) but because it contains little controversial vocabulary and because some administrators feel it has such a simplistic message that it can easily be understood by most teens and preteens. (42)

Doubtless the novella is economically written, and because of its brevity, it is arguably the first exposure many student readers have to Steinbeck's more lengthy—and, some critics would say, more weighty—writings. Serving as the bridge text and introduction to Steinbeck's fiction, one would assume *The Pearl* should be given serious critical consideration rather than dismissal as merely a light read, simple parable, or literary failure.

Initial Critical Receptions: Mediocrity, Brevity, and Women's Fare

In fact, there are American literary scholars specializing in Steinbeck's works who have either ignored *The Pearl,* clustered it with other shorter pieces of Steinbeck's works (such as *Of Mice and Men),* or scorned it altogether. In the late 1960s, Steinbeck scholar Warren French denigrated it by asserting "its mediocrity, implying that *The Pearl* was probably initially constructed 'to tap the rich resources of the never-to-be-underestimated magazines for the homemaker'" (qtd. in Meyer 43). This statement was made in reference to its initial publication as a short story ("The Pearl of the World") when it was published it in *Woman's Home Companion* in 1945. French clearly points to the inherent sexism of the period that designated those writings aimed for a female audience as carrying little-to-no literary merit. Consequently, it was deemed lesser-than Steinbeck's other, longer works.[1]

Indeed, while *The Pearl* frequently has been dismissed *because of* its brevity and simplicity, its seeming unassumingness belies the heft of its messages and its literary and narrative skillfulness. What nearly a century of criticism on the work has shown, as well, is that there are more messages in *The Pearl* than the overt and didactic takeaways that some critics have reduced it to: *Greed will lead to destruction,* and *Moral good will eventually triumph over evil.* While these morals or themes may be appropriate assessments, readers who plumb the text will find a variety of critical interpretations. Furthermore, increasingly, readers attuned to realism properly interrogate the idea that Kino's act of returning the pearl to the sea even qualifies as a good that triumphs over evil.

Hollywood Embraces *The Pearl*

When the short story, "The Pearl of the Sea" was popularly received by the readers of *Woman's Home Companion,* Steinbeck expanded it in 1947 and simplified its title to its final *The Pearl.* All along, however, Steinbeck recognized the story's potential and, with Jack Wagner, wrote a movie script for a Hollywood adaptation that debuted in 1947 as a tie-in with the newly revised book (Simmonds 17). The film was titled *La Perla* and released by RKO to popular, if not critical acclaim—much like most of Steinbeck's work. *La Perla* won a Golden Globe in 1949 for Best Cinematography and later went on to win four Ariel Awards in Mexico in 1948, including Best Director and Best Actor.

While the film is award-winning in both the United States and in Mexico, what may be more socially and culturally important about the adaptation also makes it very much aligned with Steinbeck's ethos. The movie was entirely filmed on site in Mexico, starred Mexican actors in its roles, and used Latinx professionals (Emilio Fernández, director) (IMDb). The film has been deemed significant because of the social message inherent in its production. In 2002, the film was entered into the National Film Registry by the Library of Congress for "being culturally, historically, or aesthetically significant" (*Revolvy*). When it was released, the film and the novella were both critically recognized and criticized for their artistic elements—or lack thereof.

In his film review for the *New York Times,* Bosley Crowther in 1948 praised the film for its cinematography, acting, and "simplicity and strength." Crowther begins:

> An exceptional motion picture, both in content and genesis, is the beautiful and disturbing filmization of John Steinbeck's novelette, *The Pearl*, which reached an appropriate showcase at the Sutton Theatre yesterday. *Exceptional* it is in genesis by virtue of the fact that it was made in Mexico by a Mexican company with Mexican actors who speak English throughout. And *extraordinary* it is in content through the benefit of a story of *primitive power*, told with *immaculate integrity* through an *eloquent* camera. [emphasis mine]

While the film was lauded for its "extraordinary . . . primitive power," and "immaculate integrity," with "eloquent" cinematography, its dark themes were not hidden. Crowther continues:

> *The Pearl* is no glamour picture . . . nor is it a genial entertainment for the tired businessman's night out. It is a stern, bitter, brutal, and fatalistic dramatization of a tragic folk tale, bleak in its ultimate conclusions about the enslavement of underprivileged man. And although it is richly rewarding, pictorially and dramatically, to the aesthetic sense, it is likely to leave the emotions exhausted and depressed.

Midway through his review, Crowther identifies "one philosophical weakness" in the film's screen writing:

> The story as told on the screen is the evident irresolution in the symbolism of the pearl. If this gem represents material riches to its owner—as, at times, it appears—then his passionate struggle to hold onto it has all the ugliness of greed. But if it stands for the means to a better living, education and spiritual growth, as the ultimate catastrophe makes cogent, then the conflict has social scope. The lack of clear symbolism confuses sympathy and roils the significance of the gesture of surrender and clenching of fists at the end.

Multimedia Tie-ins: A Story Meant to Be Heard

Despite some negative critical commentary at its release, the movie became a popular success and brought much attention to the book. Audience members who saw the film increasingly purchased and read the novella as viewership of the film grew. The dual release was promotional genius and a great success. Steinbeck was a Hollywood professional by now, having written and/or collaborated on several screenplays by this time, so his gamble was not a risky one. He had already produced the following screenplays:

- *Of Mice and Men* (1939)
- *The Grapes of Wrath* (1940)
- *The Forgotten Village* (1941)
- *Tortilla Flat* (1942)
- *The Moon Is Down* (1943)
- *Lifeboat* (1944)
- *A Medal for Benny* (1945)

Steinbeck knew how Hollywood worked, and he knew how to write fiction that had filmic elements and would translate to the screen.

As viewers flocked to the theaters and readers purchased the novella, a flurry of critics and scholars dismissed the latter. (Dr. Melinda Knight discusses the span of critical commentary later in this volume in her Critical Overview of *The Pearl*.) Woodburn Ross assessed *The Pearl* as "not important," and French called it nothing more than "paste" (qtd. in Bates 42). Even Steinbeck's original preface *seems* to discourage intense probing by what many interpret as a call for more simplistic, dualistic readings:

> "In the town they tell the story of the great pearl—how it was found and how it was lost again. They tell of Kino, the fisherman, and of his wife, Juana, and of the baby, Coyotito. And because the story has been told so often, it has taken root in every man's mind. And, as with all retold tales that are in people's hearts, there are only good and bad things and black and white things and good and evil things and no in-between anywhere."

"If this story is a parable, perhaps everyone takes his own meaning from it and reads his own life into it. In any case, they say in the town that ..."

This oral nature of the preface, trailing off as a storyteller would when beginning the exposition of a story is an indicator that Steinbeck wants readers to *hear* the story and to recognize its openness and indeterminacy. Rather than reading folktale/parable and probing the uses, purposes, and intents of the genre, many readers have been content to read the story for its straightforward messages of the universal battle of good vs. evil.

With symbolic messages such as good vs. evil, *The Pearl* is often designated as either a folktale or a parable. These two genres are occasionally belittled by the uninformed for what many consider their primitive and unsophisticated storytelling techniques. Regardless of any critical dismissal, parables can contain complex, powerful, and moving narratives:

> [T]hey speak to the viewer without merely using words, and often move the heart before engaging the mind. The person can describe how they are being impacted by what they hear and see, but not always explain why it has that effect on them. The power inherent in most works of art is that they reach into the human soul and demand a response. You cannot stay neutral, and even so, you have chosen to respond. Parables are powerful because they demand a response and this creates change. The purpose of the parable is not to punish the listener by asking— "What have you done?" Rather, it provokes them to ask, "What kind of person am I becoming?" (*The Baker Encyclopedia*)

In the traditional reading of *The Pearl,* by the end of the story, if nothing else, Kino must have asked himself this very question and found he didn't like what he saw reflected back at him. After yielding to his more base and violent nature (which leads to the loss of Coyotito, his son) Kino has his epiphany and attempts to reverse the course of his actions by throwing away the pearl:

And then Kino laid the rifle down, and he dug among his clothes, and then he held the great pearl in his hands. He looked into its surface and it was gray and ulcerous. Evil faces peered from it into his eyes, and he saw the light of burning. . . . And the pearl was ugly it was gray, like a malignant growth. And Kino heard the music of the pearl, distorted and insane. (117)

Cathartically, Kino's viewer/readers empathize and grow with him. Such is the purpose of a well-written parable/folktale, even if critics summarily dismiss works that appeal primarily to the emotions.

Tragedy, the Universal Story, and Artistic Skill

Barclay Bates argues, convincingly, that, along with being a parable, *The Pearl* can be read as a modern-day Greek tragedy. Referencing numerous readings of *The Grapes of Wrath* and *Of Mice and Men,* Bates cites critics such as: Joseph Warren Beach's statement that there is "a chorus in an ancient tragedy"; Burton Rascoe's contention that Steinbeck "may be, before he is finished, a greater poetic dramatist than Sophodes" and that there is "a Greek choral chant" in *Of Mice and Men*; and Joseph Fontenrose's analysis that *Of Mice and Men* is "very like a tragedy by Sophocles or Ibsen in its dramatic economy" (41). After summarizing a host of critical assessments on Steinbeck's penchant for the tragic, Bates contends that despite Kino's lack of social status he has cunning and natural intelligence, and these qualify him as an Aristotelian hero. Consequently, Bates asserts "*The Pearl* has not only tragedy's chorus and various foreshadowings but also its major figures and something rather like its cosmology" (42). The cathartic process of the literary tragedy is a powerful experience.

This universality of *The Pearl* (with its tragic outcomes, corporate and political greed, and oppression of the poor and downtrodden) comes to the fore in 2019 as this volume goes to press. Surely these messages—once vital to Steinbeck as he fought for migrant workers, immigrant populations, and marginalized populations—are as applicable today (in this time of Brexit, intense American nationalism, xenophobia, and immigrant detention centers) as they were in the early twentieth century.

Recognizing the novella's universality and layered textures in 2005, Michael Meyer wrote a reassessment of *The Pearl* and called for a renewed consideration of the story as worthy of literary analysis and exegesis:

> I believe that truly in-depth conversations about the novel have become few and far between; instead, educators have become comfortable with traditional interpretations of the work and have failed to explore other potential readings with their students . . . these teachers have continued to center in on a supposed "absolute" message that the author was trying to convey rather than to consider a multiplicity of intent. (42)

Meyer goes on to challenge contemporary readers, teachers, critics, and scholars to probe *The Pearl* with "more attention to the nuances suggested by the text" (42). Meyer identified these subtleties and categorized them in the following categories:

- Analogues/Comparative studies—exploring of *The Pearl* and how it parallels other texts and "works of art" (42)
- Techniques—critiquing *The Pearl* for its "various artistic techniques" including irony, imagery, symbols, ambiguity, and style (45)
- Philosophy—reading *The Pearl* to explore its philosophical underpinnings as espoused, for example, in *The Log from the Sea of Cortez* (50)
- Biographical/Historical Approaches—locating *The Pearl* within both its historical period and within Steinbeck's life experiences (52)
- Themes—probing *The Pearl* for its thematic areas and social concerns (such as immigrants/immigration, politics, gender roles, materialism, greed, religion and spirituality) (52–53)

Steinbeck's *The Pearl* Today

In 1983, The Steinbeck Center Foundation was established to raise awareness and funds to build a museum dedicated to the life and works of Steinbeck. The National Steinbeck Center was opened to the public in 1998: "Today, Steinbeck's status has risen in Salinas, and the writer who vowed to put his slice of central California on the map of the world—and did so—who was awarded the Nobel Prize for Literature in 1962; and who put the city of Salinas on the map of the world is a favored son" (National). As the literary world celebrated Steinbeck's 100th birthday in 2017, cities and schools across the United States selected *The Pearl* as its common reading text. This spurred a slew of newspaper articles, reprintings, and festivities. Steinbeck's legacy as a local and national treasure is solidified.

As recently as June 2019, Penguin Classics published a new Spanish edition of *The Pearl,* and to celebrate this publication the National Steinbeck Center held a series of events to honor Steinbeck's novella. They dubbed the series Pearl Week and festivities included:

- Excerpts from *The Pearl* manuscript on display
- Special foreign editions on display in exhibit
- Scavenger hunts
- A presentation on the science of pearls
- A private screening of the 1947 film of *The Pearl*
- A dramatic reading of *The Pearl* in both Spanish and English

From a short, seemingly simple retelling of an overheard myth on an ocean expedition, *The Pearl* has defied expectations, resisted criticism, and has flourished.

Note

1.   However, it must be said that Steinbeck's 1945 novel *Cannery Row* was considered a critical and popular failure which, by comparison, makes *The Pearl* that much more palatable for several critics.

Works Cited

"About John." National Steinbeck Center. n.d. www.steinbeck.org/about-john/.

Bates, Barclay W. *"The Pearl* as Tragedy." *California English Journal,* vol. 6, no. 1, 1970, pp. 41–45. files.eric.ed.gov/fulltext/ED039246.pdf.

Crowther, Bosley. "The Screen in Review." *The New York Times,* 18 Feb. 1948, p. 36. archive.nytimes.com/www.nytimes.com/ref/membercenter/nytarchive.html.

Elwell, W. A., and Beitzel, B. J. *Baker Encyclopedia of the Bible.* "Parables." Baker Book House, 1988. storage.cloversites.com/gladtidingsmissionarysociety/documents/ProbPowrPrbls.pdf.

La Perla (The Pearl). Directed by Emilio Fernández. 1947. IMDb. www.imdb.com/title/tt0037981/.

La Perla. (The Pearl). Directed by Emilio Fernández. 1947. *Revolvy.* www.revolvy.com/page-The-Pearl-(film).

Meyer, Michael. "Diamond in the Rough: Steinbeck's Multifaceted Pearl." *The Steinbeck Review,* vol. 2, no. 2, 2005, pp. 42–56. *JSTOR,* www.jstor.org/stable/41581982.

Simmonds, Roy. "Steinbeck's *The Pearl*: A Preliminary Textual Study." *Steinbeck Quarterly,* vol. 22, Winter-Spring 1989, pp. 16–34. dmr.bsu.edu/digital/collection/steinbeck/id/1628/.

Steinbeck, John. *The Pearl.* Bantam Books, 1986.

Steinbeck, John. *The Pearl.* 1993. Amazon.com. www.amazon.com/Pearl-John-Steinbeck/dp/014017737X/ref=sr_1_2?crid=2FHIT2RF238NR&keywords=the+pearl+by+john+steinbeck+paperback&qid=1562606003&s=books&sprefix=%22the+pearl%22%2Cbeauty%2C123&sr=1-2.

Steinbeck, John. *The Pearl.* Barnes & Noble. www.barnesandnoble.com/w/pearl-john-steinbeck/1002075636?ean=9780140177374#/.

Biography of John Steinbeck

Laura Nicosia and James F. Nicosia

John Ernst Steinbeck, Jr. was born in Salinas, California, on February 27, 1902, to John Ernst Sr. (owner of a feed and grain store, and a member of the Masons) and Olive Hamilton Steinbeck (a teacher and a member of the Order of the Eastern Star). His parents were the first-generation descendants of German (father) and Irish (mother) immigrants. and their success story of rising to a comfortable socioeconomic class helped Steinbeck to become "a particularly American artist" who was aware of his privilege and access (Millichap 1).

His birth comes just after the American frontier reached the Pacific coastline, and his young adulthood at the beginning stages of a modern America heading toward the Great Depression (1929–1939) and the Dustbowl catastrophe of the American Plains (1930s). Neither of these events nor their wide-ranging implications were lost on young John, and his writing repeatedly revealed a sensitivity to economic and ecological concerns.

John was John and Olive's only son, and the third of their four children in the following order: Beth, Esther, John III, and Mary. He grew up in Salinas—a place of natural beauty with green rolling hills, agricultural richness, access to the Pacific coast, and a diverse population of haves (white business owners) and have-nots (mostly marginalized immigrants who worked the fields).

He spent a seemingly happy childhood with weekend trips to the coast and was gifted with a red pony (that he named Jill) as a birthday present, which became the inspiration for his *The Red Pony* in 1937. His mother, a school teacher, had made sure that he always had access to the best of American and British books, and he read voraciously. As he says in his essay, "The Golden Handcuff," "My mother was a lady with a high church attitude toward culture. She always knew what she liked and, to a surprising degree, what she liked turned out to be art. As a medium-sized kid I was taken to The City [San Francisco] to be blooded with culture" (*America 50*).

Steinbeck frequently retreated to his room to write poems and short stories that countered what he called "Salinas thinking" when he declared his vocation at 14 years old (qtd. in Shillinglaw). In his senior year of high school, the well-read, popular, self-proclaimed rebel Steinbeck was elected class president (Millichap), perhaps fostering his willingness to stand up for his principles and be a voice for others.

Earlier in his writing career, while reflecting on his frequent trips to the Pacific coastline where his family vacationed on weekends in Pacific Grove, Steinbeck wrote: "'I remember my childhood names for grasses and secret flowers' . . . 'I remember where a toad may live and what time the birds awaken in the summer—and what trees and seasons smelled like'" (qtd. in Shillinglaw). His attention to details and his heightened senses had a powerful effect on his later writings and became evidenced in his tales of ecological stewardship that later would be revisited and cultivated after meeting Ed Ricketts.

In 1919, after graduating high school, at his parents' urging, Steinbeck registered at Stanford University and began taking classes. He did not, despite attending Stanford on-and-off for over six years, earn a degree. His first love was writing and that continued to be his vocation during his college career. But during his off times from his university studies, Steinbeck worked with farmhands and migrant laborers to earn money. By forging those connections with the oppressed laborers, and his "early sympathy for the weak and defenseless, deepened his empathy for workers, the disenfranchised, the lonely and dislocated, an empathy that is characteristic in his work" (Shillinglaw).

After several years of various jobs, Steinbeck met and married his first wife, Carol Henning (a native of San Jose), in 1930 when he was 28 years old. They later occupied the family's coastal vacation home in Pacific Grove, where they lived rent-free while John pursued his writing. Carol supported the young couple during those early years by working several odd jobs, helping him edit his manuscripts, create titles, and encouraging him to attend meetings at the Carmel's John Reed Club—known at the time for targeting its Marxist philosophies toward writers, artists, and intellectuals (Shillinglaw).

Over the following decade, Steinbeck wrote several of his California and labor-oriented novels: *The Pastures of Heaven* (1932), *To a God Unknown* (1933), *The Long Valley* (1938), *Tortilla Flat* (1935), *In Dubious Battle* (1936), *Of Mice and Men* (1937) and *The Grapes of Wrath* (1939). It was during these years that Steinbeck developed a mature writer's voice, style, and philosophy. Shillinglaw offers that by 1933, Steinbeck became aware of an:

> essential bond between humans and the environments they inhabit. In a journal entry kept while working on this novel—a practice he continued all his life—the young author wrote: "the trees and the muscled mountains are the world—but not the world apart from man—the world and man—the one inseparable unit man and his environment. Why they should ever have been understood as being separate I do not know."

Perhaps a natural outgrowth of his deep and long-lived friendship with marine biologist Ricketts, who founded the Pacific Biological Laboratories located on Cannery Row in Monterey, Steinbeck grew both worldly wise and more focused. Steinbeck met Ricketts in 1930, and the latter exposed Steinbeck to music, philosophy, Buddhism, the poetry of Walt Whitman, and the power of friendship (Shillinglaw). Even more importantly, though certainly not easily proven, is that Ricketts' influence was influential on Steinbeck's writing style, voice, and even character development. Shillinglaw writes:

> Ricketts was remarkable for a quality of acceptance; he accepted people as they were and he embraced life as he found it. This quality he called non-teleological or "is" thinking, a perspective that Steinbeck also assumed in much of his fiction during the 1930s. He wrote with a "detached quality," simply recording what "is."
>
> The working title for *Of Mice and Men*, for example, was "Something That Happened"— this is simply the way life is.

Furthermore, in most of his fiction Steinbeck includes a "Doc" figure, a wise observer of life who epitomizes the idealized stance of the non-teleological thinker: Doc Burton in *In Dubious Battle*, Slim in *Of Mice and Men*, Casy in *The Grapes of Wrath*, Lee in *East of Eden*, and of course "Doc" himself in *Cannery Row* (1945) and the sequel, the rollicking *Sweet Thursday* (1954). All see broadly and truly and empathetically. Ed Ricketts, patient and thoughtful, a poet and a scientist, helped ground the author's ideas. He was Steinbeck's mentor, his alter ego, and his soul mate.

With Ricketts' and Carol's influences, by the mid-1930s, Steinbeck had his first publishing success with *Tortilla Flat* and what followed was a succession of three acclaimed labor-related books: *In Dubious Battle* (1936), *Of Mice and Men* (1937), and *The Grapes of Wrath* (1939) (which led him to be investigated by the FBI for "suspected Communist leanings" ("Biography: John Steinbeck").

The two discovered in each other similar interests and philosophical foundations. Perhaps coincidentally, perhaps not, in the late 1930s, both Ricketts and Steinbeck produced their magnum opuses. Ricketts published the definitive California oceanographic study, *Between Pacific Tides,* with Jack Calvin, in 1939, only months after Steinbeck's *The Grapes of Wrath*. Soon after, in spring 1940, Ricketts and Steinbeck chartered a marine expedition of six weeks and 4,000 miles in the Pacific, during which they would collect numerous specimens for observation and discussion. The following year, they published together the narrative and scientific results of that voyage in *Sea of Cortez*. In the narrative section of *Sea of Cortez,* Steinbeck records the inspiration for the story that would become "The Pearl of the World" in 1945, and, in 1947, *The Pearl.* In the story he heard on this voyage, Steinbeck recounts the myth of an Indian boy from La Paz, Mexico, who discovers an exceptional pearl that he expects will change his life.

By then, John Steinbeck was already a household name. The publication of *The Grapes of Wrath* in 1939 had been monumental in several ways. On its first print run, it sold out nearly 20,000 copies in advance of publication and continued to sell on average 10,000 copies a week in its first few months in print (Shillinglaw).

Still, the book was not without its controversies, and that perhaps intensified its popularity. In 1939, America was still gripped by the Great Depression, and a novel that gave voice to and championed poor, dispossessed farmers may have been the last thing most of America wanted to confront. "[T]he book about dispossessed farmers captured the decade's angst as well as the nation's legacy of fierce individualism, visionary prosperity, and determined westward movement," says Shillinglaw. Some called the Joad family's narrative a "dirty, lying, filthy manuscript" (Shillinglaw). It was often banned, and conservative religious groups attacked some of the novel's words and images as being unfit for print. Regardless, the book continued to sell, and won the Pulitzer Prize for Steinbeck in 1940. It continues to sell in 2019 as a narrative exposing the dangers of unchecked capitalism.

By 1941, Steinbeck's marriage to Carol failed and led to divorce. Shortly after, John met and married his second wife, Gwendolyn "Gwyn" Conger. The couple had two sons, Thomas and John Steinbeck Jr., who would be Steinbeck's only children ("Biography: John Steinbeck"). During the war years of 1943–1945, Steinbeck became exceptionally patriotic and wrote war propaganda on behalf of the United States government and military. Soon later, he was hired as a war correspondent by the *New York Herald Tribune,* and went on several trips overseas (England, North Africa, and Italy) to cover the everyday lives and deaths of American soldiers overseas.

After the war, Steinbeck released "The Pearl of the World" in the December 1945 issue of *Woman's Home Companion.* The story that he had heard years earlier on his Pacific expedition with Ricketts had stayed with him, and it found its final form as *The Pearl,* in 1947, to coincide with the film version being released at the same time. Several months later, however, Steinbeck's best friend Ricketts was hit by a train as he attempted to cross the tracks in Monterey, California, and died on May 11, 1948. This devastated Steinbeck, and shattered his spirit. Upon returning to New York after Ricketts' funeral, his wife of six years, Gwendolyn, asked for a divorce. These two distressing events led to a period of depression for Steinbeck, which caused him to return to California and take up residence again in the cabin in Pacific Grove ("Biography: John Steinbeck").

In 1949, he met Elaine Scott, who would become his third wife. They moved to the east coast and took residence in New York City—where Steinbeck lived until his death. In 1951, he began his writing of *East of Eden*, the novel he intended to be his magnum opus. It was

> in part, based on Steinbeck's maternal family history. Stories of the Hamilton family are paired with the a "symbolic story" of the Trask family, a rewriting of the Cain and Abel biblical story. In this epic novel of intertwined stories, Steinbeck captures his own history as well as the history of the Salinas Valley—and he also grapples with the pain and consequences of his divorce from his second wife. ("Biography: John Steinbeck")

The novel was immediately adapted to film, directed by Elia Kazan, and starred the novice actor in his debut role, James Dean.

John and Elaine traveled the world as he continued to write in ensuing years. He earned the Nobel Prize for Literature in 1962 for his body of work (amidst some controversy). Later, in 1964 he was awarded the Presidential Medal of Freedom by President Lyndon B. Johnson ("Biography: John Steinbeck").

His last book was *America and Americans*, a 1966 collection of essays about the "American character and the common good. Topics considered include ethnicity, race, and the environment" ("Biography: John Steinbeck"). Like many of Steinbeck's works, it was in many ways ahead of its time for its attitude and subject matter. Concerning ecology and race as it does, *America and Americans* is a text highly applicable to twenty-first-century America, though it has yet to be rediscovered by Steinbeck readers.

In 1967, John Steinbeck again served as a war reporter, this time for *Newsday,* and traveled to Vietnam to cover the war in a series called "Letters to Alicia." He visited combat zones, "manned a machine-gun watch position while his son and other members of the platoon slept," and grew increasingly skeptical about the United States' role in the Vietnam War ("Biography: John Steinbeck"). His failing health, however, culminating in a series of mini-strokes, prevented him from becoming vocal or writing extensively about his disenchantment and disillusionment with the war.

John Ernst Steinbeck died at his home in New York City on December 20, 1968.

Works Cited

"Biographical Context: John Steinbeck." *Steinbeck in the Schools.* San Jose State University. sits.sjsu.edu/context/biographical/index.html.

"Biography: John Steinbeck." National Steinbeck Center. www.steinbeck. org/about-john/biography/.

Millichap, Joseph R. "John Steinbeck." *Critical Survey of Long Fiction, Fourth edition,* Jan. 2010. ezproxy.montclair.edu:2048/ login?url=http://search.ebscohost.com/login.aspx?direct=true&db=l fh&AN=103331CSLF15830140000493&site=eds-live&scope=site.

Shillinglaw, Susan. "Biography in Depth: John Steinbeck, American Writer." *Steinbeck in the Schools.* San Jose State University. sits.sjsu. edu/context/biographical/in-depth/index.html.

Steinbeck, John. *America and Americans, and Selected Nonfiction,* edited by Susan Shillinglaw and Jackson J. Benton. Viking, 2002.

CRITICAL
CONTEXTS

Historical Context of *The Pearl*: Steinbeck's Vision of Mexico

Melinda Knight

John Steinbeck was fascinated by all things Mexican. He traveled frequently to Mexico, lived for three and a half months in Mexico City in 1935, and roughly a third of his works have Mexican settings, or characters, or both.[1] He became especially interested in Emiliano Zapata and the Mexican Revolution, which began in 1910 and lasted until 1920. His novella *The Pearl* is set in Mexico, as are two films for which he wrote screenplays—*The Forgotten Village* (1941) and *Viva Zapata!* (1952). To understand *The Pearl,* it is important to consider several factors of the historical that influenced Steinbeck and his work. First are political and social developments in Mexico between its Independence from Spain in 1821 to the beginning of the Mexican Revolution in 1911. Mexico at this time experienced extreme income inequality, including severe poverty and harsh living standards for its indigenous peoples.[2] The second is his relationship with Edward F. Ricketts, including the ways in which their creative and scientific efforts complemented each other. Finally, the legend on which Steinbeck based the novella, which was originally discussed in a work he co-authored with Ricketts, sheds further light on Steinbeck's vision of Mexico.

Mexico in the Nineteenth and Early Twentieth Centuries

The region that became known as Mexico has a long and rich history, having been populated for more than 13,000 years before the arrival of Spaniards in 1519. The Spanish conquistador Hernán Cortés led an expedition that resulted in the fall of the Aztec Empire and the incorporation of large parts of what was called "New Spain" under the dominion of Spain in 1521. Several centuries later, Mexico embarked on a long struggle for independence from Spanish rule, beginning in 1810, when Father Miguel Hidalgo y Costilla called upon his parishioners to join the revolt against the colonial government in his famous *Grito de Dolores* (Cry of Dolores). With the signing of the Treaty of Córdoba in 1821, Mexico declared its independence. The country was ruled by a monarchy for the next two years, a period referred to as the First Mexican Empire. In 1824, a new federal constitution established the Republic of Mexico.

The next fifty years were extremely chaotic. Within a few decades of its establishment, the Republic of Mexico was engaged in war with both the United States and France, all while dealing with conflicts over how the newly established nation-state should be organized. The new republic was attempting to maintain control over its government and land, but continual encroachment by colonial powers kept everything in a state of flux. The Mexican-American War in 1846 to 1848, known in Mexico as the Intervención estadounidense (United States intervention in Mexico), resulted from the U.S. annexation of Texas in 1845. The war ended with the Treaty of Guadalupe Hidalgo in 1848, which ceded almost half of Mexico's territory to the United States, including the areas now known as the states of California and New Mexico.

The period known as *La reforma*, from 1854 to 1876, represented a struggle between liberals and conservatives over the further transformation of Mexico into a nation-state. They clashed over the role of the Catholic Church, corporate or communal ownership of land, the role of the military, and the rights of indigenous peoples. Essentially, the conservatives wanted a centralist state ideally controlled by a monarchy, whereas the liberals advocated for a modern nation-state based on liberal principles. The conservatives were defeated on the battlefield, and Benito Juárez, the first Mexican leader of indigenous descent, was elected president in March of 1861.

Juárez soon faced new challenges, as France invaded Mexico later that year ostensibly to collect some national debts. The Mexican army then defeated the French invaders in the Battle of Puebla on May 5, 1862—a date commemorated as Cinco de Mayo.[3] The victory in Puebla was short-lived, as the French soon returned with military reinforcements. The French joined forces with local conservatives who had lost to Juárez's forces, and together they succeeded in establishing a monarchy in Mexico, under Maximilian I, known as the Second Mexican Empire. However, this move did not stop the fighting between the sides supporting monarchy and democracy. In 1867, the liberal forces won out, executing Maximilian I and reinstating Benito Juárez. The Restored Republic lasted from 1867 to 1876, and Juárez remained in office until his death in 1872. He was praised for having resisted foreign intervention, though he was criticized for attempts to change the constitution. Juárez was succeeded by Sebastián Lerdo de Tejada in 1872, who was then overthrown in a coup led by General José de la Cruz Porfirio Díaz Mori in 1876. In the era known as the *Porfiriato*, Díaz was elected president seven times between 1877 and 1911.

Díaz's dictatorship was one of the longest in Latin American history. He held sole power for thirty-four years, except for a four-year period when he ceded power to a trusted ally, Manuel González Flores. At this time, Díaz could not be re-elected, since his coup against Lerdo de Tejada was based on a principle of no re-election. Díaz is widely credited for putting Mexico on the path to modernization, and his presidency produced significant economic growth and relative political stability. He was particularly known for inviting foreign capital, which funded a network of national railroads, revitalized mining, expanded the textile industry, and also introduced commercial agriculture.

The modernization did not, however, lead to industrialization, as Mexico supplied raw materials, agricultural products, and cheap labor supervised by foreigners in exchange for goods manufactured elsewhere (Fehrenbach 470). The land reforms, which were targeted at both the Catholic Church and the *ejidos*, communally owned land of indigenous groups, led instead to the creation of vast *haciendas,* of which there were some ten thousand by the end of the century controlling at least half the available crop land. The haciendas were large estates that included plantations or working mines or other industrial enterprises, but always with significant land holdings. This system became an extension of colonialism, whereby natural resources are sent out of the country and returned as finished goods from a mercantile economy.

Indigenous peoples made up about 40 percent of Mexico's population in 1900, but the ruling class was mostly comprised of Spaniards considered white. Most indigenous peoples lived in the central and south of Mexico on communal lands and spoke upwards of sixty languages. Beginning in the 1850s, during *La reforma*, the government began dividing the ejidos into smaller farms or confiscated them for the use of the *hacendados* (owners of the haciendas) or transferred outright to foreign investors. Díaz and his supporters also reasoned that the indigenous peoples would prefer to be yeoman farmers, rather than holding lands communally, but that notion of individualism met with Indian resistance. This process of land was accelerated during the Porfiriato.

By 1910, some ninety percent of the rural population had lost their lands, and at least half of Mexico was owned by a few thousand families and foreign companies. A surplus of labor combined with harsh working conditions and a lack of available land meant that the rural population, which was in the majority, had produced a humanitarian disaster. Historians agree that the rural standard of living was worse in 1910 than it was a century earlier when Father Hidalgo issued his Grito de Dolores. Indigenous peoples from entire villages had become tenants on the haciendas or became *jornaleros,* day laborers at very low wages, a fate also shared by mestizo peasants. Díaz was almost eighty in 1910, and while he had originally indicated that he would retire, he decided to run for election again. When results came in, they were announced as showing a massive though clearly fraudulent victory over his opponent Francisco Madero. Madero promptly called for a revolt, thus beginning the first phase of the Mexican Revolution. Díaz was forced to resign in 1911, and he fled to Spain.

The Mexican Revolution was the product of widespread anger about the policies that favored hacendados, industrialists, and foreign capitalists. Zapata's demand for land reform, principles he later incorporated in his 1911 *Plan de Ayala,* directly opposed the appropriation of land previously held communally by indigenous peoples. Although Zapata was assassinated in 1919 and did not live to see the success of the revolution, his ideas influenced Mexico for the next century. In *The Pearl*, Steinbeck's protagonist Kino shows readers the effects of disenfranchisement and lack of opportunity for indigenous peoples and others excluded from wealth and power under Díaz and earlier governing systems. The *Porfiriato* thus forms the historical backdrop for Steinbeck's *The Pearl*.

Steinbeck's Friendship with Ed Ricketts

The second major historical context necessary to understand Steinbeck's *The Pearl* is the relationship between Steinbeck and marine biologist Ed Ricketts. Steinbeck was interested in marine science even before he met Ricketts; and, in fact, some scholars have proposed that Steinbeck was "at heart a scientist," viewing "human beings as part of a group that had to be considered, ultimately, within a general ecological perspective" (Parini 37). Ricketts served as inspiration for characters in seven of Steinbeck's works, most notably as Doc in *Cannery Row*.

Steinbeck and Ricketts met in 1930 and discovered that they shared similar interests in thinking about individual and group behavior, albeit from different backgrounds. In a general zoology course he took at the Hopkins Marine Station near Monterey in 1923, Steinbeck became fascinated with the concept of the superorganism—a whole that is more than the sum of its parts—as discussed in the works of biologist William Emerson Ritter. Ricketts, who came to California in 1923, had studied at the University of Chicago with ecologist W. C. Allee, who theorized that animals behave differently as individuals than they do in groups, so that organisms that cooperate with each other ensure survival. The two spent countless hours in Ricketts' biological supply house, Pacific Biologicals, discussing the works of these two groundbreaking scientists, one a biologist (Ritter) and the other an ecologist (Alle).

Ricketts and Steinbeck were both working on their masterpieces at the same time. While receiving his only income from products of his laboratory, Ricketts spent years studying marine invertebrates of the California Coast and ultimately published *Between Pacific Tides,* co-authored by Jack Calvin, in 1939, the same year as Steinbeck's *The Grapes of Wrath. Pacific Tides* even today is considered the definitive study of oceanography in California. Ricketts and Steinbeck then decided to collaborate on a handbook for nonspecialists about marine life in the San Francisco Bay. They never completed this project, but it paved the way for the more ambitious collecting expedition they undertook in 1940 to the Gulf of California.

Ricketts and Steinbeck chartered *The Western Flyer* and over six weeks in March and April covered 4,000 miles and collected specimens at some thirty stations along the route. The result of that journey was the publication in 1941 of *Sea of Cortez*. This book is part travelogue and part catalogue of marine life and anticipates the later work of such naturalists as John McPhee and Bill McGibbon. It consists of a narrative, an explanation of preparing specimens (including photographs), and an appendix of more than 300 pages, which provides a detailed catalog of what was collected. The narrative part was presented as a collaboration, although it was based on journals kept not by Steinbeck but by Ricketts and Tony Berry, the captain of the ship (Astro 13). Ten years later, Steinbeck published the narrative separately, under his name, as *The Log from the Sea of Cortez*.

In many respects, Steinbeck was following the grand tradition of Spanish expeditions to the American Southwest and northern Mexico. As he explains in the introduction, "We made a trip into the Gulf; sometimes we dignified it by calling it an expedition" (*Sea of Cortez* 1). Expeditions sponsored by the Spanish crown would chronicle all the activities, including how the money was spent but also significant information about flora and fauna and descriptions of indigenous peoples. One of the most famous of these is Eusebio Francisco Kino's *Historical Memoir of Pimería Alta*, a work that resonates in the name Steinbeck chose for his protagonist in *The Pearl*.

The narrative in *Sea of Cortez* also contains philosophical digressions and most important, the germ of the story that became "The Pearl of the World," which first appeared in the December 1945 issue of *Woman's Home Companion* and later issued in book form as simply *The Pearl* in 1947. The book appears to be as much about Mexico as it is about a study of marine biology, for every chapter describes the location and the people who inhabited it, very much in the spirit of the grand narratives of an earlier time.

The Legend of the Pearl

In *Sea of Cortez,* Steinbeck retells a legend of an Indian boy who discovers "a pearl of great size, an unbelievable pearl" (102). The legend is set in La Paz, about which Steinbeck says "everyone in the area" knows its "greatness" (*Sea of Cortez* 101) and a place from which came the pearls on "the robes of the Spanish kings and the stoles of the bishops in Rome" (102). Steinbeck describes La Paz as "very venerable in the eyes of Indians of the Gulf," and while other cities may have been "busier" or "gayer," La Paz is *"antigua"* (102). The "pearl oysters drew men from all over the world" and "in all concentrations of natural wealth, the terrors of greed were let loose on the city again and again" (102). This vision of La Paz corresponds with the ways in which the raw materials, including metals and minerals, produced great profits for foreign investors and also how lands were plundered and taken from peasants and indigenous peoples throughout Mexico.

In the legend Steinbeck recalls, the Indian boy knew the value of the pearl and dreamed of being drunk all the time, of marrying whom he chose, and buying his way out of purgatory and moving closer to paradise, along with some of his dead relatives. Interesting about this description is the allusion to the role of agave in Mexico, which is used to make tequila. In 1900, Mexico produced far fewer foodstuffs than four centuries earlier, even though its population was roughly the same (Fehrenbach 466). So many fields formerly devoted to maize were instead converted to the more profitable agave.

The Indian boy in the legend tries to sell the pearl but is offered far less than it is worth; in fact, no one will give him a fair price, the same way no one paid for the lands confiscated from indigenous peoples throughout Mexico. The brokers are all, in effect, in cahoots. In despair, he takes the pearl to the beach and hides it under a rock but then is clubbed by greedy men and tortured again when he runs

---

away. Finally, he throws the pearl back into the ocean, and he "was a free man again with his soul in danger and his food and shelter insecure" (104).

Steinbeck speculates on the veracity of the legend: "This seems to be a true story, but it is so much like a parable that it almost can't be," for this "Indian boy is too heroic, too wise" (104). And then he further concludes that the "story is probably true, but we don't believe it" for it is "far too reasonable to be true" (104). Presumably, Steinbeck was told the story in Spanish, but we never see an original, so he has become, in effect, a translator of a local folktale.

Steinbeck retells this story in the novella *The Pearl*, and in the epigram he repeats the suggestion that if "this story is a parable, perhaps everyone takes his own meaning from it and reads his own life into it." Steinbeck also writes to his agent Elizabeth Otis that the legend is "a black-white story like a parable" (Benson 564). Although some have seen this epigram as referring to the parable in Matthew 13:45–46, Steinbeck does not mention it in the *Sea of Cortez*; and if anything, the one in the novella is the reverse of the one in the gospel of Matthew. The biblical parable likens the pearl to the kingdom of heaven, as a merchant of pearls would sell everything to buy this one pearl of value. On the other hand, some have seen the novella as conveying autobiographical concerns about the price of success (Parini 319).

A different reading is possible when considering Steinbeck's understanding of the historical context of Mexico in the 1900s and the social situation of indigenous peoples. Just as in the legend, Kino, the protagonist in *The Pearl*, is refused a fair price, and he is eventually forced to throw the pearl into the ocean, after losing his son and becoming a murderer himself. Kino never received anything of value for the pearl; instead of gaining riches, his life is ruined. Because Kino never became wealthy, it is hard to see the story as a parable about the destructive power of wealth. Instead, it seems to be a confirmation of the ways in which the indigenous peoples of Mexico were robbed of whatever they possessed of any value.

It is worth noting how Steinbeck adapts or changes the folklore material of the legend and how his characters resist or transcend stereotypical representations of Mexican peoples. The Indian boy in the legend becomes an Indian family, with Kino as the fisherman, Juana his wife, and Coyotito as the injured son in need of medical help they cannot afford. The transformation of a boy into a family unit further emphasizes the plight of indigenous peoples, who have no recourse for what has happened to them other than to eventually engage in the armed struggle led by the revolutionaries Pancho Villa and Emiliano Zapata. Class and race combine to provide no alternatives for families like Kinos, and any attempt to move upward would be met with failure.

Steinbeck was well aware of the racial and class hierarchies in Mexico. In his narrative *Zapata,* he notes that "pure" Spaniards from Spain are at the top, followed by "pure" Spaniards born in Mexico, and then those of mixed Spanish and Indian ethnicity, mestizos. But of the Indians themselves, Steinbeck writes that the "Indian was not even a citizen" but is instead viewed as "a native animal" (Zapata 20). This view is echoed in *The Pearl*, when Kino knows that "all of the doctor's race spoke to all of Kino's race as though they were simple animals" (9). When Kino goes to the doctor's door to get help for Coyotito, who has been bitten by a scorpion, the servant refuses to answer him in the "old language," presumably an indigenous one. The doctor asks his servant whether he has "nothing better to do than cure insect bites for 'little Indians,'" for he is a "doctor, not a veterinary," further emphasizing the view of indigenous peoples as animals (11).

Not having any luck with the doctor, Kino and Juana decide to try to find a magnificent pearl to pay for the doctor's services. They take their canoe to the "bed that had raised the King of Spain to be a great power in Europe in past wars, and had decorated the churches for his soul's sake" (16). They find the "pearl of the world" and immediately start dreaming of what else they could do besides cure their son. Both imagine having new clothes to replace those that clearly marked their ethnicity and class: shoes, not sandals, a hat of felt, not of straw. Kino imagines even having a rifle. As Kino dreams of all the material goods his newfound wealth will bring, he also considers how Coyotito will become literate: "My son will read and open the books, and my son will write and know writing" (26). As one critic has observed, Steinbeck clearly wanted the reader to see *The Pearl* as a Mexican story, for he uses the formal syntax of Spanish, and not colloquial English (Augenbraum 59). Kino's hope for his son is a direct translation from Spanish: "Mi hijo leerá y abrirá los libros. Y mi hijo escribirá and sabra escribir." When the priest comes to visit he uses the archaic English "thou," which is equivalent to the Spanish "tú," the informal "you." Race, again, enters the story when Kino and his brother Juan Tomás walk into town to sell the pearl, for they both squinted their eyes, "as they and their grandfathers and their great-grandfathers had done for four hundred years," as "Kino's people had learned only one defense—a slight slitting of the eyes and a slight tightening of the lips" (46).

As we know, Kino and Juana lose their son, who is shot by one of the trackers looking for them, and also the pearl, which they very publicly throw back into the ocean. By analyzing the significance of Mexico as setting and the social situation of the Indian family, one can view *The Pearl* as an allegory of ethnic relations in Mexico in the revolutionary period. Just as Steinbeck collected stories of migrants in California and transformed them into his great novel *The Grapes of Wrath,* so he took the legend of the Indian boy and his fabulous pearl and used it to produce a work that highlighted the oppression of indigenous peoples in *The Pearl* and the origins of the Mexican Revolution. Understanding the historical context, Steinbeck's friendship with Ricketts, and the origins of the folktale about a pearl demonstrates Steinbeck's great feeling for Mexico and why the country and its people have played such important roles in his works.

Notes

1. Steinbeck's relationship with Mexico also continues to be of great interest to scholars of Mexican culture, as indicated in two recent books published in Spanish, by Adela Pineda and Rogelio Martínez.
2. Throughout this chapter, I am using the term *indigenous peoples* to refer to the inhabitants of Mexico before the arrival of the Spanish conquistadors. This term more accurately represents the

first population, as opposed to *Indians*, a term that originated with Christopher Columbus, who mistakenly thought he had reached the East Indies. Steinbeck, however, called them Indians, and his term will be used for quotations from the novella.

3. Cinco de Mayo has since become a celebration of Mexican culture especially in the United States. Cinco de Mayo is only a minor holiday in Mexico, whereas the most important public holiday is Independence Day, celebrated on September 16—the date that marks the start of war against Spain in 1810.

Works Cited

Astro, Richard. *John Steinbeck and Edward F. Ricketts: The Shaping of a Novelist*. U of Minnesota P, 1973.

Augenbraum, Harold. "Translating Steinbeck." *The Steinbeck Review,* vol. 14, no. 1, 2017, pp. 52–64. *JSTOR,* www.jstor.org/stable/10.5325/steinbeckreview.14.1.0052.

Benson, Jackson J. *The True Adventures of John Steinbeck, Writer: A Biography*. Viking, 1984.

Fehrenbach, T. R. *Fire and Blood: A History of Mexico*. Macmillan, 1973.

Kino, Eusebio Francisco. *Kino's Historical Memoir of Pimería Alta: A Contemporary Account of the Beginnings of California, Sonora, and Arizona.* 1683–1711. Translated by Herbert Eugene Bolton, U of California P, 1948.

Koth, Karl B. "Crisis Politician and Political Counterweight: Teodoro A. Dehesa in Mexican Federal Politics, 1900–1910." *Mexican Studies/Estudios Mexicanos*, vol. 11, no. 2, 1995, pp. 243–271. *JSTOR,* www.jstor.org/stable/1051922.

Martínez, Rogelio. *México en la obra de John Steinbeck [Mexico in the Work of John Steinbeck]*. Palibrio, 2017.

Parini, Jay. *John Steinbeck: A Biography*. Henry Holt, 1995.

Pineda Franco, Adela. *Steinbeck y México: Una mirada cinematográfica en la era de la hegemonía estadounidense [A Cinematic Look in the Era of America Hegemony]*. Bonilla Artigas Editores, 2018. Pública cultura 6.

Ricketts, Edward Flanders, and Jack Calvin. *Between Pacific Tides.*3rd ed., Stanford U P, 1939.

Sams, Edward Boyer. "The Haunted Tree: Two Versions of John Steinbeck's *The Pearl*." *The Steinbeck Review*, vol. 11, no. 2, 2014, pp. 189–96. *JSTOR*, www.jstor.org/stable/10.5325/steinbeckreview.11.2.018.

Steinbeck, John. *The Pearl*. 1945. Penguin, 1992.

_____. "Zapata: A Narrative, in Dramatic Form, of the Life of Emiliano Zapata." *Zapata*, edited by Robert E. Morsberger, Viking, 1993, pp. 16–199.

_____. *Sea of Cortez: A Leisurely Journal of Travel and Research, with a Specific Appendix Comprising Materials for a Source Book on the Marine Animals of the Panamic Faunal Province*. Viking, 1941.

Steinbeck, John, and E. F. Ricketts. *The Log from the* Sea of Cortez: *The Narrative Portion of the Book,* Sea of Cortez *(1941)*. Viking, 1951.

Critical Reception of John Steinbeck's *The Pearl*: How a Neglected Novella Became a Classic

Melinda Knight

John Steinbeck was a controversial figure in his own lifetime. Each new work was both praised and attacked. He hardly liked his critics, for he called them "curious sucker fish who live with joyous vicariousness on other men's work and discipline with dreary words the thing which feeds them" (*Journal* 165). He says he read the reviews at one time, and then he put the criticisms "all together" and found that "they canceled each other out and left" him "nonexistent" (qtd. in Kalb 8). Despite the lack of critical consensus about his literary merit, Steinbeck was enormously popular and successful. The success of *Tortilla Flat* (1935) and *Of Mice and Men* (1937) anticipated the national sensation of *The Grapes of Wrath* in 1939, which in 1940 won the Pulitzer Prize and was made into an enormously popular film, widely considered one of the best American movies of all time. All three novels focused on ordinary people and their struggles in everyday life during the Great Depression—migrant workers, manual laborers, the under-employed. As a result, criticism has veered between those who viewed Steinbeck's work as sensational propaganda to those who appreciated or scorned what they saw as social criticism to those argued for its literary merit.

After the great successes of his novels in the 1930s, some critics believed that the quality of Steinbeck's work declined after World War II. However, his 1947 novella *The Pearl* has remained widely taught in public American secondary schools. To understand how and why *The Pearl* has been so highly regarded by educators, it is useful to consider the various trends in how the novella has been received, both in its own time and with subsequent generations of scholars and critics. The most significant commentary on *The Pearl* to explain its continued popularity in secondary school curricula comes from contemporaneous reviews, literary criticism since publication, and guides intended primarily for teachers.

Contemporaneous Reviews

The novella was originally published in the December 1945 issue of *Woman's Home Companion* as "The Pearl of the World." Critic Warren French has suggested that the novella first appeared in a women's magazine because it was so mediocre that it was apparently intended "to tap the rich resources of the never-to-be-underestimated magazines for the homemaker" (137). The novella was released in book form in 1947 simply as *The Pearl* to coincide with the release of the RKO film version, also scripted by Steinbeck. Interesting about the film version is that Steinbeck insisted on an all-Mexican cast, who spoke in English. According to biographer Jay Parini, the novella and film, "in both incarnations went relatively unnoticed," although Steinbeck's agent told him the book sold over two thousand copies in January 1948 (317).

Despite the perception that *The Pearl* was not widely discussed when it was published, quite a few reviews appeared in newspapers, trade journals, and subscription magazines in 1947 and 1948. Like other Steinbeck works, the novella received mixed reviews. Most contemporaneous reviews indicated that the work derived from an "old Mexican folk tale," but only a few of them explained that Steinbeck said he first heard the tale on the marine biology expedition he undertook with his friend Ed Ricketts and out of which came their remarkable work, *Sea of Cortez*, in 1941. Very few reviews noted the multiple meanings of "Mexican" in discussing the origins, for Steinbeck makes it very clear his protagonist is an Indian, one of the indigenous peoples, as opposed to one of the colonizers. Maxwell Geismar, for example, mentioned the "very good" description of "village life and Mexican types," and he also noted that the "whites" were "always complete villains" (14). This critic, however, was disappointed that Steinbeck displayed more the "sense of a fabulist or a propagandist" than the "insight of a writer," and he lamented the "reversionary tendency" to previous "pagan excursions" (14). From this review, Geismar would seem to prefer that Steinbeck write more about poor white people, instead of connecting the themes of labor and exploitation to race and nationality.

Other contemporaneous reviews were less ambivalent and downright hostile. In 1947 a writer in *Time,* for example, titled the review "Counterfeit Pearl" and claimed that the novella will "seem a little jewel only to those readers who find important meanings in calculated ambiguities" and who mistake "manipulated sentimentality for emotion." In a similar vein, Stevie Smith, in the *Spectator,* concluded that Steinbeck was "not quite at home with his old Mexican 'folk' story and a better description would be 'fake'" (570). Another anonymous reviewer in the *New Statesmen and Nation* agreed that the novella was "effective, if not entirely original," but any pleasure for the reader would be "offset by the desperate archaism and the portentous reflections" (401) of Steinbeck's prose. The reviewer also noted that the author repeatedly employs "the misuse of the conjunction 'and' with which to start a sentence" and writes sentence phrases such as "'a town is a thing like a colonial animal'" (401). The reviewer concluded by asking why Steinbeck "must employ this patronizing, semi-Biblical jargon" for, after all, he is not "Miss Pearl Buck" (401). A third contemporaneous reviewer, John Farrelly in the *New Republic,* also criticized Steinbeck's efforts to have his characters be described and speak in their own vernacular. Farrelly believed that the characters in *The Pearl* speak in "that kind of monumental grunt which has become, in our fiction, the conventional *patois* of the noble savage and proletariat" (28). He further suggested that Steinbeck's "lackluster, almost iambic, prose" resulted from "the boredom of the writer" (28).

More sympathetic reviews from 1947 appeared in *The New York Times.* Carlos Baker called Steinbeck a "mature and skilled writer," one "who needed no more than time and the broad outlies of this folk tale to fashion a work which fits as neatly in the list of Steinbeck's books as the last gem in a carefully matched necklace" (52). Also, in the *Times,* Orville Prescott argued that the novella is "much the best book which Mr. Steinbeck has written since *The Red Pony* and *The Grapes of Wrath*" (21). He much preferred the novella to the "wretched novels" (28) Steinbeck had been writing at the same time the story was first published in *The Woman's Home Companion.* Other favorable reviews appeared by Edward Weeks in *The Atlantic* and Thomas Sugrue in *The New York Herald Tribune.* Sugrue's review is one of the earliest to discuss biblical connections in *The Pearl,* comparing it to the story of a pearl in the Gnostic fragment "Acts of Thomas," often called the "Hymn of the Soul," in which is told a story of a pearl (4), thus anticipating subsequent criticism focusing on biblical connections. Short positive notices appeared in the trade publications *Library Journal* and *Booklist,* and *The Pearl* was "briefly noted" in *The New Yorker.*

Literary Criticism Since Publication

In the late 1940s, *The Pearl* receded into critical memory, overshadowed by Steinbeck's more well-known works. That changed in 1958, with the publication of Peter Lisca's *The Wide World of Steinbeck,* the first book-length study of the author's works since Harry Thornton Moore's pioneering monograph in 1938, which, of course, did not include anything after *The Grapes of Wrath.* Lisca has been widely considered the first professional Steinbeck scholar, ending, as John Ditsky argued, the days in which Steinbeck was no longer "at the mercy of newspaper and magazine critics" (7). Lisca gave Steinbeck's writings serious, sustained critical attention, treating them as significant contributions to literature and culture. He devoted an entire chapter of his book to *The Pearl,* particularly noting Steinbeck's success in urging "the reader to look beyond the physical events into their spiritual significance" (220). Like Sugrue in 1947, Lisca also connected *The Pearl* with the gnostic fragment the "Hymn of the Soul." He also pointed to the author's "tendency to think of groups as unit animals" (228), theories that reflected the thinking of both Steinbeck and his close friend marine biologist Ed Ricketts and that appeared in *Sea of Cortez* along with the folktale that inspired *The Pearl.*

Once scholars started paying serious attention to Steinbeck's work, the 1960s and 1970s brought more critical attention to *The Pearl*, including both positive and negative appraisals. French, who had long been a champion of Steinbeck's body of work, nevertheless denounced *The Pearl* in his 1961 book-length study of Steinbeck, calling it "defective," a "betrayal," and, perhaps worst of all, in his opinion, an "easy read" possessing very little substance (137). Two years later, Joseph Fontenrose praised *The Pearl,* seeing it as an example of where "biology takes the place of history" (140). Levant, in another full-length study, in 1974, called *The Pearl* a "triumph, a successful rendering of the human experience in the round" (197).

Critics have never come to a consensus about what *The Pearl* represents, but the fact that they were talking about this novella with such detail and attention means that it and Steinbeck were being considered important. Like all works that become part of whatever canon is in operation at the time, debates over interpretation tend to become narrower. In the case of *The Pearl,* critics have often differed over whether the novella is a teleological parable (Krause 4) or a non-teleological parable (Metzger 98). Simply put, to view a work as a teleological parable assumes that there is an end goal in mind from the beginning—in other words, an intended purpose, where everything is happening by design, for a particular moral reason. But viewing the same parable as non-teleological assumes that individuals are making decisions based on the circumstances with which they are presented, as opposed to an end design that is predetermined.

Krause, in support of the teleological, referred to the theme of *The Pearl* as the prophetic and age-old Chaucerian folk-tale motif: *Radix malorum est cupiditas* (desire is the root of all evil), and he came firmly down on the side of the teleological (3). The debate over whether Steinbeck was intending to write a teleological or a non-teleological story depends on how a crucial passage in the *Sea of Cortez* is interpreted: "non-teleological ideas derive through 'is' thinking associated with natural selection as Darwin seems to have understood it" (135). In other words, non-teleological thinking asks not "why" but "what" and "how" (*Sea of Cortez* 141). As Richard Astro has demonstrated, Ricketts and Steinbeck together collaborated on the philosophical musings contained in the *Sea of Cortez.* Krause believed strongly that "moral knowledge" was at stake, as there could be no understandable reason for Kino's ridding himself of the pearl" (6), whereas for Fontenrose, the supposed moral dilemma is "the way things are" (114). Fontenrose specifically argued that *The Pearl* evolved from Steinbeck's experiences as a marine biologist:

> As one might expect in a tale that grew out of *Sea of Cortez,* Steinbeck's interest in biology is more evident than in his other novels of the forties. Here is the town that "is a thing like a colonial animal," and which "has a whole emotion," and through which news travels swiftly by mysterious channels. . . . And in the town as ecological unit each kind of inhabitant—pearl fishers, pearl buyers, Spanish aristocrats, beggars, ants, dogs—has its niche, its particular means of preserving itself. And each individual must stay within the niche of his kind and not encroach on another's. (114)

For Fontenrose, the argument was settled, as an individual could not by himself oppose biology.

The year 1966 marked a significant advancement in Steinbeck scholarship, when Tetsumaro Hayashi and Preston Beyer founded the John Steinbeck Society and the journal *Steinbeck Quarterly.* Hayashi, along with Richard Astro, organized the first conference devoted to Steinbeck at Oregon State University in 1969, and the proceedings were published in a collection edited by Astro and Hayashi. These events marked a completion in a shift begun by Lisca, who claimed that Steinbeck was an important author who deserved a place in the canon of American literature. *Steinbeck Quarterly* was eventually replaced by *The Steinbeck Review*, and the Center for Steinbeck Studies was established at San Jose State University in 2003.[1] International conferences are regularly held on particular areas of interest to Steinbeck scholars, and there are several excellent bibliographies of scholarship on *The Pearl* including John Ditsky's study of Steinbeck's critics and Jackson Benson's analysis of the short novels.[2] Several broad themes have emerged in scholarship since the professionalization of Steinbeck studies some fifty years ago: comparative studies, imagery and symbols in the context of morality, psychoanalytic approaches, rejection of materialism, Steinbeck and the natural world or the environment, and some recent studies that reinterpret his connection with Mexico.

Comparative studies appeared early on, as many commentators saw the need to compare Steinbeck to Hemingway, who was writing at the same time. Krause took a different approach, in discussing *The Pearl* in relation to Mark Twain, arguing that Steinbeck "wrote a potent fable of self-damnation that traces a pattern of moral deterioration closely resembling the one Twain had engineered in 'The Man That Corrupted Hadleyburg'" (3). Hayashi, among his many contributions to Steinbeck studies, edited a collection of comparative studies, making connections between *The Pearl* and works by William Faulkner, Ernest Hemingway, and Émile Zola, among others (*Literary Dimension*). Mimi Gladstein's more recent comparative study has taken an extensive look at the similarities between *The Pearl* and Hemingway's *The Old Man and the Sea,* which was written in Cuba in 1951 and published in 1952. Both plots derived from stories the authors had heard earlier in their lives, and both were also made into films. Gladstein saw how "both writers use the technique of a formal-sounding, grammatically correct sentence structure to suggest the sense the characters are not speaking in English" (14), thereby refuting commentators who disparaged the quality of Steinbeck's prose, who ignored what he was trying to accomplish. Harold Augenbraum has also demonstrated that Steinbeck's syntax for Kino in *The Pearl* often represents a direct translation from Spanish (59). Although both authors won the Nobel Prize for Literature after publication of what Gladstein calls these "fish stories," only "Hemingway's was mentioned as a contributing factor" (20). Other comparative studies have restricted their analyses to the works of Steinbeck. For instance, Kyoko Ariki, in comparing *the Pearl* to the short story "Flight," has noted Steinbeck's "growing concern for the persecuted Indians and, on a broader scale, for persecuted people in general" (94).

Symbols and imagery have long been considered in interpreting *The Pearl.* Hayashi regarded it as "a novel of disengagement on at least two levels," for " it traces the symbolic journey and withdrawal of the novel's protagonist, Kino, first from the environment of society, his family, and even from his own proper place in the natural scheme; and, secondly, from the charm of the Pearl of the

World" ("Novel" 84). As Hayashi noted, the pearl "becomes Kino's new God;" and he loses the real pearl, which is his son (84). In a study focused on talismanic symbols, Todd Lieber argued that the pearl, which "first has a purely material value and significance for Kino" soon becomes "talismanic of his individual being, his soul, and it takes on a spiritual significance" (269). Kino's action in relinquishing the pearl thus "involves an acceptance of selfhood at the same time it involves a recognition of the unity of all individual beings within the larger pattern of existence" (270).

The Pearl is often read as a rejection of materialism and a concern about the price of success (Parini 319) or, as Linda Wagner-Martin has argued, a parable about the American dream. She pointed out how Steinbeck changed the folktale he heard in La Paz from the "pearl satisfying Kino's individual pleasure to it becoming a vehicle for the education of their child, and (one assumes) for the family's rise in social and economic position" (96). Adrienne Warfield has also seen *The Pearl* as depicting the negative effects of modernization, with a further emphasis on "knowledge divorced from human relationships and ethical concerns" (106). Like many other commentators, she has drawn attention to biblical symbolism to "convey the dangers and illusory nature of knowledge" (108). Another interesting interpretation about how Steinbeck rewrote the folktale is offered by Edward Sams, who has suggested that Steinbeck was influenced by a supposed curse that haunted a house he bought in Monterrey, California, and in which he was living at the time he might have been writing *The Pearl*.

For psychoanalytic interpretations, there are several excellent readings that rely on the impact of Carl Jung on Steinbeck's work. Biographer Jackson Benson reported the lifelong influence of Jung on Steinbeck, particularly the ways in which the "collective unconscious" could relate to myth and evolutionary biology (207). Robert DeMott listed nine different books by Jung in his checklist of Steinbeck's reading. DeMott further argued that Steinbeck arrived at his interest in Jung independently of his first meeting with Ricketts but that his interest intensified as a result of their conversations (62–63). Critic John Timmerman argued that Jung's influence is more evident in *The Pearl* than in any other work by Steinbeck, even though the novella has been "virtually ignored in psychoanalytic terms" (144). The fundamental premise underlying Jung's theory of the shadow is that the conscious and unconscious are always in conflict, even when one adopts a mask, what Jung termed the "persona." Timmerman concluded that this general premise, "an individual's conflict between the socially acceptable persona and unconscious desires" (146), is reflected in Kino, especially in the dream sequences. Kino stares at the pearl and imagines the acquisition of power (148), and the shadow thus becomes the unconscious self. Michael Meyer has taken a different approach to a Jungian interpretation, seeing the persona confronting the shadow not as a conflict between light and dark, but rather as an "inextricable union of good with bad and bad with good," so that the relationship is paradoxical ("Wavering Shadows" 133). Meyer further points to Steinbeck's concept of the whole, as articulated in *Sea of Cortez*. Perhaps also in the realm of psychoanalytic interpretations is an interesting theory put forth by Edward Sams, that Steinbeck was influenced by the legend of a haunted house in which he was living at the time he was writing *The Pearl*. Steinbeck had purchased the house, named the Lar-Soto Adobe, and apparently knew that it was considered haunted because a cursed child was buried under a large cypress tree on the property. Sams has argued that Steinbeck's retelling of the folktale is "darker than the original" because of his knowledge about the curse, and so the death of a child came to appear in *The Pearl* (189).

Steinbeck's connection to nature in *The Pearl* has also received considerable attention. Louis Owens, in his study of Steinbeck's "re-vision" of America, organized his book around the scenic elements from the natural environment. In particular, he looked at the importance of the mountains as the setting for *The Pearl*, both thematically and symbolically (36). He saw the work as a "parable of man achieving greatness through the courage to challenge the unknown" (45), and Kino "triumphs in defeat" (46). Kiyoshi Nakayama, in another environmental study, examined Steinbeck's uses of the land, the sea, and people in translating what he saw and described in *Sea of Cortez* to the retelling of the folktale he heard on the voyage. Nakayama has presented an alternative view of what has often been judged a tragic ending. He made the suggestion that instead of facing future misfortune and death, Kino "will contribute to his people," for "the Indians need someone to protect them or at least someone to prevent them from being cheated" (206). In Nakayama's view, Kino can "be a Zapata of La Paz, the leader of the people Steinbeck and Ricketts define in *Sea of Cortez*" (207). Nakayama has connected an environmental view to political action, and in the process has rejected any classification of the novella as simply a "parable, a symbolic tale, a realistic novella, or humanistic short fiction" (207). The environment has thus functioned as a microcosm in which the protagonists live as a "family of the world" and in which "Kino as hero" could become a leader and guardian "of the people like Emiliano Zapata" (208). Striking about this interpretation is how this critic has argued for seeing how the novella works in multiple and complex ways, with no single reading providing answers. That, perhaps, is one way to view a classic, and in this review of critical reception one can see how a work originally written off as insignificant or worse yet as inferior has come be widely appreciated, studied, and taught.

Guides for Teachers

Because *The Pearl* is widely taught in secondary schools, it is useful to consider some of the approaches recommended. The *English Journal*, the National Council of Teachers of English publication for high school teachers, has featured several articles for using *The Pearl* in secondary education. The earliest of these, by Harry Morris, has been widely cited for "putting the stamp of allegory on a modern novel" (488). More recently, Rose Reissman advocated for finding news links to the setting, characters, and themes of *The Pearl* in current newspapers and magazines. Two handbooks designed for students are also useful. Martha Heasley Cox, the founder of the Center for Steinbeck Studies at San José State University (which is now named for her), focused especially on symbols and images. She also indicated the novella has been interpreted in a number of ways—a search for values, a search for a man's soul, and, most commonly, a rejection of materialism (123). Cynthia Burkhead, for example, has followed the traditional approach of setting, plot, structure, characters, and major themes, of which the latter include destructive power of wealth, natural hierarchy of life, and appearance versus reality. She also offered an archetypal approach and a reading of the novella that subverts the myth of the American Dream—the assumption that if one works hard enough success will follow.

One of the most interesting recent analyses of *The Pearl* has focused on the musical references. Roger Caswell, a middle-school teacher in Kansas, has argued that the novella "almost cries for popular music as part of its instructional delivery" (62). He reported that his students discover Steinbeck's rhythm of phrasing. Fontenrose had earlier noted how Steinbeck used a fugal technique in which the various songs, such as the Song of Evil and the Song of the Family in *The Pearl,* have similar elements (42–43). Steinbeck himself was fascinated with classical music and particularly Bach's *Art of the Fugue.* Michael Meyer discussed using music in teaching *The Pearl*, and he has also provided a wide variety of teaching approaches, including discussion questions, writing activities, and research assignments that can be used in both secondary and college classrooms ("Diamond"). He was especially concerned that French's initial judgment of the novella as being defective would discourage teachers at all levels from teaching *The Pearl.* That clearly has not happened, as this review of critical reception has shown.

The Pearl remains an important text for critics, teachers, and students. The novella is open to multiple interpretations, making it a truly modern work. For students it offers multiple opportunities to study and appreciate literature, including learning about such terms as imagery, irony, parable, and tragedy. Reading *The Pearl* in our own time, in the twenty-first century, also provides new perspectives on the impact of colonialism and movements to restore the rights of indigenous peoples.

Notes

1. Archives of the *Steinbeck Quarterly* are available online at Ball State University, and the *Steinbeck Review* is published by the Center for Steinbeck Studies and can be accessed through *JSTOR* or *Project MUSE*.

2. Note that these bibliographies cover material up to 1990 (Benson, *Short Novels*) or the end of the twentieth century (Ditsky).

Works Cited

Ariki, Kyoko. "From 'Flight' to *The Pearl*: A Thematic Study." *Steinbeck Review*, vol. 1, no. 1, 2006, pp. 85–95. *Project MUSE*, muse.jhu.edu/article/218342. doi:10.1353/str.2007.0002.

Astro, Richard. *John Steinbeck and Edward F. Ricketts: The Shaping of a Novelist.* U of Minnesota P, 1973.

_____. "Steinbeck's Post-War Trilogy: A Return to Nature and the Natural Man." *Twentieth Century Literature*, vol. 16, no. 2, 1970, pp. 109–22. *JSTOR*, www.jstor.org/stable/440865.

Astro, Richard, and Tetsumaro Hayashi, editors. *Steinbeck: The Man and His Work, Proceedings of the 1970 Steinbeck Conference Sponsored by Oregon State and Ball State Universities.* Oregon State U P, 1971.

Augenbraum, Harold. "Translating Steinbeck." *The Steinbeck Review*, vol. 14, no. 1, 2017, pp. 52–64. *JSTOR*, www.jstor.org/stable/10.5325/steinbeckreview.14.1.0052.

Baker, Carlos. "Steinbeck at the Top of His Form." Review of *The Pearl*, by John Steinbeck. *The New York Times*, 30 Nov. 1947, p. BR4. www.nytimes.com/1947/11/30/archives/steinbeck-at-the-top-of-his-form-the-pearl-by-john-steinbeck-with.html.

Benson, Jackson J., editor. *The Short Novels of John Steinbeck: Critical Essays with a Checklist to Steinbeck Criticism.* Duke U P, 1990.

_____. *The True Adventures of John Steinbeck, Writer: A Biography.* Viking, 1984.

"Briefly Noted." Review of *The Pearl*. *The New Yorker*, vol. 27, Dec. 1947, 59.

Burkhead, Cynthia. *Student Companion to John Steinbeck.* Greenwood P, 2002.

Caswell, Roger. "A Musical Journey Through John Steinbeck's *The Pearl*: Emotion, Engagement, and Comprehension." *Journal of Adolescent and Adult Literacy*, vol. 49, no. 1, 2005, pp. 62–67. Wiley Online Library. International Literary Association. ila.onlinelibrary.wiley.com/doi/pdf/10.1598/JAAL.49.1.7. doi:10.1598/JAAL.49.1.7.

Center for Steinbeck Studies, and Project MUSE. *The Steinbeck Review.* Scarecrow P, 2004. JSTOR. jstor.org/journal/steinbeckreview.

"Counterfeit Jewel." Review of The Pearl. Time, 22 Dec. 1947, p. 92.

Cox, Martha Heasley. "The Pearl." *Study Guide to Steinbeck: A Handbook to His Major Work*, edited by Tetsumaro Hayashi, Scarecrow P, 1974.

DeMott, Robert J. *Steinbeck's Reading: A Catalogue of Books Owned and Borrowed.* Garland, 1984.

Ditsky, John. *John Steinbeck and the Critics.* Camden House, 2000.

Farrelly, John. "Fiction Parade." Review of *The Pearl. New Republic,* vol. 117, 22 Dec. 1947, p. 28.

Fontenrose, Joseph Eddy. *John Steinbeck: An Introduction and Interpretation.* Holt, Rinehart and Winston, 1963.

French, Warren. *John Steinbeck.* Twayne, 1961.

Geismar, Maxwell. "Fable Retold." Review of *The Pearl. Saturday Review,* vol. 30, 22 Nov. 1947, pp. 14–15. www.unz.com/print/SaturdayReview-1947nov22-00014a02/.

George, Stephen K. "A Taoist Interpretation of John Steinbeck's *The Pearl.*" *The Steinbeck Review*, vol. 1, no. 1, 2004, pp. 90–105. *JSTOR*, www.jstor.org/stable/41581951.

Gladstein, Mimi. "Fish Stories: Santiago and Kino in Text and Film." *The Steinbeck Review*, vol. 6, no. 2, 2009, pp. 10–21. *JSTOR*, www.jstor.org/stable/41582112.

Hamby, James A. "Steinbeck's *The Pearl*: Tradition and Innovation." *Western Review: A Journal of the Humanities*, vol. 7, no. 2, 1970, p. 65.

Hayashi, Tetsumaro. "The Pearl as the Novel of Disengagement." *Steinbeck Quarterly,* vol. 7, nos. 3–4, 1974, pp. 84–88.

Hayashi, Tetsumaro, editor. *A New Study Guide to Steinbeck's Major Works, with Critical Explications.* Scarecrow P, 1993.

_____. *Steinbeck's Literary Dimension: A Guide to Comparative Studies.* Scarecrow P, 1973.

Kalb, Bernard. "Trade Winds." *Saturday Review,* vol. 36, 27 Feb. 1954, p. 8.

Karsten, Ernest E. "Thematic Structure in *The Pearl.*" *The English Journal,* vol. 54, no. 1, 1965, pp. 1–7. *JSTOR,* www.jstor.org/stable/810934.

Kingery, Robert E. Review of *The Pearl. Library Journal,* vol. 72, 1 Nov. 1947, p. 1540.

Krause, Sidney J. "*The Pearl* and 'Hadleyburg': From Desire to Renunciation." *Steinbeck Quarterly,* 7, no. 1, pp. 3–17. Ball State University. dmr.bsu.edu/digital/collection/steinbeck/id/3460/rec/24.

Levant, Howard. *The Novels of John Steinbeck.* U of Missouri P, 1974.

Lieber, Todd M. "Talismanic Patterns in the Novels of John Steinbeck." *American Literature,* vol. 44, no. 2, 1972, pp. 262–75. *JSTOR,* www. jstor.org/stable/2924509.

Lisca, Peter. *The Wide World of Steinbeck.* Rutgers U P, 1958.

Metzger, Charles R. "Steinbeck's *The Pearl* as a Nonteleological Parable of Hope." *Research Studies,* vol. 46, 1978, pp. 98–105.

Meyer, Michael. "Diamond in the Rough: Steinbeck's Multifaceted Pearl." *Steinbeck Review,* vol. 2, no. 2, 2005, pp. 42–56. *JSTOR,* www.jstor. org/stable/41581982.

_____. "Wavering Shadows: A New Jungian Perspective in Steinbeck's *The Pearl.*" *Steinbeck Review,* vol. 1, no. 1, 2004, pp. 132–45. *JSTOR,* www.jstor.org/stable/41581954.

Moore, Harry Thornton. *The Novels of John Steinbeck: A First Critical Study.* Normandie House, 1939.

Morris, Harry. "'The Pearl': Realism and Allegory." *The English Journal,* vol. 52, no. 7, 1963, pp. 487–505. *JSTOR,* www.jstor.org/ stable/810771.

Nakayama, Kiyoshi. *The Pearl* in the *Sea of Cortez:* Steinbeck's Use of Environment. *Steinbeck and the Environment: Interdisciplinary Approaches,* edited by Susan F. Beegel et al., U of Alabama P, 1997, pp. 194–208. ebookcentral.proquest.com/lib/cornell/detail. action?docID=438121.

"New Novels." Review of *The Pearl. New Statesmen and Nation,* vol. 36, 6 Nov. 1948, 400–01.

Owens, Louis. *John Steinbeck's Re-vision of America.* U of Georgia P, 1985.

Parini, Jay. *John Steinbeck: A Biography*. Henry Holt, 1995.

Prescott, Orville. Review of *The Pearl,* by John Steinbeck. *New York Times*, 24 Nov. 1947, p. 21.

Reissman, Rose C. "'News Links' to Literature: Bridging the Gap between Literature and the News." *The English Journal*, vol. 83, no. 1, 1994, pp. 57–58. *JSTOR*, www.jstor.org/stable/820959.

Review of *The Pearl*. *Booklist,* 15 Dec. 1947, p. 152.

Sams, Edward Boyer. "The Haunted Tree: Two Versions of John Steinbeck's *The Pearl*." *The Steinbeck Review*, vol. 11, no. 2, 2014, pp. 189–96. *JSTOR*, www.jstor.org/stable/10.5325/steinbeckreview.11.2.0189.

Smith, Stevie. "Short Stories." Review of *The Pearl*. *Spectator*, vol. 181, 20 Oct. 1948, p. 570.

Steinbeck, John. *Journal of a Novel: The East of Eden Letters*. New York: Viking P, 1969.

_____. *The Pearl*. 1947. Penguin, 1992.

Steinbeck, John, and Edward F. Ricketts. *Sea of Cortez: A Leisurely Journal of Travel and Research, with a Specific Appendix Comprising Materials for a Source Book on the Marine Animals of the Panamic Faunal Province*. Viking, 1941.

Steinbeck Quarterly. Ball State University Digital Media Repository, dmr.bsu.edu/digital/collection/steinbeck.

Sugrue, Thomas. "Steinbeck's Mexican Folk-Tale." Review of *The Pearl*. *The New York Herald Tribune Weekly Book Review,* 24, Dec. 1947, p. 4.

Timmerman, John H. "The Shadow and the Pearl: Jungian Patterns in *The Pearl*." Benson, *Short Novels,* pp. 143–160.

Wagner-Martin, Linda. *Steinbeck: A Literary Life*. Palgrave Macmillan, 2017.

Warfield, Adrienne A. "Steinbeck and the Tragedy of Progress." *A Political Companion to John Steinbeck*, edited by Cyrus Ernesto Zirakzadeh and Simon Stow, U P of Kentucky, 2013, pp. 98–116.

Weeks, Edward. Review of *The Pearl,* by John Steinbeck. *Atlantic Monthly*, Dec. 1947, p. 138.

"So That One Beautified the Other": An Ecocritical Perspective on Character and Place in John Steinbeck's *The Pearl*_____

Kyler Campbell

Early in Steinbeck's novella *The Pearl*, the protagonist Kino finds himself in a position of immense privilege. In his brush house, squatting next to his wife and surrounded by his neighbors, he holds in his hand the largest pearl ever found in the waters off the coast of La Paz (23). As he ponders his once hidden treasure and the opportunities (or disasters) that it may bring him, he hears the ringing melody of the song of the pearl and the song of the family blending together "so that one beautified the other" (24). At this moment in his story, Kino recognizes that two seemingly unconnected ideals have been married together into something much more awe-inspiring and life changing, something that he knew would change the rules of his life and give him a deeper understanding of the world around him.

In a similar way to Kino, the reader is sitting over Steinbeck's hidden treasure of a novella and is presented with two striking literary elements. While these two pieces may seem unconnected at first glance, they are so intrinsically woven together that they exist, much as Kino's song of the pearl and the family, in harmony, complimenting each other and revealing new depths of literary merit together. And while there is a well-rounded critical discussion of *The Pearl*, there is some territory that lies uncharted and ready to beautify our understanding of Kino and the characters surrounding him. That discussion is concerned with Steinbeck's blending of place and character within his novella, and it is guided by the burgeoning field of ecocriticism.

Ecocriticism is concerned with the representation of the natural world within literature. It essentially represents the intersection of character and place, noting how these elements can serve to complement or beautify one another. By considering the juxtaposition of key literary elements in *The Pearl*, readers can reap the benefits of a strong union that looks at character, plot, and, most importantly, setting not as separate entities, but as interconnected threads spinning new revelations along a well-trodden path.

The Ecocritical Perspective

But before diving into the nuances of Steinbeck's novella, the principles of ecocriticism should be established clearly, and readers should be familiar with the values it seeks to uncover within any given text. The foundation of these principles is simply how the natural elements are presented within the story and what sort of detail the author places into those elements. Scott Russell Sanders argues that ecocritical perspective starts with the "acknowledgment of a nonhuman context" (183) with the eventual goal, according to Buell, being that of charting the "kinship between nonhuman and human" (182). This allows the reader to analyze character actions, as one would normally do in a more straightforward character analysis, and it also gives the reader the opportunity to experience the text as a complete piece of literature, by incorporating how setting affects those actions.

The first order is to dispel a common presupposition: The setting of a literary work is merely a backdrop for the primary action. Instead, ecocriticism recognizes that the natural world is "the energizing medium from which human lives emerge and by which those lives are bounded and measured" (Sanders 183). This idea of setting as secondary or even tertiary is something that would not be considered to be true in the everyday world (a child growing up in rural West Virginia is undoubtedly shaped by that environment as much as one growing up in southside Chicago). Therefore, why should this be true in good fiction? Neil Evernden argues that true art makes the natural world "personal—known, loved, feared, or whatever, but *not neutral*" (100), meaning it cannot serve as *just* a setting. In transformative art, the environment itself becomes a character. In the case of *The Pearl,* this most often shows up in the way that Steinbeck describes the environment. For example, as Kino, Juana, and Coyotito begin their trek through the mountains in order to escape the trackers, the reader should note that the wind "pelted them with bits of sticks, sand, and little rocks" and that they walk underneath stars sitting "cold in a black sky" (68). The environment in this scene is a projection of the characters internal struggle, the world against them, on their journey into unknown entirely alone. The setting here is not just a backdrop but a dynamic piece of the larger story. Just as in our own world, the characters in any well-developed piece of literature are seen as "individual-in-context, individual as a component of place, defined by place" (Evernden 103). And so, it becomes clear to us as readers that setting is not merely setting; it is a defining principle of characterization.

Once it is established that characters are defined by place, the reader can now pay attention to how the characters interact with their environment. There are two distinct methods to this interaction: commoditization and harmonization. For example, if a character seeks to bend nature to her will, her perspective is to commoditize nature, creating a relationship in which "literally everything, is one way or another answerable to human need" (Phillips 218). However, the opposite perspective is what Evernden describes as a "subtle diffusion" (97) into the environment. This occurs when characters find themselves not seeking to dominate nature but viewing themselves as another integral part of the ecosystem. It is the difference between a hierarchy over the environment and a relationship with the environment based on mutual respect. Ecocriticism would argue that this sort of character seeks to harmonize with nature. In the novella, this is present in Juana's homemade poultice for Coyotito's wound, made from seaweed (15). This remedy is based on the natural elements within the characters' environment and demonstrates her deep knowledge of her surroundings and a sort of harmony with them. While these two perspectives are opposite ends of a dramatic spectrum, they can be used to demonstrate a shift in character attitudes or beliefs (as will be seen later).

Beyond these basic principles, ecocriticism is largely undefined territory. There are a few terms that exist as part of an agreed upon lexicon, and those will be discussed a bit later as they become relevant to the analysis. However, to get a "lay of the land" as it were, the discussion must move right into Kino's journey within the novella.

The Myth of the Pastoral

In the opening scene of *The Pearl,* Steinbeck presents the reader with a pristine and idealistic beach landscape. The ecocritical perspective designates this type of landscape as pastoral, or untouched. While most readers may be familiar with the general idea of pastoral landscapes, Ecocriticism focuses more heavily on the pastoral's impact on character development.[1]

The idea of a pastoral landscape is rooted in the migrations that founded the United States. Settlers in urbanized landscapes across Europe dreamed of an escape from the crowded civilizations and a return to a "more 'natural' state of existence" (Buell 31). Hence, the pastoral idea of the American landscape is a common theme in early American literature and often serves as a starting point for an ecocritical discussion of a balance between man and his natural environment. But the pastoral landscape is more complex than that. It was the early colonizers who, when they arrived on the shores of the new world, found that nature is not always so nurturing. Buell argues that "there is always the chance that the [pastoral] text will tempt the reader to see all sugar and no pill" (41–42). This is to say that the pastoral landscape is often a veneer of simplicity, a thin veil created by idealistic interpretations of man's relationship with the landscape[2]. He believes himself to be the master of his domain or, on the other side of the argument, a child seeking a "return to the primal warmth of womb or breast in a feminine landscape" (Kolodny 173). However, both of these assumptions are often misguided and dangerous. As he is first presented in the novella, Kino is entranced by this very idea, the pastoral beauty of his home and the world he inhabits.

In the opening pages of *The Pearl*, Steinbeck sets a stage that is, in a word, orderly. Kino is surrounded by a world built on a certain structure. The sun is rising on time, the pigs and the birds are going about their normal business, and everything seems to move in a predictable fashion (3). Kino even goes so far as to refer to the scene as "very good," emulating God's succinct summary of creation in the book of Genesis (1). Nature even seeks Kino's approval and comfort within the first few pages as well in the form of a goat who "sniffed at him," and the moth that "blustered in to find the fire" (2). These images are all indicative of a landscape that seeks out Kino for needs that the natural elements do not provide. He is the source of comfort and warmth, the bringer of fire, and the center of all action and curiosity in this world.

However, it is only a few lines later that Steinbeck sends the pastoral ideals of Kino's home into a tailspin. In the midst of these creatures who flock to Kino for recognition or comfort of some kind, Kino watches with "the detachment of God while a dusty ant [tries] to escape the sand trap an ant lion had dug for him" (3). Barclay Bates suggests that Kino is ignorant to "the natural events which make dear his standing in the cosmos as they foreshadow his fate" (42). In this the reader finds an ecocritical essential: the merging of literary device and environmental representation. Natural elements become foreshadowing of Kino's eventual fall into the trap of greed or materialism. In this way Steinbeck demonstrates a commitment to "reanimating and redirecting the reader's transactions with nature" (Buell 97), not merely relegating the natural elements to backdrops or set pieces, but using them to affect strong literary ties to character and destiny. In this scene, the reader is presented with a dispelling of the pastoral myth. While the landscape appears to value Kino's place in its order, it also predicts and parallels his eventual fall from status and grace, indicating that his environment is neither for him nor against him. It is governed by rules and systems set in place that are beyond his control, much like the culture with which he finds himself in conflict later in the novella.

The other trap of the pastoral mindset lies in applications of moral values to natural elements. For example, humans tend to regard certain animals or insects as good or bad depending on their level of threat to our survival. Within the first chapter of *The Pearl,* the reader can clearly see that Kino himself has applied moral principles to natural elements. As the scorpion makes its way toward his son, Kino finds himself off guard and "a new song [has] come, the Song of Evil" (5). While this is a natural response for a man who is charged with protecting his family, it is rather unnatural in the sense of Kino's place in his environment. He has been lulled into a false sense of security by his pastoral home and has tricked himself into believing that this landscape contains elements of good and evil, when in reality, the elements themselves are only natural. But Kino's view, and our own as the readers, on the pastoral prevents us from predicting a common situation, that is when "man's nurturing environment threatens to stop nurturing and to start killing" (Fromm 34).

In the sense of morality, the scorpion is no more evil than the "little splash of morning waves on the beach" can be morally justified as "very good" (Steinbeck 1). They are both part of the same environment and therefore only behave in a manner fitting their design. The only reason Kino classifies some natural elements as "good" is because they are not seeking to harm him. The scorpion in the story is not an agent of darkness, but merely an animal that strikes out of fear or self-defense. However, its actions are physically harmful to Kino and his family, and so he hears the Song of the Enemy in his fit of rage (6).

Because of this tragedy, readers are tempted to view Kino as a victim of evil or bad luck. In actuality, he is not a victim at all, but is subject to the idealness and terror of his own environment. It is merely his perspective that affects his moral judgment on the environmental factors around him.

Urban Complexity

The second of Steinbeck's major environments is one that is wholly unnatural, that is the town of La Paz. While it may seem counterintuitive to look to a manmade civilization through the view of ecocriticism, the reality is that "civilized" structures often provide a deeper analysis of the cultures they emanate from, more specifically in their treatment and views on the natural world around them. Evernden highlights the core conflict between man and nature, which is when the former seeks "only the consumption of landscape as a commodity" (102). Cultures who often accept this viewpoint see themselves (and their social and moral ideals) as the center of existence; they operate as if their own needs or wants are of primary concern rather than considering themselves as part of a larger ecosphere that requires balance and harmony. Because of this mindset, cultures will often distance themselves from the natural world, favoring the manufactured existence over the "horror and revulsion" of the wilderness that surrounds them (Sanders 184).

In fact, it is the lack of natural elements within the town of La Paz that brings the ecocritical perspective into focus. Instead of waves lapping at the shore and stars gleaming in the dawn light (as in Kino's home on the beach), Steinbeck describes a "town of stone and plaster" (21), a stark contrast to the pastoral richness of Kino's beach home. Also referenced are the city's "harsh outer walls" and "inner cool gardens" as Kino and his family make their way to see the doctor (8). As mentioned previously, a hallmark of the ecocritical approach lies in noticing and excavating the conflict between man and his environment. In this case, the depiction of the city's walls and gardens plays a key role in demonstrating the town's desire for control and power over their environment. Karsten suggests that "they corroborate the picture of the town as protective and withdrawn from life and nature and suggest that the people are almost as lifeless and unnatural as their gardens" (3). The people become "unnatural" in that they have separated themselves from their natural environment in order to create their own manufactured "ecosystems" (for example, the Priest's self-interested brand of religion, the Doctor's destructive habits, and Pearl Buyers' economic monopoly).

These "ecosystems" have been twisted so that they do not promote balance like the natural ones, but a strong desire for control. Unlike the natural order seen in Kino's pastoral home, where elements deemed both "evil" and "good" occur outside of Kino's control, the Priest's false piety is unnatural and manufactured in order to benefit himself and his own interests (Steinbeck 21). The Doctor poisons Coyotito not out of self-defense (like the scorpion in the beginning), but out of greed. In the same way, the pearl buyers' game of low ball offers for Kino's massive treasure is the result of a manufactured monopoly designed not out of some ecological drive, but out of a desire for economic control and perhaps even cruelty. The initial buyer's slip of the hand when handling his coin underneath the desk is evidence of that very act of hiding and creating artificial dramatizations to maintain their own illusion (49). Because of their separation from the natural balance of nature, the core principles of the town now encourage commoditization of resources and promote values of artificiality and deceit.

In discussing the extent of their desire for control, the townspeople's decision to pen in the natural world and harness its beauty and utility for their own enjoyment is the simplest kind of colonial metaphor. However, it does not become less important when discussing the moral complexities that Kino finds himself the victim of throughout his journey. Karsten writes again that if these ecological boundaries are suggestive of the town's view on human relationships, then readers must call their normalcy into question (3), meaning that the townspeople's understanding of social orders is directly represented by those "harsh outer walls" and "caged birds" (Steinbeck 8). As demonstrated by the Doctor, the town's chief value is self-interest; therefore, whatever is outside of the self, is of no value, which in the case of the novella, would include Kino and his people.

For the Doctor, the indigenous peoples are a part of the natural world that the town has walled itself away from. Kino's "own brown skin" is even a product of a communal relationship with nature, a higher dose of melanin to protect his tribe from their long days in the sun (83). This is contrasted heavily with the doctor's features, the "puffy little hammocks" in which his eyes rest and his voice that had grown "hoarse with the fat that pressed on his throat" (10). These traits point the reader to a man not in commune with the natural world, but a manufactured world with the goal of providing escape from any natural dangers or labor. This, in turn, emphasizes a harsh dynamic between the two people groups of the town: the indigenous people rugged and in tune with natural rhythms of the sun and tide against the Doctor's civilization walled off against any outside interference and existing to serve their own pleasure.

However, when the artificial "ecosystem" set up within the culture of La Paz is threatened with imbalance, it reacts to correct the problem, namely Kino's refusal to sell the pearl to the Pearl Buyers. Juan Tomás remarks that he, Kino, and everyone they know "are cheated from birth to the overcharge of [their] coffins," and in the midst of that system, Kino has gone against "the whole structure, the whole way of life" (54). In doing so, Kino has upset the status quo of the town's desire for control over those outside its boundaries and imbalanced the structure of their lives. It is because of this very action that he is forced to flee with his family away from the only home he has known.

Regression in the Natural Order

Steinbeck's third unique landscape is the most foreign to the protagonist and the one that seems most at odds with Kino's well-being. Far from the sheltering pastoral landscape of his home, Kino finds himself, along with Juana and Coyotito, being pursued into a "dry creaking" sort of landscape, marked by "naked granite mountains, rising out of erosion rubble and standing monolithic against the sky" (76). The craggy landscape of the final act proves to be an antithesis to the opening beach scene in that the illusion of the comfort and provision of the pastoral ideal has been completely dismantled. And in its place, is the full capability of the natural environment: a catalyst that forces an individual to adapt their methods and morality in order to ensure their own survival.

The clearest depiction of this capability is that of the "lean little spring" that feeds into "the little pools" near the bottom of the mountain range (79). These pools are presented in two seemingly paradoxical ways. Here Steinbeck shows the duality of nature, providing the opportunity for refreshment and at the same time leaving the probability for calamity and death. The pools are home to all manner of life, a place where all local things "come to drink and to hunt" (80). The land provides life-giving nourishment but does not seek to shelter its inhabitants from dangers that may befall them, Kino and Juana included. The watering holes are at the same time "places of life" and "places of killing" (79). A far cry from the pastoral beach, Kino finds himself in an environment that is indifferent to his survival, and seeks only natural balance. It does not find him to be the center of interest or comfort (as his beach home did) but provides opportunity for him to adapt his standards of behavior in order to survive. And as he traverses the land, attempting to evade his own predators (the trackers pursuing him and his family through the mountains), this instinct begins to seep into Kino's behavior and perspective, making him perhaps more beast-like than he thought possible.

Throughout the novella, Steinbeck chooses to connect Kino and his people to the natural order of things around them, chiefly the animal order. When refusing to treat his son, the doctor remarks that he is "a doctor—not a veterinary" (11). In addition, there are many references of Kino snarling, baring his teeth, or even hissing like a snake (5, 51, 59). These inclusions would suggest, as Harry Morris argues, that "Kino is identified symbolically with low animal orders: he must rise early and he must root in the earth for sustenance" (490). And this is not just at the end of his journey but throughout. However, it can be argued that Kino begins the novella at the height of his humanity. It is only after he finds the pearl that he slips down the natural order, becoming more animal-like and losing that which makes him distinctly human.

Arguably, Kino's state in his pastoral home is the peak of his humanity. In the opening pages, the reader finds a man who is entranced by the pleasant and comforting rhythm of the Song of the Family, "clear and soft" (2) in his ears. He is contented and enamored with his life, not consumed by the visions of misleading possibilities and false futures he later finds in the pearl (24–25). In this way it is Kino's contentment that sets him above the "low animal orders" who exist without any sense of higher purpose, only living for "sustenance" (Morris 490). This contentment extends to his environment as well. Early on he watches without interfering as a "dusty ant frantically [tries] to escape the sand trap an ant lion had dug for him" (3). Kino recognizes the order of his ecosystem and does not try to save the ant or interfere in this natural process.

This is directly contrasted later on when, by his placing his foot in the path of the marching ants (70), he asserts his own need for control and dominance. In this scene, Kino no longer feels the "detachment of God" (3) when looking over the insects in front of him. Instead, Kino "put his foot in their path" (70). Kino's intervention in the natural state of things, when compared to his earlier observation of a more brutal natural process, is indicative of his changing nature. In this moment, his pride awakens in him the need to assert his dominance over the natural world. Kino then watches helplessly as the "column climb[s] over his instep and continue[s] on its way" (70). Kino's interference is a manifestation of his newfound survival instinct. Just as when he first spots the scorpion climbing down Coyotito's crib and leaps into action, he moves from contented and balanced to predatory and willful. The stark difference between the two is motivation. He acts against the scorpion in order to save his son, however, he interferes with the ants' marching out of his own need for control and dominance. Much like the inhabitants of La Paz with their walls and gardens, he now sees himself as dominant over the natural processes. This is the interruption of the natural order, and he now starts on the path to losing what was once his higher place within his ecosystem. At this moment, he begins his final transformation.

As the novella progresses, Kino's contentment clearly breaks down and becomes replaced by a man-made paranoia. His time in the city begins to degrade his psyche as he is latched onto by the "evil limbs of greed and hatred and coldness" (43). However, it is the way Steinbeck weaves together natural elements in his descriptions of Kino that indicate the protagonist's shift from humanity into the animal kingdom. Arguably, it is the environment in which he finds himself that perpetuates this change in him. The brutality of the mountainous terrain brings out the animal instincts within Kino. Before attacking the group of trackers, Kino removes his clothes as they "would show up against the dark night" and realizes that "his own skin [is] a better protection for him" (83). This act of camouflage is reminiscent of some wild predator utilizing his own natural coloring to blend in with his environment in order to take down his prey. His Song of the Family, once clear and soft (2), is now "fierce and sharp and feline as the snarl of a female puma" (84). As he stalks through the craggy landscape he finds himself as a predator, once prey to the control of the town's own manufactured ecosystem and the will of the trackers on his trail, but now on the hunt.

Combined with the rise in aggression and brutality throughout the novella, most notably his attacking Juana (59), the change within his character becomes evident: an evolutionary regression from contented man into instinctual predator. However, once his assault begins, Steinbeck's descriptions of Kino's actions change, shifting from animalistic to something else entirely. As he leaps into action, dispatching the trackers one by one, Kino is described as "a terrible machine," his movements and actions "cold and deadly as steel" (86, 87). This sort of language does not fit within previous descriptions that evoke associations of the natural world. Kino has, in this passage, become something unnatural, a machine that moves from victim to victim with efficiency and poise, situated to enact its will without remorse or hesitation.

This is Kino's arc: a metaphysical transformation down the natural order of things from contented father and husband to predator, and finally to a sort of murder machine. Among the natural order of ecosystems, machines are wholly unnatural. In fact, they tend to regularly disrupt the order of ecological existence. Here Kino's journey is completed. He is no longer part of the natural order in which he once found himself. He is something outside of naturalness, not driven by the morality of a man or the instincts of an animal, but by the programming of a machine. And this programming is only broken by the horrific outcome to his story. He is fully mechanical until he hears "the cry of death" (87), snapping him back into his humanity and out of his murderous machinations. The death of his only son breaks the unnatural order he finds himself a part of, careening him back into a natural existence, and he once again regains his place in the world he has always inhabited.

And what has brought him to this transformation? His love for the pearl and his desire to protect the false futures it promises him inspire his rampage. However, the physical environment is also evidence of this process. It is within this environment, one that encourages such a strong predatory instinct within its inhabitants, that Kino begins to assimilate those same traits. His arc is not merely the rise and fall of a tragic hero who cannot recognize that it is "his pride that brings him disaster" (Bates 43), but a man who gives up his humanity and becomes wholly unnatural, an anomaly that exists outside of the natural order that he once looked upon with detachment and contentment.

His Misfortune and His Life

In a moving scene of dialogue to his brother, Kino refers to the pearl as "my misfortune and my life" (66). Having trekked through the uncharted territory of this ecocritical approach, this statement becomes all the more poignant to Kino's story. While a traditional literary character analysis does give the reader an idea of the truth in that statement, by looking at Kino's journey through this ecocritical lens, his transformation becomes infinitely more harrowing and saddening. His pain is intensified, and his fall from grace hits the reader a bit harder. While there is value in the "immense knowledge that he has gained about good and evil" (Morris 494), the ecocritical perspective shows the metaphysical depths Kino has plumbed in order to gain that knowledge. The reader sees a father and husband, once contented with his meager existence, become a man consumed with a desire for control who slips down and out of the natural order. This merging together of place and character shows us an important truth about an important work of American fiction: *The Pearl* is not merely a story of misfortune and hard lessons learned; it is a tale about the deepest truths of our humanity and our willingness to trade that humanity for the chance at a better life.

Notes

1. While the definition of a "pastoral landscape" is ever evolving, the simplest form of the idea is that of a rural land that evokes simplicity and openness, specifically appealing to urbanites who may be fed up with their own surroundings.

2. The term "man" in this context refers to humanity as a whole, not necessarily one specific gender.

Works Cited

Bates, Barclay W., and Redlands California Association of Teachers of English. "*The Pearl* as Tragedy." *California English Journal*, vol. 6, no. 1, 1970, pp. 41–45. Institute of Education Sciences. files.eric. ed.gov/fulltext/ED039246.pdf.

Buell, Lawrence. *The Environmental Imagination: Thoreau, Nature Writing, and the Formation of American Culture*. Belknap P of Harvard U P, 1996.

Evernden, Neil. "Beyond Ecology: Self, Place, and the Pathetic Fallacy." *The Ecocriticism Reader: Landmarks in Literary Ecology*, edited by Cheryl Glotfelty and Harold Fromm, U of Georgia P, 1996, pp. 92–104.

Fromm, Harold. "From Transcendence to Obsolescence: A Route Map." *The Ecocriticism Reader: Landmarks in Literary Ecology*, edited by Cheryl Glotfelty and Harold Fromm, U of Georgia P, 1996, pp. 30–39.

Howarth, William. "Some Principles of Ecocriticism." *The Ecocriticism Reader: Landmarks in Literary Ecology*, edited by Cheryl Glotfelty and Harold Fromm, U of Georgia P, 1996, pp. 69–91.

Karsten, Jr. Ernest E. "Thematic Structure in *The Pearl*." *The English Journal*, vol. 54, no. 1, 1965, pp. 1–7. *JSTOR*, www.jstor.org/ stable/810934.

Kolodny, Annette. "Unearthing Herstory: An Introduction." *The Ecocriticism Reader: Landmarks in Literary Ecology*, edited by Cheryl Glotfelty and Harold Fromm, U of Georgia P, 1996, pp. 170–181.

Morris, Harry. "*The Pearl*: Realism and Allegory." *The English Journal*, vol. 52, no. 7, 1963, pp. 487–505. *JSTOR*, www.jstor.org/ stable/810771.

Phillips, Dana. "Is Nature Necessary?" *The Ecocriticism Reader: Landmarks in Literary Ecology*, edited by Cheryl Glotfelty and Harold Fromm, U of Georgia P, 1996, pp. 204–222.

Sanders, Scott Russell. "Speaking a Word for Nature." *The Ecocriticism Reader: Landmarks in Literary Ecology*, edited by Cheryl Glotfelty and Harold Fromm, U of Georgia P, 1996, pp. 182–195.

Steinbeck, John. *The Pearl*. 1947. Penguin, 1992.

Pearls, Marlin, and Small Tragedies: Steinbeck's *The Pearl* and Hemingway's *The Old Man and the Sea*

James Plath

Few texts invite comparison as much as John Steinbeck's *The Pearl* (1947) and Ernest Hemingway's *The Old Man and the Sea* (1952). Both are postwar novellas that remain widely taught in secondary schools because of their brevity and simply written, yet richly textured parable-like narratives; both are lyrical stories that revolve around poor fishermen who work out of small villages just south of the United States (in Steinbeck's Mexico and Hemingway's Cuba); both were first published in popular magazines of the day ("The Pearl of the World" in the December 1945 *Woman's Home Companion,* and "The Old Man and the Sea" in the September 1, 1952 *Life*); both were "comeback" books, following, as they did, in the wake of Steinbeck's disappointing *Cannery Row* and *The Wayward Bus* and Hemingway's heavily mocked *Across the River and Into the Trees*; both were expansions of brief stories the author had heard years earlier; and each is the product of a writer who would go on to win the Nobel Prize (Hemingway in 1953, and Steinbeck in 1962).

When *The Old Man and the Sea* was first published, Steinbeck wrote a friend, "Just read Hemingway's new book. A very fine performance. I am so glad. The obscene joy with which people trampled him on the last one was disgusting. Now they are falling too far the other way almost in shame" (Steinbeck *Letters* 429). That combination of profuse admiration and slight resentment had been a part of Steinbeck's response to Hemingway ever since he first read "The Killers" the summer of 1929 at his wife Carol's request. Hemingway was "the finest writer alive" he declared then, at the same time vowing never to read him again (Benson 156). Yet, as biographer Jay Parini notes, Steinbeck was consciously influenced by Hemingway, having realized that the flowery writing of his first novel, *Cup of Gold* (1929), was not just about the past—it *was* the past, and Hemingway's spare style of writing was the future. "What he hoped to write from now on was lean, muscular prose—not a copy of Hemingway's style, exactly, but his own equivalent," Parini explains (86).

A decade later, Steinbeck would still find much to admire in Hemingway's writing, even if he was scornful of his rival's pursuit of headlines and celebrity (Benson 547). He was impressed enough by Hemingway's Spanish Civil War story "The Butterfly and the Tank" to write Hemingway that it was "one of a very few finest stories in all time" (Baker 337). That, in turn, led to the authors' first meeting—though biographers can't agree on which of the writers' mutual friends should get the credit (or blame) for bringing them together. It happened the spring of 1944 at Tim Costello's famed New York City restaurant, with Steinbeck and Hemingway part of a larger group that included Costello, wartime photojournalist Robert Capa, and writers John O'Hara, John Hersey, and Vincent Sheean. According to one witness, some of the men were standing at the bar and O'Hara was "proudly showing Hemingway his walking stick, a gift from Steinbeck, which was a blackthorn that had been handed down from his grandfather" (Benson 548). Hemingway doubted that it was blackthorn and bet him fifty dollars that he could prove it by breaking it over his own head. O'Hara took the bet, but when Hemingway destroyed it "O'Hara was mortified, while Steinbeck, who had withdrawn into himself for most of the evening, looked on and thought the whole thing was unnecessarily cruel and stupid" (Benson 548). "After that evening," Benson reports, "Hemingway seemed to stick in his craw, and he worked up an enormous hostility toward the man and his work, which he maintained for several years, a competitive hostility that one would think more typical of Hemingway than of Steinbeck" (548).

Hemingway, meanwhile, was ever conscious of his literary rivals and well aware of Steinbeck and his oft-chosen form of the small book. In fact, when Hemingway wrote his editor, Max Perkins, in 1938 about a new collection that was taking shape, he argued that there is "enough new stuff in the book to make a book a good deal longer than *Of Mice and Men*, say" (*Selected Letters*

474). Less than two years later he used Steinbeck as a benchmark again when he wrote of his Spanish Civil War novel *For Whom the Bell Tolls*, "There is a chance the Book of the Month will take the book. If they do, they will print a hundred thousand and Scribner's a hundred thousand and we will be off in a cloud of Steinbecks" (*Selected Letters* 511). Ever conscious of Steinbeck's popular appeal and commercial success, Hemingway was referring to *The Grapes of Wrath*, which had been cited by *The New York Times* as the best-selling book of 1939, with an initial print run of 430,000 copies ("1939 Book Awards" 1).

While Steinbeck admitted to being influenced by Hemingway—even saying, at one point, "I suppose I shall be imitating Hemingway" (Parini 97)—the latter generally steered clear of acknowledging influences. Yet there are enough similarities between *The Old Man and the Sea* and *The Pearl* to suggest that Hemingway may well have had Steinbeck's slender parable in mind as he mounted his own literary comeback with a slender parable of his own. It would not have been the first time that Hemingway, "for whom writing was a competitive sport" (Reynolds 252), would use a rival's book for inspiration. When he had written a draft of *The Sun Also Rises* more than two decades earlier he told F. Scott Fitzgerald in a letter, only half-joking, that he intended it as "a Greater Gatsby" (*Selected Letters* 231). No such letter exists with *The Old Man and the Sea*, but the books were written a few years apart at a time when the authors were acutely aware of each other's work, and their novellas written in parabolic style marked a new direction for both men.

A number of Steinbeck scholars have remarked just how different *The Pearl* was from Steinbeck's previous novels. As Benson summarizes, others before it "reflected closely the personality and the imagination of the man . . . and dealt intimately with many of the people he cared about deeply. . . . *The Pearl*, by contrast, was a work of imagination which had extraordinary distance from its author" (564). Likewise, critics were quick to notice what a departure *The Old Man and the Sea* was from Hemingway's other fictions, which were also heavily autobiographical. With the old fisherman Santiago, Hemingway offered for the first time a hero who wasn't a thinly disguised version of himself or a close friend, as was the case with Jake Barnes (*The Sun Also Rises*), Nick Adams (short stories), Frederic Henry (*A Farewell to Arms*), Harry Morgan (*To Have and Have Not*), Robert Jordan (*For Whom the Bell Tolls*), or Colonel Richard Cantwell (*Across the River and Into the Trees*). For the first time, Hemingway's hero was based more on hearsay, on someone else's experience—a more purely imagined book, as it was with *The Pearl*.

Each novella's mythic-parabolic-folkloric quality is reinforced by the use of an omniscient "communal" narrator. Steinbeck further emphasizes the mythic nature of the work by focusing on the timeless element of fishing for pearls: "For centuries men had dived down and torn the oysters from the beds and ripped them open, looking for the coated grains of sand" (17). That sense of ancient tradition, of near-ritualistic work, is given additional weight by Steinbeck's continued reference to songs: "Kino's people had sung of everything that happened or existed. . . . and the songs were all in Kino and his people" (18). Whether a Song of Family or a Song of Evil (5, 6), they are "songs" that push the reader beyond the more familiar narrative territory of realism. Kino's recognition not only of a "God" but "gods" adds another layer of generational ancientness to the book (18, 17).

With Hemingway, the sense of the mythic or folkloric is created by his biblical evocation of forty days of fishless fishing with the boy, Manolin, and his further use of threes—another number of biblical significance. Santiago's eyes were "the same color as the sea" and his scars were "as old as erosions in a fishless desert" (10)— Hemingway's way of tying his character to a sense of the ancient and timeless. In addition, as one Hemingway scholar summarizes, Santiago's "constant association with the king of ballplayers and the king of beasts adds to the man's heroic proportions" (Gurko 151)—and also contributes to the novella's mythic dimension. As Parini notes of *The Pearl*, "An atmosphere of unreality permeates the story, a mood engendered by the light of the gulf, which flickers on the world as if it were a movie screen. Kino is Everyman, and his journey is the classic hero's journey in search of fortune" (319)—

more elements that add to the sense of the mythic-folkloric. Robert W. Lewis, Jr. sees the same technique at work in Hemingway's story and concludes, "The persistent use of sight-and-light imagery indicates that the strangeness of the old man is in his supernatural sight . . . and his friendship with the light-giving stars, sun, and moon." That deliberately crafted "strangeness" or supernatural element is what helps Hemingway to convey to readers, even without giving notice in an epigraph as Steinbeck had done, that *The Old Man and the Sea* should be read as a parable.

Critics, already conditioned perhaps by Steinbeck's novella, pick up on this, with one calling the novella "a parable about human existence" and noting that the same time Hemingway was writing it he penned two fables for *Holiday* magazine, "The Good Lion" and "The Faithful Bull" (Hays 102). Delbert E. Wylder was one of the earliest scholars to delve deeply into the idea of *The Old Man and the Sea* as fable, pointing out that the "quality of fable is introduced early in the work, not only through the omniscient author's description of the old man, but in the description of the comparative serenity of the man's existence," despite the younger fishermen who laugh at his misfortune (33). Hemingway had not worked in the mythic-parabolic mode before that, he had never created characters that were so instantly sympathetic, and he hadn't injected religion into his fiction to such a degree that fellow novelist and Nobel laureate William Faulkner would remark in his review of *The Old Man and the Sea*, "This time, he discovered God, a Creator. Until now, his men and women had made themselves, shaped themselves out of their own clay; their victories and defeats were at the hands of each other, just to prove to themselves or one another how tough they could be. But this time, he wrote about pity: about something somewhere that made them all . . ." (5).

Hemingway's expansion of his own anecdotal story follows the same narrative strategy Steinbeck used in rewriting the folktale he had heard—not only to make the story more dramatic, but also to make the main character more sympathetic. Although Steinbeck said he "tried to write it as folklore, to give it that set-aside, raised-up feeling that all folk stories have" (*America and Americans* 160), as one biographer notes, "Unlike the characters in most folktales or allegorical stories, Steinbeck's Kino and Juana have distinctive personalities and cannot be simply regarded as stock figures from the classic repertoire of peasant types" (319). Kino is young, hot-headed, and stubbornly conscious of his manhood. "He had said 'I am a man,' and that meant certain things to Juana. It meant that he was half insane and half god. It meant that Kino would drive his strength against a mountain and plunge his strength against the sea" which would "surge while the man drowned in it" (58). Kino also stands out because he seems more sensitive to the "music" of his people than the others. So, too, was Hemingway's fisherman both typical of his folkloric kind and also distinctly individual. Santiago carries himself with the same dignity in poverty that Kino displays, and just as readers are told that the mother of his child "had prayed that they might find a pearl with which to hire the doctor to cure the baby" (16), Santiago offers the same kind of prayers to God—a plea, or bargain—when he is alone in his skiff and desperately in need of his own "pearl." When he finally feels "a light delicate pulling and then a harder pull" on his line, he prays, "God help him to take it" (42).

Steinbeck developed an outline for *The Pearl* during the month of January 1944 while in Mexico working on *Cannery Row* and magazine articles that would pay for his trip (Benson 542). The plot of *The Pearl* was based on a story he had heard many years earlier. In that story, it's an Indian boy who finds "a pearl of great size" and value, but the boy immaturely thinks that the pearl's great wealth will enable him "to marry any one of a number of girls, and to make many more a little happy, too" (qtd. in Parini 318). Arrogantly, the boy even expects the pearl to buy him out of purgatory for whatever mischief he might make as he revels in his fortune. But when he tries to sell it, dealers try to cheat him. After that he's attacked and almost killed by a group of men, which makes him think he was better off without the pearl. So he tosses it back into the sea. (Parini 318). To create a more sympathetic main character, Steinbeck made Kino a young father with a baby boy he hovers over—especially after a scorpion stings the boy and it becomes his quest to find a pearl so big that he can afford the doctor who refused to treat the boy without sufficient payment. Facing a life-or-death situation, Kino's motivation for wanting to find a great pearl is unselfishly parental, while the poverty that keeps him from leading a life that readers might consider "normal," and the dignity with which he carries himself, also make him sympathetic.

The Old Man and the Sea was based on a story Hemingway heard and briefly mentioned in a non-fiction piece published in *Esquire* in 1936. In that story, an old man fishing alone in a skiff hooks into a big marlin and is pulled out to sea. "Two days later the old man was picked up by fishermen sixty miles to the eastward, the head and forward part of the marlin lashed alongside." Sharks had attacked the man who, when rescued, was half out of his mind (Hemingway *By-Line* 239). As Steinbeck did, Hemingway gives the man a boy to focus all his care and attention on for the first third of the book. Readers are told that the "boy," who is old enough now to buy and drink beer, first began going out in Santiago's skiff as his apprentice when he was only five years old. "The old man had taught the boy to fish and the boy loved him" (10). As with Kino, the old man's poverty is entwined with his bad luck—for it can only be called bad luck when someone as skilled and knowledgeable a fisherman as Santiago fails to catch fish. Symbolically, the sail of his skiff was "patched with flour sacks and, furled, it looked like the flag of permanent defeat" (9). But the eighty-four fishless days are not as hard for him to bear as the forty-four days he had to endure without the boy, whose parents made him switch to a luckier boat. "The boy keeps me alive," Santiago laments (106). Structurally, it also gives Santiago someone to talk to in the first fourth of the novella—just as Kino has Juana to talk to in *The Pearl.* Alone in his skiff, Santiago repeatedly talks about how much he misses the boy—so much so that while "it was considered a virtue not to talk unnecessarily at sea and the old man had always considered it so and respected it," he could not keep himself from talking aloud about the boy after he could no longer fish with him (39). Numerous critics have commented on the tender relationship between the old man and the boy he loves like his own son. Though unspoken, it is clear that

Santiago's primary motivation for breaking that bad-luck streak is to get the boy back again.

Steinbeck wrote the drama (screenplay) first for several of his novellas, and he did so again with *The Pearl,* imparting it with a simple but effective three-act structure that's the standard in Hollywood. In Act I (Chapters 1–2)—the "set-up"—readers are introduced to the characters and the problem. Pearl fisherman Kino, whose only valuable possession is a much-repaired canoe inherited from his father and grandfather, must find a pearl so the doctor will treat his baby before the scorpion's poison can work through his little body. Though Kino is part of a community of fishermen who, on that day, had already gone out and were "clustered in the haze, riding over the oyster bed" (16), Steinbeck sets Kino apart from the rest. With Juana also onboard, Kino paddles far from the other fishermen, determined that his skill and knowledge of oysters will lead him to success. Steinbeck gives details that support Kino's skill and knowledge—he moved "cautiously so that the water would not be obscured with mud and sand," and "in his pride and youth and strength, could remain down over two minutes without strain, so that he worked deliberately, selecting the larger shells" (17–18). But Steinbeck also introduces the idea of luck. After the baby is stung, Kino "knew that Juana was making the magic of prayer, her face set rigid and her muscles hard to force the luck, to tear the luck out of the gods' hands" (18). Act I ends with Kino finding a pearl "large as a sea-gull's egg": Flushed with excitement, "He looked past his pearl, and he saw that the swelling was going out of the baby's shoulder, the poison was receding from its body. Then Kino's fist closed over the pearl and his emotion broke over him. He put back his head and howled" (20).

In Act II (Chapters 3–5)—the confrontation(s)—news spreads that "Kino had found the Pearl of the World"; as a result, "All manner of people grew interested in Kino—people with things to sell and people with favors to ask" (23). The priest comes, the doctor visits (and scams him by giving "medicine" that may have made the baby's condition worse), and someone tries to rob him in the dark. Kino takes the pearl to dealers, who conspire to lowball him on what they will pay. Then there's a second mysterious scuffle in the dark as Kino tries to protect his property, and Juana begins to think he should throw it back in the sea, for all the trouble it's causing. In fact, she takes the pearl from where Kino had hidden it and is poised to throw it into the sea herself when he "caught her arm and wrenched the pearl from her" (57). He strikes her, and she "knew there was murder in him"—after which he's attacked by more men. This time he kills a man with his knife, and Act II ends with two sad realizations: "There was nothing to do but save themselves" (59), and "This pearl has become my soul," Kino said. "If I give it up I shall lose my soul" (65). To expand the folktale and make it more dramatic, Steinbeck replaced a single attack by multiple people with a series of attacks that grow progressively worse, beginning with a vague scuffle in the dark, then a second scuffle with a knife slashing at nothingness, and yet a third attack by several shadow-figures, during which Kino "felt his knife go home, and then he was swept to his knees and swept again to the ground" (58).

Act III (Chapter 6)—the resolution—pushes the drama to its conclusion. In *The Pearl*, two trackers and a man on horseback with a rifle pursue Kino, Juana, and the baby, who have fled inland on foot after the canoe was sabotaged and their brush house set on fire. Kino has become like a hunted animal (70, 72) and cornered, he decides that for them to survive he must leap for the gun held by the man on horseback and kill him. He does so, just as the baby cries in the distance and the man fires in that direction. Kino is triumphant, but not before the marksman is able to shoot the top of the baby's head off. It ends, finally, in loss and with the pearl thrown back from whence it came—reclaimed by the sea—and with a tragic irony, insomuch as the baby that Kino was trying to save by the find of a great and expensive pearl was instead killed because of that pearl.

Prior to *The Old Man and the Sea*, Hemingway's novels could not be broken down easily into a cinematic three-act structure, but that structure is clearly evident in his novella—even though there are no chapters or divisions. As Steinbeck had done, in Act I Hemingway introduces his characters and the chief problem. Though the situation is not as high-stakes as Kino's, Santiago

---

nonetheless is a very old man with very bad luck who struggles to fish alone because of his age. The first act establishes the close bond between Santiago and the boy Manolin, as well as the central problem: the bad luck that has taken the boy from him temporarily and threatens to do so permanently. The first act also establishes that Santiago is different from the other fishermen, that he is, in his own words, "a strange old man" (14). Unlike younger fishermen who use motorboats and buoys, Santiago fishes the old way, rowing his skiff. He is also more skilled and knows "many tricks," like how to let "the current do a third of the work" and how to keep his lines "straighter than anyone" (14, 30, 32). He eats turtle eggs for strength and shark liver oil for his eyes (37). While others fish in the usual places within sight of each other, Santiago uses the current to go far out, farther than anyone had gone before. Act I ends after the big fish is hooked and the "boat began to move slowly off toward the north-west" (45).

Act II is the main confrontation, the old man's epic battle with the great eighteen-foot marlin using only a braided handline in a flimsy wooden skiff that's shorter than the fish. During the three-day battle, Santiago laments having been born with only one good hand, wishes he had the boy to help and to share the experience, bargains more with God, dreams of lions, and thinks back to when he was younger and had more strength, and finds inspiration in wanting to be "worthy of the great [New York Yankees slugger Joe] DiMaggio who does all things perfectly even with the pain of the bone spur in his heel" (68).

For Act III, Hemingway did as Steinbeck and took a single group attack and turned it into a progression of attacks that grew more serious and consequential. First comes a lone speedy Mako shark (100–01), and Santiago kills the attacker but loses his harpoon. He is conscious of his own manhood and his diminishing strength, thinking, "I may not be as strong as I think. . . . But I know many tricks and I have resolution" (23). After a while, two shovel-nosed "hateful sharks" (107) attack, and the old man fights them off by stabbing at them with a knife lashed to an oar. After more time passes, another shovel-nosed shark comes "like a pig to the trough if a pig had a mouth so wide that you could put your head in," and Santiago "drove the knife on the oar down into his brain. But the shark jerked backwards as he rolled and the knife blade snapped" (111). Tired and now defenseless, Santiago thinks, "I am too old to club sharks to death. But I will try it as long as I have the oars and the short club and the tiller" (112). Like Kino, he has been backed into a corner, metaphorically speaking. Having found his own version of the Pearl of the World that the priest in Steinbeck's story called "a great fortune" (27)—a great fish that Santiago calls "my fortune" (95)—Santiago is so invested in protecting his prize that he is willing to do anything. "I'll fight them until I die" (115), he says, in an echo of a desperate Kino. Just as Kino fought the "sharks" that would steal his prize, Santiago battles them fiercely. But he, too, is overwhelmed. Around midnight, they "came in a pack and he could only see the lines in the water that their fins made" and he "clubbed at heads and heard the jaws chop and the shaking of the skiff as they took hold below. He clubbed desperately at what he could only feel and hear and he felt something seize the club and it was gone" (118). The sharks stop attacking when there is "nothing more for them to eat." Just as the sea reclaimed Kino's pearl, it reclaimed Santiago's great fish. And as in *The Pearl*, *The Old Man and the Sea* ends in irony, for after Santiago makes it back to his village and lies exhausted in his shack, tourists who see the skeleton of the great fish are addressed by the proprietor at La Terraza trying to explain the attack, and they mistakenly think the great fish Santiago caught is a shark.

Thematically, both novellas offer riffs on the "be careful what you wish for" maxim, with what begins as a blessing turning into a curse. Kino finds "the greatest pearl in the world" (20) and "There has never been such a fish" as the marlin Santiago catches (123). Both men repeatedly look at their treasures, Kino staring into the pearl and seeing his future (23–24) and Santiago, who "looked at the fish constantly to make sure it was true" (99–100). Yet, as quickly as their bad luck turned phenomenally good, it turns phenomenally bad for both men. And both men distinguish between luck and chance. "Chance was against [every shell in his basket containing a pearl], but luck and the gods might be for it" (18), Kino thinks. For him, "the pearls were accidents, and the finding of one was luck, a little pat on the back by God or the gods or both" (17). Santiago also distinguishes between luck and chance. He tells Manolin, "If you were my boy, I'd take you out and gamble. . . . But you are your father's and your mother's and you are in a lucky boat" (13). Both men also question the idea of luckiness. "It is not good to want a thing too much," Kino thinks. "It sometimes drives the luck away. You must want it just enough, and you must be very tactful with God or the gods" (19). Likewise, alone with the great fish and realizing his situation, Santiago thinks, "Maybe I'll have the luck to bring the forward half [of the marlin] in. I should have some luck. No. . . . You violated your luck when you went too far outside" (116). Both Steinbeck's and Hemingway's characters begin to think, when their luck changes for the very worst, that maybe their pursuit of the pearl or the fish was somehow linked to sin. "This pearl is like a sin!" Juana declares (37), while an exhausted Santiago thinks, "Perhaps it was a sin to kill the fish. I suppose it was even though I did it to keep me alive and feed many people. . . . Do not think about sin. It is much too late for that" (105). While much has been made of Santiago's mantra, "A man can be destroyed but not defeated" (103)—which expresses a frequent theme of Hemingway's, that of winning for losing or losing for winning—even that line seems a variation of Kino's: "A plan once made and visualized becomes a reality along with other realities—never to be destroyed, but easily to be attacked" (28).

In a final irony that feels like a postscript, both *The Pearl* and *The Old Man and the Sea* have engendered comparisons to the author's personal circumstances. Steinbeck's biographer concludes, "The autobiographical impulses behind *The Pearl* are not hard to discern; this is clearly a story about the price of success. . . . Steinbeck's own pearl was his gift of narrative, his ability to express himself in language; he had been tempted by the world and its rewards; he had won some things but lost so much more" (Parini 319–20). Likewise, as Katharine T. Jobes summarizes, "*The Old Man and the Sea* has been interpreted not only as a parable about the heroic capabilities

of man in general, but also as Hemingway's private parable" (5)—
an interpretation first offered by the same *Life* editors who published
Hemingway's novella: "Perhaps the old man is Hemingway himself,
the great fish is this great story and the sharks are the critics" (20).
Or perhaps, as a dismissive Hemingway once famously wrote a
critic shortly after publication of *The Old Man and the Sea*, "All the
symbolism that people say is shit" (*Selected Letters* 780).

Perhaps. But there are enough similarities between *The Old
Man and the Sea* and *The Pearl* to suggest that this new fictional
territory for Hemingway may well have been inspired by his rival
on the West Coast . . . who got there first.

Works Cited

"1939 Book Awards Given by Critics: Elgin Groseclose's 'Ararat' Is
Picked as Work Which Failed to Get Due Recognition." *The New
York Times*, 14 Feb. 1940, p. 25. www.nytimes.com/1940/02/14/
archives/1939-book-awards-given-by-critics-elgin-groseclose-
ararat-is.html.

Baker, Carlos. *Ernest Hemingway: A Life Story.* Charles Scribner's Sons,
1969.

Benson, Jackson J. *John Steinbeck, Writer: A Biography.* Penguin, 1984.

Cohen, Milton A. "Styles." *Ernest Hemingway in Context.* Edited by
Debra A. Moddelmog and Suzanne del Gizzo. Cambridge U P, 2013.
pp. 109–18.

Faulkner, William. Rev. of *The Old Man and the Sea. The Old Man and
the Sea: Modern Critical Interpretations.* Edited by Harold Bloom.
Chelsea House, 1999, p. 5.

"A Great American Storyteller." *Life*, vol. 33, no. 9, 1 Sept. 1952, p. 20.

Gurko, Leo. "The Old Man's Heroic Struggle." *Readings on Ernest
Hemingway: The Old Man and the Sea.* Edited by Bonnie Szumski.
The Greenhaven Press Literary Companion to American Literature.
Greenhaven P, 1999, pp. 147–56.

Hays, Peter. *Ernest Hemingway.* Frederick Ungar/Continuum, 1990.

Hemingway, Ernest. *By-Line: Ernest Hemingway: Selected Articles and
Dispatches from Four Decades.* Edited by William White. Charles
Scribner's Sons, 1967.

_____. *The Old Man and the Sea.* 1952. Scribner Classic/Collier edition. Collier, 1986.

_____. *Selected Letters: 1917–1961.* Edited by Carlos Baker. Charles Scribner's Sons, 1981.

Hendrickson, Paul. *Hemingway's Boat: Everything He Loved in Life, and Lost, 1934–1961.* Alfred A. Knopf, 2011.

Jobes, Katharine T. *Twentieth Century Interpretations of The Old Man and the Sea: A Collection of Critical Essays.* Prentice-Hall, 1968.

Parini, Jay. *John Steinbeck: A Biography.* Henry Holt and Co., 1995.

Steinbeck, John. *America and Americans and Selected Nonfiction.* Edited by Susan Shillinglaw and Jackson L. Benson. Viking, 2002.

_____. *The Pearl.* 1947. Steinbeck Centennial Edition. Penguin, 2002.

_____. *Steinbeck: A Life in Letters.* Edited by Elaine Steinbeck and Robert Wallsten. Viking, 1975.

Wylder, Delbert E. "*The Old Man and the Sea* as Fable." *Readings on The Old Man and the Sea.* Edited by Bonnie Szumski. The Greenhaven Press Literary Companion to American Literature. Greenhaven P, 1999, pp. 32–41.

CRITICAL
READINGS

Of Mollusks and Men: An Ecocritical Approach to *The Pearl*_____

Lowell Wyse

In the second chapter of *The Pearl,* John Steinbeck depicts the gray-green underwater realm in which his protagonist, Kino, is about to find and harvest the exceptional oyster that contains "the pearl of the world" (27). To construct this crucial scene, Steinbeck focuses on the oyster beds themselves before turning to the biological process of pearl formation:

> The gray oysters with ruffles like skirts on the shells, the barnacle-crusted oysters with little bits of weed clinging to the skirts and small crabs climbing over them. An accident could happen to these oysters, a grain of sand could lie in the folds of muscle and irritate the flesh until in self-protection the flesh coated the grain with a layer of smooth cement. But once started, the flesh continued to coat the foreign body until it fell free in some tidal flurry or until the oyster was destroyed (20).

Through a combination of experience, strength, and intuition (along with, the story suggests, great need and desire) Kino extracts a particularly "ancient" oyster from its hiding place under a rocky overhang and rises to the surface to face a different future (22).

For all the rightful attention directed to the titular pearl in Steinbeck's story, comparatively little has been said about the oyster that produced it. Scientifically speaking, pearl oysters are a group of tropical bivalve mollusk in the family *Pteriidae.* They live attached to hard surfaces like rocks and are characterized by dual valves (two pieces of hard shell connected by an elastic ligament), a large central muscle that operates the hinge-like structure, and the cilia-covered gills through which they feed on tiny organic particles ("Oyster"). Two species are indigenous to the region that Steinbeck was writing about, Mexico's Gulf of California. The primary species, known as mother-of-pearl (*Pinctada mazatlanica*), produces pearls that are "typically baroque [non-spherical] or semi-baroque, with a silver to dark grey body color and strong overtones of blue, lavender, and green," while the rainbow mabe (*Pteria sterna*) "produces smaller but rounder pearls, in a variety of natural hues," most commonly purple and violet (Cariño and Monteforte 88). As Steinbeck was well aware, the natural beauty of these pearls, as well as the oyster shells themselves, made them a prized commodity in Europe for four centuries, beginning in the mid-1500s.

Such background information may seem secondary to the understanding of a fictional story that, on its surface, is clearly about enduring human themes like morality, wealth, violence, and community. However, as this essay will demonstrate, another option is available, an interpretive approach that takes its cues from history, science, geography, and the author's own philosophies of life and literature. Following Steinbeck's invitation in the prologue to read this legend-turned-novella as a "parable," I suggest we read it not as a parable of what can happen when the life of one family is touched by greed, "evil," or perhaps just bad luck, but in environmental terms, as an exploration of the relationship of human beings in the natural world. Reading the text in this way, from an *ecocritical* perspective, reveals new dimensions of the plot and characters, as well as a final twist on the story's basic meaning that connects it to contemporary environmental thinking.

What Is Ecocriticism?

Ecocriticism emerged as a distinct field of literary studies in the 1990s and has been flourishing ever since. Like feminist criticism and Marxist criticism before it, ecocriticism developed from a position of political activism, like an academic branch of the environmental movement. Just as feminism combats sexism and Marxist theory takes on capitalism, ecocriticism's fundamental challenge is to "unthinking anthropocentrism" (Bertens 204), the idea that humans are the dominant species whose existence is the most important thing in the world. By focusing on literary representations of the natural world and human relationships within it, ecocritics can be said to interrogate the division between nature and culture that (in the Western tradition) imagines people as somehow separate from nature.

To be sure, ecocriticism is an umbrella term that accounts for a wide array of critical and theoretical practices. Indeed, as Dana Phillips has argued, it is perhaps better defined by its inherent contradictions and ironies than by any convenient shorthand.[1] Yet as ecocriticism continues to spread, arguably in response to the global environmental crisis, it is worth considering what it actually means to read ecocritically. What kinds of things should readers pay attention to when they put on their green-tinted lenses?

One way to think about this question is to ponder what Lawrence Buell, in the early days of ecocriticism, identified as the properties of an ideal ecocritical text:

1. The nonhuman environment is present not merely as a framing device, but as a presence that begins to suggest that human history is implicated in natural history.
2. The human interest is not understood to be the only legitimate interest.
3. Human accountability to the environment is part of the text's ethical orientation.
4. Some sense of the environment as a process rather than as a constant or a given is at least implicit in the text. (*Environmental* 7–8)

Although this list is not comprehensive and its aims are somewhat simplistic, it does indicate some things that ecocritics tend to analyze—namely, textual portrayals of the natural world and the ways that humans think about it. These points of analysis, I would argue, are the foundation of most scholarship on literature and the environment, the practical basis of what was famously (if vaguely) defined as an "earth-centered approach" to literature (Glotfelty xix).

Perhaps unsurprisingly, Buell's list bears a strong resemblance to much of Steinbeck's fiction, and the history of Steinbeck studies suggests a commitment to understanding the environmental implications of his works. In 1997, the year after the foundational *Ecocriticism Reader* was published, the collection *Steinbeck and the Environment* was released, building on past scholarship while blazing new trails that critics continue to follow.[3] In recent years, critics have moved beyond Steinbeck's attention to landscapes, species, and biological processes to explore connections in his works to specific strains of environmental thought, such as deep ecology and ecofeminism, as well as to environmental writers like Wendell Berry.[4] Such research demonstrates not only the growing interest in environmental readings of Steinbeck that mirrors the rise of ecocriticism, but also the diversity of approaches that fit under the ecocritical canopy.

Setting and Geography
In addition to interpretations of environmental themes and depictions, ecocriticism may also benefit from a sense of historical and geographical contexts. This practice allows us to think about the setting in a text from the standpoint of environmental history. Steinbeck's fiction in particular is often remembered for its evocative "sense of place," especially in works like *Of Mice and Men, Cannery Row,* and *East of Eden*, which are set in the region of central California that encompasses the Salinas River Valley and the coast of Monterey Bay. Indeed, this area, which includes the city of Salinas, where the author was born and laid to rest, is often referred to today as "Steinbeck Country." Although it is not set in California, *The Pearl* evokes a similarly memorable setting, owing, in part, to Steinbeck's own experience in the region where the story takes place.

Like the author's beloved Salinas Valley, Baja California is a "strip angled against the Pacific" (Steinbeck, *Travels* 173), in this case a long, slender peninsula extending nearly a thousand miles southeast from the mouth of the Colorado River near the United States–Mexico border. The arid peninsula runs between the Pacific Ocean to the west and the Gulf of California (which Steinbeck called the Sea of Cortez) to the east. A few references to Mexican history and culture (e.g., pesos as currency) occur in the story, and several place names (specifically the cities of La Paz and Loreto) correspond to the geography of Baja California and identify this as the setting.

Steinbeck traveled to this region on several occasions, most famously during his 1940 expedition to the Gulf with his friend, Ed Ricketts, memorialized in *The Log from the Sea of Cortez* (1951). *The Pearl*'s primary setting is the city of La Paz, which lies on a bay toward the southeast end of the peninsula and remains the largest city in the region. Steinbeck described it as a place where "the Gulf and the town were one, inextricably bound together..." (*Log* 204). He also noted that the town was imbued with a "'home' feeling": "We had never seen a town which even looked like La Paz, and yet coming to it was like returning rather than visiting" (104-105). He would return in time, notably in 1947 to complete the film version of *The Pearl*. Perhaps most importantly, La Paz is where Steinbeck claims to have heard the local legend that would become the basis of his pearl story.

The reason La Paz exists is evident from its natural geography: it is nestled into a north-facing bay that Steinbeck called "secluded and protected" (*Log* 76). For centuries, indigenous people (including the Pericú, Guaycura, and Cochimí) lived in and around this bar-built estuary, where a small river empties into the Gulf, creating habitat for many species of fish, oysters, and other marine animals. Upon their arrival in the 1530s, the Spanish recognized the economic and military value of the area; Hernán Cortés himself claimed the site for the Crown in 1535, perhaps even motivated by the pearls he received as gifts from the Aztec emperor Montezuma, which may have come from La Paz Bay (Donkin 308). Only after many decades of violent conflict was the town christened, somewhat ironically, *La Paz* (City of Peace), permanently settled (in 1811), and named the capital of Baja California Sur (Nakayama 195). Yet, it was likely the humble oyster that gave the city its staying power. From the late 1500s through the early 1900s, La Paz was a global hub of pearl harvesting, perhaps even, as Steinbeck claimed, "the great pearl center of the world" (*Log* 85).

The World in the Text

With all this in mind, we can begin to look at Steinbeck's depiction of the natural world in the novella, as one might analyze a landscape painting; as a representation, it may bear some resemblance to a real place, but it is also imaginatively depicted. The sheer persistence of spatial and biological references supports an argument for the environment's importance in the text. Frequently these descriptions provide not only a sense of place—things like sights, sounds, and smells—but a kind of ecological orientation within the living world. When Juana and Kino cross the desert with Coyotito, for example, Steinbeck writes about the life that surrounds them:

> This land was waterless, furred with the cacti which could store water and with the great-rooted brush which could reach deep into the earth for a little moisture and get along on very little. . . . Little tufts of sad dry grass grew between the stones, grass that had sprouted with one single rain and headed, dropped its seed, and died. Horned toads watched the family go by and turned their little pivoting dragon heads. And now and then a great jackrabbit, disturbed in his shade, bumped away and hid behind the nearest rock. (81)

Here Steinbeck offers a description of a particular landscape that is bolstered by a sense of its ecology, of how plants and animals have adapted to survive there and live in relation with each other and the whole ecosystem.

No matter the specific setting—from the aquatic spaces of the estuary to the shelter of the mountain waterfall—Steinbeck carefully populates his narrative with living things in an almost documentary way. These descriptions often convey some ecological reality, such as how the mountain spring serves as a support system for an entire ecosystem:

> The animals from miles around came to drink from the little pools, and the wild sheep and the deer, the pumas and raccoons, and the mice—all came to drink. . . . Beside this tiny stream, wherever enough earth collected for root-hold, colonies of plants grew, wild grape and little palms, maidenhair fern, hibiscus, and tall pampas

grass with feathery rods raised above the spike leaves. And in the pool lived frogs and waterskaters, and waterworms crawled on the bottom of the pool. Everything that loved water came to these few shallow places. (84)

Kino and Juana, of course, locate this refuge for exactly the same reason: the possibility of water in an extremely arid landscape. In this sense, they (or we as humans) are depicted as no different from the (other) animals, and an element of physical setting can be said to contain a broader ecological insight. From just these two examples of Steinbeck's environmental descriptions, readers can see that nature is an important element of the story and deserving of closer attention.

Humans in Nature

This practice of writing the biological world suggests that Steinbeck considered nature more than just a backdrop in his fiction. Indeed, nature imagery was one of the primary ways he both situated human characters within the natural world and commented on their role within it. Much of his work, as Jason Horn writes, "develops characters in relation to their environment and implicitly argues for a clearer understanding of how humans might best live within the limits of their natural surroundings. . . . To be human, for Steinbeck, was to be a part of the larger ecological scheme, to be a living being linked to all life and to the earth itself" (315).

From the outset of *The Pearl,* Steinbeck closely associates his protagonist with nature. The first few pages consist of Kino's waking up and taking note of his surroundings: "The roosters had been crowing for some time, and the early pigs were already beginning their ceaseless turning of twigs and bits of wood to see whether anything to eat had been overlooked. Outside the brush house in the tuna clump, a covey of little birds chittered and flurried with their wings" (5). In just the few moments after getting out of bed, he notices two species of ant, a yellow-eyed goat, a spotted dog, a flock of wild doves, and a moth flying into the fire (5-6). Kino is closely attuned to nature, and from an ecocritical standpoint, we might say that his awareness doubles as the reader's awareness.

Later, when Kino is stricken with anxiety after failing to sell his great pearl, he sits on his mat considering what to do. Again, an awareness of his surroundings comes to him, this time as a kind of stabilizing force:

> His senses were burningly alive, but his mind went back to the deep participation with all things, the gift he had from his people. He heard every little sound of the gathering night, the sleepy complaint of settling birds, the love agony of cats, the strike and withdrawal of little waves on the beach, and the simple hiss of distance. And he could smell the sharp odor of exposed kelp from the receding tide. (59)

This "deep participation with all things"—or what, elsewhere in the novella, he refers to as "the *Whole*" (6)—is Steinbeckian code for a kind of ecological holism, the sense in which humans are deeply and intricately connected with the natural world and all its processes. It figures here, in the description of Kino, as a kind of ancestral gift, something inherently (and perhaps problematically) indigenous.[5]

The connectedness of human characters with nature in *The Pearl* deepens as the story turns from one of conflict over economic assets (i.e., the pearl) to one of survival in the elements. Yet, in a sense, this is a survival story from the beginning. The scorpion that bites the baby Coyotito and instigates the story's chain of events is a literal attack from nature against which the adults are defenseless. The scorpion attack brings out Kino's animal instincts: "Then, snarling, Kino had it [the scorpion], had it in his fingers, rubbing it to a paste in his hands. . . . His teeth were bared and fury flared in his eyes" (9). As the story continues and Kino and Juana fight to survive a barrage of external threats, both are frequently likened to animals—whether it is Kino springing "like an angry cat" (42) or Juana peering "like an owl from the hole in the mountain" (88). The comparison becomes overt after Kino kills an anonymous assailant on the beach: "He was an animal now, for hiding, for attacking, and he lived only to preserve himself and his family" (68).

Just as the plot of *The Pearl* turns on a threat from nature (the scorpion bite) that forces people into animalistic survival mode, the pearl itself also disrupts a kind of natural order. After Coyotito is stung and the doctor refuses to help, Juana and Kino seek out the pearl as an economic remedy. They both see it as an answer to their problems (and, in Juana's case, prayers). From the instant it is extracted "from the dying flesh" of the oyster (26), the pearl transforms from an element of nature to an economic asset and, eventually, an existential threat.

One aspect of this threat is communal. By changing the socioeconomic dynamics, the pearl disrupts the order of the indigenous community, which literally subsists on what the ocean provides. Historically, oysters were primarily gathered as a food source, not merely for their pearls, and fishing is so important to Kino's community that the destruction of a canoe is considered a crime more serious than murder (68). Not only Kino, but the entire community is depicted as attuned to and dependent on the natural world, to the extent that the people in their brush houses can supposedly hear a large school of fish preying on a smaller school out in the estuary (38). In responding to a threat from nature, Kino and Juana extract something valuable from it, taking what they can, not realizing how this action will alter their fortunes and those of their community, even to the point of separating them from it.

Extractive Economies

In this process, Steinbeck's protagonists participate in, expose, and at last fall victim to a system of social and environmental exploitation that had existed for centuries in the Gulf of California. For when Kino and Juana go to sell the great pearl, they encounter an obstacle in the form of the pearl buyers, who have already heard of the pearl and agreed not to pay a fair purchase price. Unable to sell it, the couple returns home, only to endure multiple attempted thefts and physical assaults, one of which ends in Kino's murdering the assailant and eventually fleeing the village with his family.

For Steinbeck, this entire grim episode would have been indicative of the system of economic inequality (another persistent theme in Steinbeck's works), whereby indigenous divers were conscripted to harvest pearls that made the Spaniards rich while doing little to help the native community. In the story, the social, economic, and racial contrast is embedded in the very spaces of the village, with the simple brush houses of the fishing village standing separate from "the stone and plaster city where the streets were a little wider and there were narrow pavements beside the buildings" (51). Tellingly, Steinbeck refers to the town as a "colonial animal" with "a nervous system and a head and shoulders and feet" (27). He liked ecological metaphors, and some of the seemingly benign biological descriptions in the novella—including ant-lions preying on ants, hungry dogs and pigs that scavenge for dead fish, and fish that feed off of rejected oysters—may even symbolize a "parasitic" relationship between the native village and the Spanish city (Karsten 3–4).

This dynamic is so central to the identity of La Paz that Steinbeck embeds it in his description of the oysters: "This was the bed that had raised the King of Spain to be a great power in Europe in past years, had helped to pay for his wars, and had decorated the churches for his soul's sake" (20). Here Steinbeck draws a direct line between the ecology of the estuary and the great wealth and great violence of imperial Europe and the colonial systems it installed around the world. The doctor initially refuses to treat Coyotito, in part, because he is "of a race which for nearly four hundred years had beaten and starved and robbed and despised Kino's race, and frightened it too, so that the indigene came humbly to the door" (14). Such authorial commentary leaves little doubt as to the origins of injustice in the region.

The environmental history of pearl fishing in the Gulf of California, and La Paz in particular, supports this interpretation of the novella while adding an ironic twist. By 1940, when Steinbeck first went to La Paz collecting marine specimens, the famed pearl oysters of the Gulf had all but vanished due to overfishing. Under the Spanish empire and, later, the Mexican government, the oyster beds of La Paz and the rest of the Gulf were periodically decimated, with near-extinction events due to over-harvesting occurring in the

1680s, 1750s, 1870s, and 1930s (Cariño and Monteforte). What began as an essentially sustainable system, with small communities of indigenous fishermen using traditional methods to harvest oysters for food, eventually became an industrialized process, employing bigger ships and mechanical diving suits for extracting more material wealth from an increasingly limited supply of natural resources. The economic model upon which these practices were based is recognizable to anyone familiar with natural resource extraction today, from the coal strip-mines of West Virginia to the vast tar sands of Alberta. Extraction is often a boom-and-bust process, with outside speculators moving in quickly and taking as much as they can get until the resources are gone and the landscapes destroyed.

This, then, is the great unrecognized irony of *The Pearl*: by the time Steinbeck visited La Paz and eventually wrote this story, there were no more pearl oysters left to write about. In their weeks of collecting marine specimens in the Gulf of California in the spring of 1940, Steinbeck, Ricketts, and their crew never found a single one (though local fishermen showed them a few). Ricketts' journal of the expedition mentions only one specimen in the region (Nakayama 197), and Steinbeck only noted, somewhat blithely, that the oysters were "growing rare" (*Log* 131). Another crew member wrote that "The oysters had a disease eight or so years before that and had just petered out. The oyster shells were thick with disease" (qtd. in Nakayama 208). Thus, although Steinbeck was writing a fictional version of a local legend that could have happened many years prior, by the time his story reached its audience the oysters themselves had already died out, and with them an important element of local culture.

Steinbeck knew the effects of overfishing from his observations of other species, like the sardines in his home area of Monterey Bay. In fact, on expedition to the Gulf, he and his friends boarded a Japanese vessel that was blatantly using destructive industrial techniques to harvest shrimp. He wrote that the Japanese shrimp boats were "dredging with overlapping scoops, bringing up tons of shrimps, rapidly destroying the species so that it may never come back, and with the species destroying the ecological balance of the whole region" (*Log* 2).

Although born too early to be considered an "environmentalist," in today's terms, Steinbeck was not afraid to speak out about environmental degradation: "We in the United States," he wrote, "have done so much to destroy our own resources, our timber, our land, our fishes, that we should be taken as a horrible example and our methods avoided by any government and people enlightened enough to envision a continuing economy" (*Log* 207). His awareness of the impact of extraction on whole habitats and individual species suggests that he might have been open to an ecocritical interpretation of his pearl parable, particularly as it relates to economic and environmental exploitation.

In a recent analysis of some of Steinbeck's other fiction, Robert Searway notes that While Steinbeck depicts rapidly encroaching threats of a modern world . . . . he also presents simple communities and the renewal of life in the preservation of natural settings. People within those communities who come to uphold regional values that protect the environment against economic exploitation serve as an antidote to encroaching global forces . . ." (176). This observation applies also to *The Pearl*, in which the values of a local community are pitted against powerful social and economic forces.

Throughout the story, Steinbeck shows Kino growing apart from the essential ethic of his community, which we might term environmental sustainability, thereby contrasting capitalist greed (embodied by the pearl buyers) with the kind of sustainable, bioregional dwelling of the oyster divers. The fact that Kino finds the pearl just when he needs it suggests that it has always been there, but it only becomes available once he adopts the outsiders' mentality of taking too much and ignoring the consequences. Kino harvests the pearl to ensure his family's survival, yet the pearl's potential economic value skews his own attitudes and the attitudes of his neighbors, disrupting the natural order and causing them to focus on the instant wealth that comes from the irresponsible extraction of natural resources. He tries and fails to beat the Spaniards at their own game. In the end, by throwing the pearl back into the sea,

Kino takes the symbolic stance of an activist, which, we could say, mirrors contemporary protests against fossil fuel companies and other unsustainable extractive industries that too often undermine communal values and local habitats.

A Twenty-First Century Lens

Reading *The Pearl* from an ecocritical standpoint, with attention to its depiction of the natural world and humans' place within it, shows how the story resonates with the environmental history of a particular place and a particular species—the pearl oysters of La Paz Bay—not to mention Steinbeck's own philosophy. More specifically, ecocriticism gives us the tools to interpret the malevolent greed surrounding the pearl as a specifically environmental (and colonial) greed, part of a long history of problematic human attitudes toward natural resources and local communities.

Strictly (and ecocritically) speaking, the pearl itself cannot be seen as evil, despite what the characters say. It is merely part of nature that is extracted from its place, forced into an exploitive economy, and ultimately returned to the oyster beds when Kino throws it in the water. After all that has happened to Kino and Juana—including the loss of their home, their livelihood (via the broken canoe), and their only child—Steinbeck seems to suggest that the ocean floor is the rightful place for the extraordinary pearl. He depicts its descent through the water in a way that recalls the scene of its discovery: "The waving branches of the algae called to it and beckoned to it. . . . It settled down to the sand bottom among the fern-like plants. Above, the surface of the water was a green mirror. And the pearl lay on the floor of the sea. A crab scampering over the bottom raised a little cloud of sand, and when it settled the pearl was gone" (97). The beautiful pearl, which began as "an accident," a grain of sand lodged in the body of a particular mollusk, sinks back into the sand it came from.

In the end, the pearl is not evil but benign, a mere object defined only by the shifting human attitudes toward it. Any perceived evil, therefore, exists not in the pearl, but in the hearts of human beings and the harmful systems they construct. In effect, Steinbeck uses the pearl as an indicator of the great human capacity not only for greed and violence, but also for strength and endurance. This contradiction makes it a potent emblem of environmental attitudes in the twenty-first century—the pearl of the world, indeed.

Notes

1. See Phillips, "Ecocriticism's Hard Problems (Its Ironies, Too)" (2013).

2. Among the more comprehensive and accessible accounts of ecocritical history and practice are Hans Bertens's chapter in *Literary Theory: The Basics* (2008), Ursula Heise's "The Hitchhiker's Guide to Ecocriticism," Greg Garrard's *Ecocriticism* (2004), and Lawrence Buell's "Ecocriticism: Some Emerging Trends" (2011).

3. *The Ecocriticism Reader: Landmarks in Literary Ecology*, edited by Cheryll Glotfelty and Harold Fromm, effectively introduced ecocriticism to the academic world. *Steinbeck and the Environment: Interdisciplinary Approaches* was edited by Susan Beegel, Susan Shillinglaw, and Wesley Tiffney.

4. See Rodney Rice, "Circles in the Forest: John Steinbeck and the Deep Ecology of *To a God Unknown*" (2011); Cynthia Bily, "You're Kind of Untouchable: Women, Men, and the Environment in *The Long Valley*" (2011); and Elisabeth Bayley, "John Steinbeck's *To a God Unknown* and Wendell Berry: An Ecocritical View" (2017). Brian Railsback's "John Steinbeck, Ecocriticism, and the Way Ahead" (2007) is another important touchstone.

5. While tying indigenous people to nature may seem positive, it may also be seen as a kind of essentialism and/or primitivism. As evidenced in *The Log,* Steinbeck undoubtedly saw indigenous people, particularly in Baja California, as different, simple, and noble, possible stereotypes that underpin *The Pearl* and warrant further analysis. For a wider consideration of Steinbeck's portrayals of Native Americans, see Louis Owens' article "'Grampa Killed Indians, Pa Killed Snakes': Steinbeck and the American Indian" (1988).

Works Cited

Bayley, Elisabeth. "John Steinbeck's *To a God Unknown* and Wendell Berry: An Ecocritical View." *Steinbeck Review*, vol. 14, no. 2, 2017, pp. 151–63. *Project MUSE*, muse.jhu.edu/article/678458. Beegel, Susan F., Susan Shillinglaw, and Wesley N. Tiffney, editors. *Steinbeck and the Environment: Interdisciplinary Approaches.* U of Alabama P, 1997.

Bertens, Hans. *Literary Theory: The Basics.* 2nd ed. Routledge, 2008.

Bily, Cynthia A. "'You're Kind of Untouchable': Women, Men, and the Environment in *The Long Valley.*" *John Steinbeck.* Edited by Donald R. Noble. Salem P, 2011. pp. 75–89.

Buell, Lawrence. "Ecocriticism: Some Emerging Trends." *At the Intersections of Ecocriticism. Qui Parle: Critical Humanities and Social Sciences,* vol. 19, no. 2, 2011, pp. 87–115. *Project MUSE*, muse.jhu.edu/article/430997.

_____. *The Environmental Imagination: Thoreau, Nature Writing, and the Formation of American Culture.* Belknap P of Harvard U P, 1996.

Cariño, Micheline, and Mario Monteforte. "History of Pearling in La Paz Bay, South Baja California." *Gems & Gemology,* vol. 31, no. 2, 1995, pp. 88–105. ResearchGate. www.researchgate.net/publication/271300925_History_of_Pearling_in_La_Paz_Bay_South_Baja_California.

Donkin, R. A. *Beyond Price: Pearls and Pearl-fishing: Origins to the Age of Discoveries.* American Philosophical Society, 1998. Google Books.

Garrard, Greg. *Ecocriticism.* London: Routledge, 2004. The New Critical Idiom.

Glotfelty, Cheryll. "Introduction: Literary Studies in an Age of Environmental Crisis." *The Ecocriticism Reader: Landmarks in Literary Ecology.* Edited by Cheryll Glotfelty and Harold Fromm. U of Georgia P, 1996, pp. i-xx.

Glotfelty, Cheryll, and Harold Fromm, editors. *The Ecocriticism Reader: Landmarks in Literary Ecology.* U of Georgia P, 1996.

Heise, Ursula K. "The Hitchhiker's Guide to Ecocriticism." *PMLA,* vol. 121, no. 2, 2006, pp. 503–16. *JSTOR*, www.jstor.org/stable/25486328.

Horn, Jason G. "John Steinbeck" *Twentieth-Century American Nature Writers: Prose. Dictionary of Literary Biography,* vol. 275, Gale, 2003, pp. 314–23.

Karsten, Ernest E., Jr. "Thematic Structure in *The Pearl.*" *The English Journal,* vol. 54, no. 1, 1965, pp. 1–7. *JSTOR,* www.jstor.org/stable/810934.

Nakayama, Kiyoshi. "The Pearl in the Sea of Cortez: Steinbeck's Use of the Environment." *Steinbeck and the Environment: Interdisciplinary Approaches.* Edited by Susan F. Beegel, Susan Shillinglaw, and Wesley N. Tiffney. U of Alabama P, 1997, pp. 194–208.

Owens, Louis. "'Grampa Killed Indians, Pa Killed Snakes': Steinbeck and the American Indian." *MELUS,* vol. 15, no. 2, 1988, pp. 85–92. *JSTOR,* www.jstor.org/stable/466974.

"Oyster." *Encyclopædia Britannica,* n.d., www.britannica.com/animal/oyster.

Phillips, Dana. "Ecocriticism's Hard Problems (Its Ironies, Too)." *American Literary History,* vol. 25, no. 2, 2013, pp. 455–67. Oxford. doi.org/10.1093/alh/ajt017.

Railsback, Brian E. "John Steinbeck, Ecocriticism, and the Way Ahead." *John Steinbeck and his Contemporaries.* Edited by Stephen K. George and Barbara Heavilin. Scarecrow P, 2007, pp. 271–79.

Rice, Rodney. "Circles in the Forest: John Steinbeck and the Deep Ecology of *To a God Unknown. The Steinbeck Review,* vol 8, no, 2, 2011, pp. 31–52. Wiley. onlinelibrary.wiley.com/doi/abs/10.1111/j.1754-6087.2011.01146.x.

Searway, Robert. "Conflicting Views of Landscape in John Steinbeck's Literary West." *The Steinbeck Review,* vol. 12, no. 2, 2015, pp. 175–89. *JSTOR,* www.jstor.org/stable/10.5325/steinbeckreview.12.2.0175.

Steinbeck, John. *The Log from the Sea of Cortez.* 1951. Penguin, 1995.

_____. *The Pearl.* 1947. Penguin, 1994.

_____. *Travels with Charley: In Search of America.* Viking, 1962.

"This Is the *Whole*": Ecological Thinking in John Steinbeck's *The Pearl*

Christopher Bowman

> And it is a strange thing that most of the feeling we call religious, most of the mystical out-crying which is one of the most prized and used and desired reactions of our species, is really the understanding and the attempt to say that man is related to the whole thing, related inextricably to all reality, knowable and unknowable. This is a simple thing to say, but the profound feeling of it made a Jesus, a St. Augustine, a St. Francis, a Roger Bacon, a Charles Darwin, an Einstein. Each of them in his own tempo and with his own voice discovered and reaffirmed with astonishment the knowledge that all things are one thing and that one thing is all things—plankton, a shimmering phosphorescence on the sea and the spinning planets and an expanding universe, all bound together by the elastic string of time. It is advisable to look from the tide pool to the stars and then back to the tide pool again. (John Steinbeck, *The Log from the Sea of Cortez* 178–179).

In the epigraph to *The Pearl*, John Steinbeck sets up the ensuing narrative as a well-known folktale, introducing the main characters—Kino, Juana, Coyotito, and, arguably, the pearl—before noting its allegorical structure, as he writes: "If this story is a parable, perhaps everyone takes his own meaning from it and reads his own life into it" (1). While Steinbeck here acknowledges the potential universality of this relatively simplistic story, it nevertheless becomes clear while reading *The Pearl* that much of its allegorical value stems from a pervasive sense of ecological awareness in the narrative. Moreover, the aftermath of Kino's discovery of the pearl highlights the risks of an industry that inherently causes ecological disruptions, and the narrative's conclusion offers incisive environmental arguments that are timely for readers in the twenty-first century, as we grapple with issues such as sustainable land use, environmental justice, and the consequences of extractive economies. With this in mind, *The Pearl*'s careful attention to an ecological sense of interconnectedness, as well as the historical background to Steinbeck's composition of the story, make it just as relevant to environmental conversations today as it was when it was published in the mid-1940s.

Although *The Pearl* first appeared in 1945 in *Woman's Home Companion*, and again in 1947 as a novella and as a film adaptation, Steinbeck first heard a version of the story years earlier during a biological research expedition to the Gulf of California (also called the Sea of Cortez), which he undertook aboard the *Western Flyer* with his close friend, marine biologist Ed Ricketts; his first wife, Carol Steinbeck; and the ship's captain and a crew of three others. Because of the records that were kept on this trip, we can be rather precise in dating Steinbeck's introduction to this folktale, which he and Ricketts describe in the March 20, 1940, entry in *The Log from the Sea of Cortez*. This story, which the crew heard as they visited La Paz, Mexico, has much in common with Steinbeck's retelling of it, with a few fundamental differences: instead of being focalized through a small family, the main character in the original story is a young, single boy. And instead of the tragic conclusion in Steinbeck's version, the boy's decision to throw the pearl back into the sea is considered a moment of freedom in the original tale, as he "laughed a great deal about" it (*Log* 85–86). As this chapter will argue, Steinbeck's decision to shift the focus from a single boy to a small family is noteworthy for an environmental reading of the story, as it facilitates the central role that his ecological philosophies play in this narrative, which parallel his biological interests that compelled him to pursue this trip to the Sea of Cortez in the first place.

Indeed, for readers more familiar with Steinbeck's classic works of fiction, his participation in scientific research in the Sea of Cortez might seem perplexing. However, this decision arose from the confluence of Steinbeck's lifelong interest in biology—cultivated, in part, by his friendship with Ricketts—and the unrelenting scrutiny that followed the immediate success of *The Grapes of Wrath* in 1939. Having brought national attention to the Dust Bowl migrants in California with that novel, Steinbeck sought to disengage from the conversation entirely, and he began to focus his time and energy on studying biology with Ricketts in his lab, Pacific Biological Laboratories, in Monterey, California. As a culmination of these studies, Steinbeck and Ricketts planned to collaborate on two book projects: first, a high school-level textbook that would document the littoral organisms of the San Francisco Bay area; second, a book on the marine life in the Sea of Cortez, located between Baja California and the mainland of Mexico.

Steinbeck's experiences working in Ricketts's lab and participating in collecting trips to the area's tide pools proved to be a breath of fresh air for him and his work. As he writes in his journal on October 16, 1939: "I have to go to new sources and find new roots. . . . I know it will be found in the tide pools and on a microscope slide rather than in men" (*Working* 106). He further declares: "The song of the microscope. There is something. Glass tubing—x-ray. These are poems worth writing. These are things that could make for rebirth" (*Working* 107). Although the planned textbook on the San Francisco Bay area never materialized, Steinbeck pursued this personal and professional "rebirth" for about six weeks aboard the *Western Flyer*, in March and April 1940. The book resulting from this trip, *Sea of Cortez: A Leisurely Journal of Travel and Research*, was published the following year, consisting of a narrative log and a biological index of the species that the expedition encountered, and was jointly credited to Steinbeck and Ricketts.[1] Although Steinbeck then pursued a number of projects related to World War II, his interest in the story of the pearl remained, and he began working on his version of it in late 1944.

Considering that Steinbeck first heard this story—or, perhaps, the "grain of sand" that he would later revise into *The Pearl*—on a research trip to collect specimens and catalogue biodiversity, it is perhaps unsurprising that the novella's plot would be pertinent to contemporary environmental discourse. Yet this relevance is more than merely a symptom of these circumstances aboard the *Western Flyer* in 1940; throughout the 1930s, Steinbeck also developed a proto-ecological theory of human behavior, which he called the "phalanx." This theory, which Steinbeck thought would explain the observable differences in human behavior across individual and collective scales, was based on the work of a host of interdisciplinary figures—including W.C. Allee, a pioneer of the field of ecology, under whom Ricketts had studied at the University of Chicago.[2]

In this theory, humans in groups function much like cells in an organism, and also have a form of species memory that manifests through our basic instincts. As Steinbeck writes in an unpublished essay, entitled "Argument of Phalanx": "Men are not final individuals but units in the greater beast, the phalanx. Within the body of a man are units, cells, some highly specialized and some coordinate, which have their natures and their lives, which die and are replaced, which suffer and are killed. In their billions they make up man, the new individual" (1). Moreover, just as Steinbeck notes that individual cells are not entirely representative of the organ or tissue that they construct, neither does an individual human encapsulate the complexity of the phalanx "organism." In fact, Steinbeck argued that humans are not necessarily aware of participating in a phalanx, which he thought was only accessible through the subconscious ("Argument" 1).

Although Steinbeck did not impose limits on the size of a phalanx—depending on the context, he thought that one might be as small as two people, or as large as an entire species—he nevertheless retained a belief that humans in groups have fundamentally distinct behaviors from individuals operating on the basis of pure self-interest. In this regard, both Steinbeck's phalanx theory and his trip to the Sea of Cortez are representative of his intellectual investments in the field of what is today called ecology, and are furthermore deeply engrained in *The Pearl* in two distinct, yet overlapping, realms: "phalanx"-like relationships between humans, such as the dynamics between Kino's family and the people of La Paz; and more traditionally "ecological" relationships between humans and their environments, such as the attunement of Kino and Juana to their surroundings throughout the narrative.

Considering the novelty of the phalanx theory, it has been widely discussed in criticism of Steinbeck's fiction—especially on texts from the late 1930s, such as *In Dubious Battle*. However, as Kiyoshi Nakayama points out, Steinbeck's concept of the phalanx is also central to understanding the ecological worldviews at the heart of *The Pearl* (199–201). In this novella, phalanxes range in size from the entire city of La Paz to the small family unit led by Kino and Juana. For example, just as Steinbeck writes that men function as cell-like units that constitute a larger organism in "The Argument of Phalanx," so, too, is La Paz described in similarly biological language, as Steinbeck writes:

> A town is a thing like a colonial animal. A town has a nervous system and a head and shoulders and feet. A town is a thing separate from all other towns, so that there are no two towns alike. And a town has a whole emotion. How news travels through a town is a mystery not easily to be solved. News seems to move faster than small boys can scramble and dart to tell it, faster than women can call it over the fences. (21)

In addition to Steinbeck's anatomical descriptions of La Paz, moments in which the entire town is promptly aware of events in the narrative occur time and again throughout the novella, which embodies the rapid transmission of information in the organismal "nervous system" that Steinbeck notes above. Examples range from an instant awareness of Coyotito being stung by the scorpion (8–11), the knowledge that the priest was visiting the family (26–27), and the immediate understanding that Kino and Juana had discovered the pearl, as "the nerves of the town were pulsing and vibrating with the news—Kino had found the Pearl of the World. Before panting little boys could strangle out the words, their mothers knew it. The news swept on past the brush houses, and it washed in a foaming wave into the town" (21). In all of these moments, La Paz is depicted as a unique and holistic entity, in which individual humans are generally defined by their participation in a broader, superorganism-like context, and which connects these individuals on a material level through their shared knowledge.

As noted above, though, Steinbeck did not limit the application of the phalanx to large groups of people, but instead also believed that it applied to "the 'two or three gathered in My name'" ("Argument" 2). In *The Pearl*, this is evident in the strong sense of family portrayed in Kino, Juana, and Coyotito, and which also expands at times to include Juan Tomás, Apolonia, and their children. In the story, the phalanx of Kino's family is clearly differentiated from the broader phalanx of La Paz, as Steinbeck writes:

> It is wonderful the way a little town keeps track of itself and of all its units. If every single man and woman, child and baby, acts and conducts itself in a known pattern and breaks no walls and differs with no one and experiments in no way and is not sick and does not endanger the ease and peace of mind or steady unbroken flow of the town, then that unit can disappear and never be heard of. But let one man step out of the regular thought or the known and trusted pattern, and the nerves of the townspeople ring with nervousness and communication travels over the nerve lines of the town. Then every unit communicates to the whole. (40)

That is, in the act of discovering the pearl, Kino and Juana develop aspirations that effectively disrupt the balance of the ecosystem of La Paz, which isolates them from their neighbors as they become separated from the "whole" of the town. With this in mind, Steinbeck's revision of the protagonist in the folktale that he heard in 1940—from one boy to a young family—adds complexity to the narrative by applying his ecological phalanx concept to the central characters, which enables a deeper tension between the family and the town.

Moreover, paralleling the instantaneous communication among the people of La Paz, much is also immediately understood between Kino and Juana. For example, early in the story, Kino is aware of Juana's care for Coyotito, which he "could see . . . without looking at them. Juana sang softly an ancient song that had only three notes and yet endless variety of interval. And this was part of the family song too. It was all part. Sometimes it rose to an aching chord that caught the throat, saying this is safety, this is warmth, this is the *Whole*" (5). Beyond their intimate familiarity, Steinbeck's choice of the word "whole" here—and, indeed, his emphasis on it via capitalization and italicization—bears important connotations for how readers are to interpret this family's bond. For in addition to his reflections on the meaning of "the whole" in the epigraph to this chapter, Steinbeck also writes in *The Log from the Sea of Cortez*: "The whole is necessarily everything, the whole world of fact and fancy, body and psyche, physical fact and spiritual truth, individual and collective, life and death, macrocosm and microcosm" (125). That is, the word "whole" is meant to be interpreted literally as everything that "is," which Kino accesses through the phalanx of his family. Just as the passage in the paragraph above describes units communicating with the "whole" of La Paz, in this passage Kino's family enables him to feel related to everything that exists, establishing a perception of ecological relatedness not just to other people, but to all things, living and nonliving, throughout the narrative.

While Steinbeck's theory of the phalanx clearly plays a central role in *The Pearl*, it should be noted that despite this philosophy having commonalities with the field of ecology, it is nevertheless not entirely compatible with contemporary ecological thinking due to its generally anthropocentric focus. However, this is perhaps largely explained by the historical context in which Steinbeck was living and writing. As Wesley N. Tiffney, Jr. notes, ecology was still a relatively young discipline in the 1930s, having arisen around the turn of the century, and contemporary concepts such as "the environment," "environmentalists," and "environmental science" moreover did not exist at the time (2–4). So, while the field of ecology has unsurprisingly advanced and developed in the decades since the late 1930s and early 1940s, which has rendered some aspects of Steinbeck's approach outdated, he was nevertheless ahead of his time, as Clifford and Mimi Gladstein argue, when they write: "A generation before such ideas were popularized, Steinbeck exhibited an ecological understanding and environmental sophistication both rare and unusual" (163). As such, although Steinbeck's exploration of the phalanx concept is generally more anthropocentric than current approaches to ecological thinking would allow, his concerns and motivations nevertheless align with the development of the discipline.

Despite this anthropocentric focus of the phalanx theory, Steinbeck was nevertheless also attentive to ecological relationships among humans and nonhumans in *The Pearl*, as he combines a biologist's attention to detail with a writer's sense of drama in his environmental characterizations in the narrative, which parallels the writing style in *The Log from the Sea of Cortez* (Gladstein & Gladstein 163). For example, while describing the estuary by La Paz, Steinbeck calls attention to a variety of species participating in a variety of behaviors throughout the ecological niches of this setting, as he writes:

> The beach was yellow sand, but at the water's edge a rubble of shell and algae took its place. Fiddler crabs bubbled and sputtered in their holes in the sand, and in the shallows little lobsters popped in and out of their tiny homes in the rubble and sand. The sea bottom was rich with crawling and swimming and growing things. The brown algae waved in the gentle currents and the green eel grass swayed and little sea horses clung to its stems. Spotted botete, the poison fish, lay on the bottom in the eel-grass beds, and the bright-colored swimming crabs scampered over them. (14)

While this passage devotes the entirety of its attention to nonhuman beings, its placement in the narrative also recontextualizes Kino and Juana as participants in their surroundings, as this description follows their rejection by the town doctor and precedes their discovery of the pearl. Considering the major implications of these events for the story's plot, Steinbeck's description of the estuary above refocuses the reader's attention to the broader ecosystem in which their story occurs. And, having established the details of this environmental setting, Steinbeck moreover portrays Kino and Juana as intimately connected to various aspects of it, including the air, the landscape, and the sea—even as he ultimately critiques the consequences of human impacts on the environment in *The Pearl*.

After Steinbeck establishes Kino and Juana's place within this ecosystem, he immediately foreshadows the discovery of the pearl through a reading of the air over the sea. As he writes: "Although the morning was young, the hazy mirage was up. The uncertain air that magnified some things and blotted out others hung over the whole Gulf so that all sights were unreal and vision could not be trusted; so that sea and land had the sharp clarities and the vagueness of a dream" (14–15). In addition to echoing the passages describing the atmospheric haze in *The Log from the Sea of Cortez* (Nakayama 198), this "uncertain air" also applies to Kino and Juana's anxieties over Coyotito's health, while additionally foreshadowing the anticipation and disbelief felt after Kino discovers the pearl. As such, the atmospheric conditions here are intimately related to the characterizations of the family, whose anxieties and triumphs are rendered legible in the sky overhead.

Indeed, this is not the only time in which Kino and Juana are fundamentally connected to the air around them. As they prepare to escape La Paz, the sky is cloudy, and the "wind blew freshly into the estuary, a nervous, restless wind with the smell of storm on its breath, and there was change and uneasiness in the air" (61). And while this sense of restless unease characterizes the time before they can leave, it is furthermore fortuitous for their escape, as Juan Tomás points out that the "wind is good" since it will eliminate their tracks (65). Of course, even as the wind aids Kino and Juana, it furthermore characterizes the frantic nature of their escape, as it is described in the language of violence and fear. As Steinbeck writes: "The wind screamed over the Gulf and turned the water white, and the mangroves plunged like frightened cattle, and a fine sandy dust arose from the land and hung in a stifling cloud over the sea" (65). And during their flight from the city into the countryside, the intensity of this atmospheric description also characterizes their haste in outrunning the trackers, before eventually transitioning into an air of calmness after night falls, and Kino and Juana are outside of the city (66–67).

In addition to these connections to the air around them, Kino and Juana are also shown to have an intimate knowledge of—or what James C. Kelley calls a "visceral understanding" of (33)—their environmental surroundings. This visceral understanding is portrayed time and again throughout the novella, such as the early scenes of their morning routine (3–6), their flight from La Paz (66–79), and

Kino's attack on the trackers (80–84). It is furthermore featured as Kino and Juana prepare to flee La Paz; as Kino attempts to sleep: "His senses were burningly alive, but his mind went back to the deep participation with all things, the gift he had from his people. He heard every little sound of the gathering night, the sleepy complaint of settling birds, the love agony of cats, the strike and withdrawal of little waves on the beach, and the simple hiss of distance" (53). While this visceral understanding of his surroundings and his "deep participation with all things" recalls Kino's connections to the "whole" discussed above, this passage elaborates on this perception with more explicit focus on Kino's relationships to nonhuman entities, which underscores the ecological sensibilities at the heart of the story.

For while Steinbeck was, indeed, preoccupied with the human behavior in the phalanx concept, he was also remarkably attentive to the implications of this connection to the "whole" thing, as he writes in *The Log from the Sea of Cortez* that on a material level, biological distinctions between different species ultimately break down as "groups melt into ecological groups until the time when what we know as life meets and enters what we think of as non-life: barnacle and rock, rock and earth, earth and tree, tree and rain and air. And the units nestle into the whole and are inseparable from it" (178). More concisely, he elsewhere simply declares that, "ecology has a synonym which is ALL" (*Log* 72). With consideration to these ecological philosophies—which have indeed become fixtures of environmental discourses over the past several decades[3]—the portrayals of Kino's sense of kinship with nonhuman beings above should be interpreted literally, as Steinbeck approached these passages with a thorough investment in notions of ecological interrelatedness that transcended conventional boundaries of life and nonlife.

It is furthermore noteworthy that Steinbeck locates this "deep participation with all things" within Kino's heritage throughout *The Pearl*. This not only conveys a deep respect for the native inhabitants of La Paz, but it is also central to Steinbeck's critiques of settler colonialism and extractive industries, which are intimately related in the story. In this regard, although Kino and Juana are shown to have a visceral understanding of their environments, they are nevertheless implicated in a larger critique of pearl diving, as the collateral damage of this activity is highlighted throughout the narrative, from the detailed passages of dead oysters discarded on the sea floor, to the systemic cheating of the pearl divers by the brokers (and the violence against Kino's family associated with this system). In these moments, this extractive industry is shown to disrupt the local ecosystems of La Paz while primarily benefitting peoples elsewhere, which parallels a common feature of contemporary neoliberal extractive industries, such as mining for precious metals, or drilling for oil, gas, and even water.

For example, the collateral damage of the pearl-diving industry is foreshadowed even as Kino finds the great pearl, during which the narrative attention is split between the pearl's beauty and the oyster's death. As Steinbeck writes: "In the surface of the great pearl he could see dream forms. He picked the pearl from the dying flesh and held it in his palm, and he turned it over and saw that its curve was perfect" (20). As an environmental parable, this attention to both the desirability of the pearl, and the inherent destruction involved in its obtainment, offers clear parallels to contemporary experiences of rural communities located near sites of resource extraction, such as mines or drilling sites. All too often, these resources are obtained by multinational corporations and sold in global marketplaces, even as the local inhabitants must coexist with the waste of these practices. As such, these descriptions of the dead, discarded oysters in *The Pearl* not only foreshadow Coyotito's heartbreaking death, but they also underscore the negative local impacts of a system structured to benefit the wealthy elite at the expense of rural communities.

This dichotomy is further reinforced by *The Pearl*'s attention to the long history of resource extraction and settler colonialism in La Paz. This history is introduced in the family's interactions with the doctor, and is furthermore highlighted as Kino begins his dive, as he looks down to the "bed where the frilly pearl oysters lay fastened to the rubbly bottom, a bottom strewn with shells of broken, opened oysters. This was the bed that had raised the King of Spain to be a great power in Europe in past years, had helped to pay for his wars, and had decorated the churches for his soul's sake" (16–17). Emphasizing the violence of this practice, as well as its longevity, Steinbeck furthermore notes that men have "dived down and torn the oysters from the beds and ripped them open, looking for the coated grains of sand" for centuries (17). In this regard, it is clear from the juxtapositions of the sea bed to the King of Spain that this disruption of the ecosystem has been a longstanding arrangement, as wealth has been extracted from La Paz while its people have remained impoverished.

Of course, the history of this colonial practice is furthermore embodied by Kino's attempts to sell the pearl to agents in La Paz, who all work for the same buyer, and who, therefore, refuse to pay a fair price for it. And when Kino rejects these unfair offers, he undermines the entire system in which this economy functions, which is furthermore described in ecological terms. As Juan Tomás argues: "We do know that we are cheated from birth to the overcharge on our coffins. But we survive. You have defied not the pearl buyers, but the whole structure, the whole way of life, and I am afraid for you" (52). While acknowledging the unjust system of the pearl trade—which the majority of the town does not realize is cheating them (51)—Juan Tomás envisions this "whole structure" as a threat, since Kino is out of place in this ecosystem as long as he possesses the pearl. Inevitably, Juan Tomás's intuitions are correct, as the "phalanx" of the town reacts with jealousy toward Kino's refusal of the buyers' offers, since the town feels personally connected to the pearl:

> The essence of pearl mixed with essence of men and a curious dark residue was precipitated. Every man suddenly became related to Kino's pearl, and Kino's pearl went into the dreams, the speculations, the schemes, the plans, the futures, the wishes, the needs, the lusts, the hungers, of everyone, and only one person stood in the way and that was Kino, so that he became curiously every man's enemy. The news stirred up something infinitely black and evil in the town; the black distillate was like the scorpion, or like hunger in the smell of food, or like loneliness when love is withheld. The poison sacs of the

town began to manufacture venom, and the town swelled and puffed with the pressure of it. (23)

Ultimately, the balance of this "ecosystem" only returns to normal when the pearl is returned to the sea, which is depicted in yet another instance of serene, descriptive nature writing. As Steinbeck writes: "And the pearl settled into the lovely green water and dropped towards the bottom. The waving branches of the algae called to it and beckoned to it. The lights on its surface were green and lovely. It settled down to the sand bottom among the fern-like plants" (87). Despite the violence that results from the pearl's discovery, the language of this final passage nevertheless suggests a resilient conclusion to the story, as this environmental parable argues for a rejection of extractive industries by those who are typically exploited by them. For although Kino imagines that this pearl will open up better futures for his family, the reality of this system is that this is never truly accessible to them.

In this regard, *The Pearl*'s sustained relevance for contemporary readers lies not only within its persistent attention to the interrelatedness of humans, nonhumans, and their environments, which indeed has its roots in ecological perspectives that have grown in popularity and influence in recent years. But the story's relevance also stems from its timely critiques of extractive economies and environmental injustices, which will grow increasingly important as we navigate the environmental challenges of the twenty-first century.

Notes

1. In 1951, the narrative portion of *Sea of Cortez* was republished separately as *The Log from the Sea of Cortez* and was attributed solely to Steinbeck.

2. As Jackson Benson reports, Steinbeck's phalanx theory was influenced by a range of intellectual figures from disciplines such as philosophy (John Elof Boodin), anthropology (Ellsworth Huntington and Robert Briffault), history (Oswald Spengler and P.D. Ouspenski), folklore and psychology (Carl Jung), biology (W.C. Allee), and physics (Erwin Schrodinger, Max Planck, Niels Bohr, Albert Einstein, and Werner Heisenberg) (265–270). See also Richard Astro's *John Steinbeck and*

Edward F. Ricketts: The Shaping of a Novelist (61–74) and James C. Kelley's "John Steinbeck and Ed Ricketts: Understanding Life in the Great Tide Pool."

3.   For example, Kelley notes Steinbeck's relevance to "deep ecology" (34), and Gladstein & Gladstein find parallels in the Gaia hypothesis (164–165). More recently, a similar critical focus has been located in conversations surrounding posthumanism and material ecocriticism.

Works Cited

Astro, Richard. *John Steinbeck and Edward F. Ricketts: The Shaping of a Novelist*. U of Minnesota P, 1973.

Benson, Jackson. *The True Adventures of John Steinbeck, Writer*. Viking, 1984.

Gladstein, Clifford Eric, and Mimi Reisel Gladstein. "Revisiting the Sea of Cortez with a 'Green' Perspective." *Steinbeck and the Environment: Interdisciplinary Approaches*, edited by Susan F. Beegel, Susan Shillinglaw, and Wesley N. Tiffney, Jr., U of Alabama P, 1997, pp. 161–75.

Kelley, James C. "John Steinbeck and Ed Ricketts: Understanding Life in the Great Tide Pool." *Steinbeck and the Environment: Interdisciplinary Approaches*, edited by Susan F. Beegel, Susan Shillinglaw, and Wesley N. Tiffney, Jr., U of Alabama P, 1997, pp. 27–42.

Nakayama, Kiyoshi. "*The Pearl* in the *Sea of Cortez*: Steinbeck's Use of Environment." *Steinbeck and the Environment: Interdisciplinary Approaches*, edited by Susan F. Beegel, Susan Shillinglaw, and Wesley N. Tiffney, Jr., U of Alabama P, 1997, pp. 194–208.

Steinbeck, John. "Argument of Phalanx," an unpublished essay in a letter to Richard Albee circa 1936, Letter obtained from the Bancroft Library at the University of California Berkeley, with the assistance of The Martha Heasley Cox Center for Steinbeck Studies, San José State University, San José, CA 95192.

_____. *The Log from the Sea of Cortez*. 1951. Penguin, 1995.

_____. *The Pearl*. 1947. Penguin, 2002.

_____. *Working Days: The Journals of The Grapes of Wrath*, edited by Robert DeMott. Penguin, 1990.

Tiffney, Jr., Wesley N. "A Scientist's Perspective." Introduction. *Steinbeck and the Environment: Interdisciplinary Approaches*, edited by Susan F. Beegel, Susan Shillinglaw, and Wesley N. Tiffney, Jr., U of Alabama P, 1997, pp. 1–7.

Steps to a Littoral Ecology: Community and Nature in John Steinbeck's *The Pearl*

Michael Zeitler

> The role of science, like that of art, is to blend exact imagery with more distant meaning, the parts we already understand with those given as new into larger patterns that are coherent enough to be acceptable as truth. (Wilson 51)

> [Y]et the impulse which drives a man to poetry will send another man into the tide pools and force him to try to report what he finds there. (Steinbeck, *The Log from the Sea of Cortez* 1)

Novelist, short story writer, journalist, and Nobel Prize winner John Steinbeck chronicled the struggles of ordinary people with compassion and an abiding commitment to social justice. His subjects were working class, often poor, at times homeless and dispossessed, and, in telling their stories, his novels helped to reshape the nation's moral and political compass. Importantly, he also framed his narratives of the human condition not solely in anthropomorphic terms, but always with an ecological understanding that emphasized the interdependence of human culture and the natural world, prefiguring by half a century many of today's most important ecological concepts.

It is not surprising, then, that Steinbeck's short allegorical novel, *The Pearl*, has its origins and finds its major controlling metaphors in the author's study of marine biology. As for its origins, Steinbeck first heard the story of the poor Indian fisherman who discovered the Great Pearl of the World in March of 1940, while documenting the marine ecology of the Pacific Coast and the Gulf of California in Baja, Mexico, with his friend and long-time intellectual collaborator, Ed Ricketts. The two men saw themselves as modern-day Darwins on their own voyage of the *Beagle*, collecting and cataloguing specimens and noting the distribution of species along the Gulf's rocky shores, open coasts, bays, estuaries, and reefs. In the words of Steinbeck biographer Jackson Benson, "For a man who all his life had felt a part of nature and who thought of nature as *All*, collecting in the Gulf was a little like the sudden hearing for a time of the heartbeat of the universe" (442). They discovered snails, sea hares, crabs, shrimp, limpets, sponges, starfish, sea worms, octopi; in all, 550 species, of which about ten percent proved to be new (McElrath 207). Between collecting excursions, they talked, speculated on science, literature, and philosophy, and drank beer with the diverse local populations, all the time observing and collecting culture with as much enthusiasm as they documented marine life. It was in such a setting, near La Paz, that a local told Steinbeck the story about a young Indian and a great pearl.

In *The Sea of Cortez*, the narrative portion of the 1941 book he co-authored with Ricketts about their expedition, Steinbeck recounts in his log entry for March 20, 1940, a short, two hundred word version of the story that would become *The Pearl*, categorizing the tale as a legend "typical of such places" (*Log* 102). True to his impulse that collecting local stories and legends is as relevant to an understanding of a cultural region as collecting marine specimens is to understanding its ecology, he prefaced his narrative with a sentence or two on the ecological history of human interactions with the sparse, arid landscape of the Baja peninsula, a habitation largely "unfriendly to colonization" by Europeans. Humans were not wanted in great numbers, he tells us. Nevertheless, they came, drawn by the potential riches of the oyster beds, for "The robes of the Spanish kings and the stoles of Bishops in Rome were stiff with the pearls from La Paz" (*Log* 102). And with the arrival of Europeans, "as in all concentrations of natural wealth, the terrors of greed were let loose on the city again and again" (*Log* 102).

From there, as Steinbeck records it, the basic facts and framework of the log entry are in the main broadly consistent with those of the novel as expanded by Steinbeck in 1944 for publication as *The Pearl*, first in the *Women's Home Companion* in December 1945 and later in book form for Viking in November, 1947: a poor indigenous fisherman finds a pearl of great size and value, dreams of the great riches it will bring, and, rather than be cheated by the local pearl buyers, refuses to sell it and hides it under a stone. That night he is beaten and searched, and even after fleeing inland, is tracked, waylaid, and tortured. Finally, and only "with his soul in danger and his food and shelter insecure" (*Log* 103) is he able to free himself by cursing the pearl and casting it back into the sea. The story, Steinbeck tells us, "seems to be a true story, but it is so much like a parable that it almost can't be" (*Log* 103).

While most critics have followed Steinbeck in seeing the tale as a parable, or at least parable-like, there has been little interpretative consensus about its exact allegorical nature (Morris 149–162, Lisca 134). Indeed, Stanley J. Krause, in his summary of *The Pearl*'s various critical interpretations over time, points out that the novel "has been regarded on the 'black' side as defeatist, negativistic, pessimistic, somber, and pathetic, tragic, a study in futility, and a rejection of the promise of salvation; while, on the 'white' side, it has been taken as heroic, a rejection of naturalism, a re-establishment of the meaning of existence, a personal victory, and a triumphant preparation for salvation" (4). In juxtaposition to the wide-ranging moral register suggested in these allegorical readings, this essay proposes instead to view the novel's plots and themes through the lens of its origins, through the lens of Steinbeck's and Ricketts' deeply ecological observations on marine biology.

A decade before the 1940 scientific expedition to the Gulf that occasioned his first acquaintance with the story of the pearl, the two men were already exploring the intertidal zones of the central California coast. Steinbeck had met Ricketts in 1930, when Ricketts' biological marine laboratory on Cannery Row in Monterey was becoming a magnet for artists, writers, scientists, and the area's bohemian population, a place where friends gathered for food, drink, music, and intellectual conversation. Something of the flavor of their youthful friendship can be found in Steinbeck's fictionalized portrayal of Ricketts as "Doc" in the novels *Cannery Row* and *Sweet Thursday*. Steinbeck already had a growing interest in marine biology and years before their first meeting had taken classes at the Hopkins Marine Lab in Pacific Grove, California. In

Ricketts he found an ideal mentor and partner. Ricketts had studied marine biology at the University of Chicago under W.C. Allee, a pioneering ecologist who investigated the effects of environmental stimuli on cooperative group behavior among invertebrates. In his 1931 *Animal Aggregations* Allee had argued the existence of "an automatic mutual interdependence among organisms ... a sort of co-operation" that is a "fundamental trait of living matter" (355). Allee concluded: "Evidently mutual interdependence, or automatic co-operation, is sufficiently widespread among the animal kingdom to warrant the conclusion given above that it ranks as one of the fundamental qualities of animal protoplasm, and probably of protoplasm in general" (357).

Allee's work was a life-long influence on Ricketts, and soon the two friends were speculating on similar socio-biological patterns in human ecology, speculations that would continue in their conversations and writings throughout the decade leading up to the 1939 publications of *The Grapes of Wrath* and Ricketts's *Between Pacific Tides*. Allee's ecological approach clearly influenced Ricketts' thinking about marine ecology. "In my book (*Between Pacific Tides*)," he wrote in his notes, "there will be frequent considerations of an ecological and sociological nature, as contrasted to the usual systematic approach. Ecology will be defined, briefly, as that science that deals with the framework of relations between an animal and its environment, both biological and physical" (qtd. in Hedgpeth, vol. 1, 33). Ricketts would employ such terms as "wave shock," "competitive exclusion," "habitat," and "food chain" long before they were common in scientific or popular usage, and the holistic language and ecological philosophy that Ricketts used to discuss marine biology would prove a formative influence in Steinbeck's thinking as well.

As early as June, 1933, Steinbeck would comment to his friend Carlton Sheffield that "the group is an individual as boundaried, as diagnosable, as dependent on its units and as independent of its units' natures, as the human unit, or man, is dependent on his cells and yet is independent of them" (*Letters* 75). Fifteen years later, in his forward to the second (1948) edition of Ricketts's classic,

Steinbeck would again reaffirm his belief that "there are answers to the world's questions in the little animals of tide pools, in their relations to one another" (*Pacific Tides* vi). Thus, while the story of Kino, Juana, and the pearl touches on such humanistic themes as ambition, community, tradition, fate, survival, and justice, Steinbeck continually frames these issues within a Darwinian natural world, a biological struggle for survival where death to one is life to another. Although Steinbeck the artist might focus on human conflicts, for Steinbeck the naturalist the unit of study cannot be the individual organism, but a complex web: an interdependent, biologically based ecosystem. As with the oyster bed, the tide pool, and mountain stream ecologies described in *The Pearl,* the human world of Indian fishermen, their families and neighbors, Spanish merchants, beggars, and the professional classes of clergy and doctors are also part of intricate webs of relationships held together by traditions, customs, beliefs, memories, and stories—whole systems of knowledge and power. These webs of interconnectivity, evolving early on in Steinbeck's writing career, derived from his collaborative biological studies and conversations with Ricketts, and formulated in his narrative commentary to the *Sea of Cortez*, collectively develop the major controlling metaphors of *The Pearl*: the biology of colonial animals such as pelagic tunicates and the theme of community, the tide pool or mountain stream organic ecosystems and the themes of interdependence and survival, and an oyster's formation of a pearl as thematic of an organism's natural resistance to alien irritants. Uniting these metaphors is an ecological imperative implied by the necessity to place the human community, together with its institutions and ideologies, within a larger biological context.

Five days after noting the legend of the pearl in his log book, Steinbeck records the following:

> There are colonies of pelagic tunicates which have taken a shape like the finger of a glove. Each member of the colony is an individual animal, but the colony is another individual animal, not at all like the sum of its individuals. Some of the colonists, girdling the open end, have developed the ability, one against the other, of making a pulsing movement very much like muscular action. Others of the colonists

collect the food and distribute it, and the outside of the glove is hardened and protected against contact. Here are two animals, and yet the same thing . . . (*Log* 164)

Here, drawn from Allee in its simple, biological form is Steinbeck's controlling metaphor for community. It is present in the opening pages of *Tortilla Flat*, where "when you speak of Danny's house you are understood to mean a unit of which the parts are men" (1). It is there in *The Grapes of Wrath*: As the migrants push westward along Route 66, the shift from the personal and individual "I" to the collective and communal "we" is given a biological metaphor: "This is the zygote. For here 'I lost my land' is changed; a cell is split and from its splitting grows 'We lost our land'" (152). The same dust-bowl refugees "scuttle like bugs," then "cluster like bugs" near water and shelter as the dark overtakes them, sharing food, stories, and hopes as each evening a new community comes to life (194).

In *The Pearl,* the small Mexican fishing village that serves as the novel's primary setting is an organic whole, coexisting with other communities in the natural world and subject to the same biological forces. And while the town is, in Joseph Fontenrose's formulation an "ecological unit" where "each kind of inhabitant— pearl fishers, pearl buyers, Spanish aristocrats, beggars, ants, dogs—has its niche, its particular means of preserving itself" (114), it is also something more than the sum of its part. "A town," Steinbeck writes in *The Pearl*, "is a thing like a colonial animal. A town has a nervous system and a head and shoulders and feet. A town is a thing separate from all other towns, so that there are no two towns alike. And a town has a whole emotion" (27). Like any living organism, the town's "pulse and vibrating nerves" (*The Pearl* 27) react to external stimuli, and its interconnected ganglia transmit information: "The news swept on past the brush houses, and it washed in a foaming wave into the town of stone and plaster" (28). Propelled by the same biological instinct for survival one finds in the natural world, a town seeks its own ecological homeostasis; "Let one man step out of the regular thought or the known and trusted pattern, and the nerves of the townspeople ring with nervousness and communication travels over the nerve lines of the town" (53). The town, on the one hand, is just one of the many multiple communities in the novel, like the oyster beds or the mountain streams. But it is "news" that swept past houses and "washed in a foaming wave" into "stone and plaster." For the human community, news is language and a signifier, like the stone and plaster, of culture and the wave is a metaphor.

The Pearl integrates into its emphasis on human interconnectivity the significance of narrative memory and storytelling—the "news" as pulsing through our interconnected ganglia—in binding us communally to one another, to nature, to the past, and to the evolutionary importance of human culture, the community without which we cannot survive. Even the "song" Kino adds to the morning sounds of awakened earth connects him as much to a cultural ancestry as to the natural habitat; "Now, Kino's people had sung of everything that happened or existed. They had made songs to the fishes, to the sea in anger and to the sea in calm, to the light and the dark and the sun and the moon, and the songs were in Kino and in his people—every song that had ever been made" (22).

Human interconnectedness is not only with the natural world but with its own past. The oyster beds supply the town with both food and revenue, and, conversely, swarms of fish live off the oysters thrown away by the pearl fishers. Yet it is Kino's canoe that represents his ability to survive as a predator in the oyster bed ecology, and the canoe is a creation of human culture, passed down as human knowledge, and thus a connection through memory to his ancestors. "And every year Kino refinished his canoe with a hard shell-like plaster by the secret method that had also come to him through his father" (19). Humans interact with their environment through culture and community, surviving, not so much individually through competition, but together through cooperation and adaptation.

For Steinbeck, thinking ecologically offers the possibility that human adaptation and cooperation are an integral part of natural selection; and, therefore, human culture has evolutionary value. Human culture and history inscribes the material objects of Kino's world, the boats, utensils, knives, guns, houses, fishing nets, and folk medicines with cultural meaning. Thus Kino, even in his desperation to escape his pursuers, will not steal a canoe, for "the killing of a man was not as evil as the killing of a boat" (80). Without a canoe, a man cannot survive, cannot feed his family. It represents the collective knowledge of the village; a culture passed down and improved upon through generations. His broken canoe symbolizes Kino's separation from his community, the seriousness of his transgression, his ambition juxtaposed against the social patterns of village life. He must steal away in the dark, as the town "closed itself against the night" (89). Without the support of the village, Kino "was an animal now, for hiding, for attacking, and he lived only to protect himself and his family" (80).

Kino's story, the story of the Great Pearl will itself enter into the interconnected ganglia of collected nerve cells, as Steinbeck emphasizes the role of narrative in transmitting cultural memories. Steinbeck both prefaces and ends *The Pearl* referencing storytelling activities that connect Kino's tale to the collective consciousness of the community. "In the town they tell the story of the great pearl," he begins, reminding us that "the story has been told so often it has taken root in every man's mind" (1). Again, at the end of the novel we are told that everyone remembers the family's return: "There may be some old ones who saw it, but those whose fathers and whose grandfathers told it to them remember it nevertheless. It is an event that happened to everyone" (114–15). Stories like Kino's function culturally as examples of folk wisdom and reinforce the traditional conduct codes necessary for the town's cohesion and survival. "As with all retold tales that are in peoples' hearts, there are only good things and bad things and black things and white things" (1).

In another passage from *The Log from the Sea of Cortez*, this one dated April 22, Steinbeck expands the community metaphor from a colonial animal to a school of hungry fish that turn as a unit and dive as a unit. Observing their behavior, Steinbeck noted:

Their functions in the school are in some as yet unknown way as controlled as though the school were one unit. We cannot conceive of this intricacy until we are able to think of the school as an animal itself, reacting with all its cells to stimuli which perhaps might not influence one fish at all. And this larger animal, the school, seems to have a nature and drive and ends of its own (*Log* 240).

Here, individuals of a species act collectively as a unit, as the pearl buyers are "only one pearl buyer with many hands" (54). Finally, Steinbeck expands the collective metaphor from the species, to the tide pool, to the sea and to life itself:

> In the little Bay of San Carlos, where there were many schools of a number of species, there was a feeling (and feeling is used advisedly) of a larger unit which was the interrelation of species with their interdependence for food, even though that food was each other. . . . And perhaps *this* unit of survival may key into the larger animal which is the life of all the sea, and this into the larger world (*Log* 241).

In *The Pearl*, the opening of chapter three captures that "feeling . . . of a larger unit" with its interrelated species. It begins at daybreak on the water's edge describing the tide pool, a sea bottom "rich with crawling and swimming and crawling things" (18). Fiddler crabs and lobsters scamper in the shallows, in the eel grass and undulating waves of brown algae are sea horses, spotted botote, and bright colored crabs. Yet Kino's world, like Darwin's, is a fierce struggle for survival. As dawn breaks over the Sea of Cortez, animals begin the hunt for food: pigs root in the underbrush, roosters feint at each other in elaborate displays, and hawks hunt mice. What is death to one is life to another. The fishing beds necessary for the survival of Kino's family are home to great fishes that eat small fishes. Kino watches with "the detachment of God" as an ant lion traps an ant. Humanity does not stand apart. A scorpion instinctually reacts to the threat of Kino's presence and attacks, stinging the baby, Coyotito. Kino, just as instinctually, crushes it, stamping his enemy repeatedly(7). For Steinbeck, "There would seem to be only one commandment for living things: Survive! And the forms and species and units and groups are armed for survival, fanged for survival, timid for it, fierce for it, clever for it, poisonous for it, intelligent for it" (*Log* 241).

Even the little mountain spring where Kino and Juana find temporary shelter is both an oasis of life and a deadly killing ground. "The little pools of water were places of life because of the water, and places of killing because of the water, too" (104). The struggle for survival is recast in narrative terms as a hunt, and the trackers hunting Kino and Juana reenact a hunter/prey relationship: "He [Kino] knew these inland hunters. In a country where there was little game they managed to live because of their ability to hunt, and they were hunting him. They scuttled over the ground like animals and found a sign . . ." (96). Indeed, as Louis Owens suggested (38), Steinbeck's descriptions of the mountain landscape in *The Pearl*— the outcropping of granite, the deep crevices, where high in the gray stone mountain a small spring bubbles from a fissure in the stone to fill a pool, then cascades a hundred feet to another pool, strewn with wild grapes, maidenhair ferns, and little palms along the banks (102)— all derive from almost identical descriptions in *The Log from the Sea of Cortez*. A few days after hearing the story of the pearl, Steinbeck and Ricketts accepted an invitation from locals to climb by mules led by Indian guides into the mountains to camp and hunt. Like Kino and Juana, they make camp in a deep cleft in the granite outcropping of the mountains south of La Paz. "In this cleft," Steinbeck writes, "a tiny stream of water fell hundreds of feet from pool to pool. There were palm trees and wild grapevines and large ferns, and the water was cool and sweet" (*Log* 162). Like Kino's trackers, Steinbeck and Ricketts rode up the mountain trail carrying rifles to hunt. Like Kino, they watched the moon rise and their Indian guides talking softly together, smoking cigarettes, half-sleeping "like restless birds" (*Log* 163).

The pearl itself is another controlling metaphor for the novel, one once again drawn from marine biology and the pearl's origins in the sea. It reflects an organism's resistance to alien irritants. Steinbeck first introduces the oyster beds as another interconnected ecology: barnacles and bits of kelp attaching to oyster shells, small crabs climbing over all of them, swarms of fish feeding in the shells thrown back into the sea by the pearl fishermen (21). Reacting as a unit to Kino's disturbance, the shells of the animals close down tighter. But, Steinbeck tells us, the pearls were accidents:

> An accident could happen to these oysters; a grain of sand could lie in the folds of muscle and irritate the flesh until in self-protection the flesh coated the grain with a layer of smooth cement. But once started, the flesh continued to coat the foreign body until it fell free in some tidal fury or until the oyster was destroyed (21).

Organisms— in all the multiple and overlapping, individual and collective meanings Steinbeck gives to the term— will react to alien irritants armed with survival mechanisms to flush them out by "tidal fury" or they die.

The reader has seen the village, described by Steinbeck as a colonial animal, react to the news of Kino's discovery: "The news stirred up something infinitely black and evil in the town; the black distillate was like the scorpion, or like hunger in the smell of food. The poison sacs of the town began to manufacture venom, and the town swelled and puffed with the pressure of it" (30). The pearl, too, has also placed its alien poison into Kino's mind and spirit, and with it a personal ambition to transcend the limits placed on him by class, race, and education now threatens to disrupt the intricate interdependencies that make up village life. Yet the priest preaches sermon on the necessity of knowing your place, and Kino's brother warns him that personal and societal survival depends upon staying within traditional structures: "We do know we are cheated from birth to the overcharge on our coffins. But we survive. You have defied not only the pearl buyers, but the whole structure, the whole way of life, and I am afraid for you" (70). Kino exists between two worlds, yet alien to each.

Kino's pearl, however, seems to have value that cannot be expressed in simple biological terms, value beyond its usefulness (or lack thereof) to an oyster or even to its role in the life of the estuary. The first discovery of pearls in the bay drew the European world to La Paz and "the terrors of greed were let loose on the city again and again" (*Log* 102). The Europeans' greed for the pearls, like the sand irritant that created them, is toxic. Viewing the pearl symbolically, as capital, as wealth, raises issues in the novel of race, class, and colonialism, and, in raising these issues within the text's overall ecological framework, points to Steinbeck's novel as a prescient work of environmental and postcolonial criticism.

Mary Klages, in *Literary Theory: The Complete Guide*, identifies multiple components of current ecocritical theory, at least four of which are evident in *The Pearl*: biocentrism, bioregionalism, place, and ecological imperialism. Biocentrism denies the Western, anthropocentric view that sees a binary opposition between the human and the natural world and prioritizes the human. Race further complicates the Western human—nature opposition, as we see in *The Pearl*. Indigenous people in the colonizers' mind are, by reason of their non-European lifestyle, metonymically connected to nature. They are part of nature and thus fall on the "wrong" side of the human-nature binary, with the non-human, with the animals. Kino, Steinbeck tells us, could kill the doctor more easily than he could talk to him, "for all of the doctor's race spoke to all of Kino's race as though they were simple animals" (12). In contrast, a biocentric view denies that humans are inherently more important than the biotic community as a whole. Klages quotes Aldo Leopold, whose *Sand County Almanac* argued for a "land ethic" that "enlarges the boundaries of the community to include soils, waters, plants, and animals" (quoted in Klages 143). A related term, bioregionalism, describes defining geographic features of dwelling, sustainability, and habitation through ecological terms. These are Ricketts' working principles in *Between Pacific Tides*, and Steinbeck's throughout his career, whether in *The Grapes of Wrath* or *The Log from the Sea of Cortez*, or *The Pearl*. The natural world, including man, Steinbeck writes, is a seamless whole:

> [S]pecies are only commas in a sentence ... One merges into another, groups melt into ecological groups until such time when what we think of as life meets and enters what we think of as non-life: barnacle and rock, rock and earth, earth and tree, tree and rain and air. And the units nestle into the whole and are inseparable from it. (*Log* 216)

In her discussion of bioregionalism, Klages differentiates between the concepts of space and place. Places, she argues, have meaning ascribed to them, spaces don't. "Places feel warm, you can smell them, recall them, think about how you feel in them" (146). Both also expose ideology and value. Europeans settling in the Americas see only empty space. They build their farms, cities, and factories and create place. At the same time, the land was not open space but inhabited. To native peoples it was place and that sense of place was first altered, and then stolen. In *The Pearl*, as Juana and Kino carry Coyotito to the doctor, "they came to the place where the brush houses stopped and the city of stone and plaster began" (10). The ubiquitous presence of living things and sense of intimacy with all life one feels in Kino's village is abruptly replaced by the man-made gardens, flagstone water fountains, and caged birds of the European city— ideologically signifying "civilization," a European place separated from the rest of the town and the rest of creation by "harsh outer walls" (10). The doctor, with his eye on a return to Paris, is utterly alienated from the natural world that surrounds him outside those harsh walls, yet, of necessity, includes him unawares.

An awareness of such conflicting ideological views in relation to the environment forms the core of what Klages defines as "ecological imperialism" and its implication of "colonizing forces taking, changing, damaging, or otherwise appropriating the environments of colonized territories, usually for political and economic gain on behalf of the colonizers, at the expense of the colonized" (149). Pearls had made Spain powerful; and Spain, in turn, altered the relationship of Kino's people to their environment and forced upon them adaptive survival strategies. Europeans had for nearly four hundred years "beaten and robbed and starved and despised Kino's race, and frightened it too, so that the indigene came humble to the door" (Steinbeck 12).

Kino attempts to restore balance by casting the pearl into the sea. Its poisonous song diminishes to a whisper and disappears even as the pearl itself sinks into the sea ferns and scampering crabs on the bay's sandy bottom. Yet, for Steinbeck, humanity's imprint cannot be so quickly erased. Even as he is hearing Kino's story for the first time that night in La Paz, before he and Ricketts have time to publish their study of the Gulf's diverse marine life or he can expand the short tale into *The Pearl*, the dynamics of human interaction are recalibrating the bay's littoral ecologies. Fleets of Japanese shrimp boats with overlapping scoops are dredging the bays for tons of shrimps and destroying species (*Log* 8). And in La Paz, the beaches where Kino's people lived and fished are being replaced by expensive hotels. "Probably the airplanes will bring week-enders from Los Angeles before long, and the beautiful poor bedraggled old town will bloom with a Floridian ugliness" (*Log* 118). Perhaps, as Steinbeck suggests in his Preface, the story might just be a parable where "everyone takes his own meaning from it" (1). Yet in the decades since the novel's publication a new and powerful global environmental consciousness has emerged, aided by writers like John Steinbeck and Ed Ricketts, making it possible to see *The Pearl*'s allegorical warnings of human "progress" and greed as a deeply ecological moral imperative.

Works Cited

Allee, W.C. *Animal Aggregations*. U. of Chicago P, 1931.

Astro, Richard, and Tetsumaro Hayashi. *Steinbeck: The Man and His Work*. Oregon State U P, 1972.

Benson, Jackson. *The True Adventures of John Steinbeck, Writer*. Penguin, 1984.

Fontenrose, Joseph. *John Steinbeck: An Introduction and Interpretation*. Holt, Rinehart and Winston, 1963.

Hedgepeth, Joel W., editor. *The Outer Shores* (2 vols.). Mad River P, 1978.

Klages, Mary. *Literary Theory: The Complete Guide*. Bloomsbury Academic, 2017.

Krause, Sydney J. "*The Pearl* and 'Hadleyburg': From Desire to Renunciation," *Steinbeck Quarterly*, vol. 7, no. 1, 1975, p. 4. Ball State University. dmr.bsu.edu/digital/collection/steinbeck/id/3460/rec/24.

Lisca, Peter. *John Steinbeck: Nature and Man*. Thomas Crowell, 1978.

McElrath, Joseph R., Jessie Crisler, and Susan Shillinglaw. *John Steinbeck: The Contemporary Reviews*. Cambridge U P, 2009.

Morris, Harry, "*The Pearl:* Realism and Allegory." *Steinbeck: A Collection of Critical Essays.* Edited by Robert Murray Davis. Prentice Hall, 1972. 149–163.

Owens, Louis. *John Steinbeck's Revision of America.* U of Georgia P, 1985.

Ricketts, Edward, and Jack Calvin. *Between Pacific Tides*, 3rd ed. Stanford U P, 1962.

Steinbeck, Elaine, and Robert Wallstein. *Steinbeck: A Life in Letters.* Penguin, 1989.

Steinbeck, John. *The Grapes of Wrath: Text and Criticism.* 1939. Edited by Peter Lisca and Kevin Hearle. Penguin, 1997.

_____. *The Log from the Sea of Cortez.* 1951. Viking, 1962.

_____. *The Pearl.* 1947. Bantam, 1956.

_____. *Tortilla Flat.* 1935. Viking, 1963.

Wilson, Edward O. *Biophilia.* Harvard U P, 1984.

The Song of Inequality: Sickness and Wealth in Steinbeck's *The Pearl*

Jericho Williams

In twenty-first century America, social concerns relating to environmental, financial, and personal health pervade media discourse. In broader terms, the effects of climate change cast a shadow over the coming century. Since the Recession of 2008, there has been an increase in wealth among a small, financial elite and more attention directed towards the thinning of a middle class and underemployment. A rise in obesity indicates an until recently unimaginable reality that young adults may not live as long as their parents' or grandparents' generations. And man-made drug epidemics, ranging from opioids marketed and distributed by pharmaceutical companies to methamphetamines produced in people's homes, have decimated the health of vast numbers of people, particularly those living in impoverished pockets of the country. A lack of access to affordable health care, or even health care at all, continues to be a concern for a significant portion of the population living in poverty and at great distances from adequate medical facilities.

For these reasons, now is the perfect moment for a renewed attention to John Steinbeck's *The Pearl*, a deceptively complex novella that confronts inequality partially from an angle of health and social wellness. This essay discusses *The Pearl* while seeking to accomplish three tasks. First, it works against readings that reduce the story to a simple parable or allegory about one man's rise and fall after stumbling upon an extraordinary pearl. Instead of seeking to fully undermine these existing interpretations, the essay calls attention to key details that also ground the novella's sense of realism. It pays closer attention to the function of poison, sickness, and medical treatment as they relate to poverty and wealth. By focusing on the conflict between Kino and the doctor rather than Kino's personal struggles after locating the pearl, the essay sheds light on the inequity that prevents a father from gaining immediate care for his son in an emergency situation, and then speculates how this trauma and the father's subsequent interactions with a corrupt doctor impact his reckless plight that comprises the remainder of *The Pearl*.

The Problem of Parable

The debate about whether or not *The Pearl* should be read as a parable has been central to critical responses to the text. Charles Metzger views the story as a parable relating the "high price of hope," noting that Kino's loss of his son and his subsequent tossing of the pearl into the sea is symbolic of all that he sacrifices for the wrong pursuits (47). More pointedly, Joseph Allegretti describes the novella as a "study of the self-defeating nature of greed" (8). Richard Astro adds that the story may be a parable of the search for happiness while transitioning from a primitive to a modern world (63). Breaking away from the commonality that links these readings of *The Pearl*, Peter Lisca notes that the story should be considered an allegory because it exceeds the typical length of a parable. In developing his argument, Lisca hints at the greater problem with either designation as parable or allegory, however, by arguing that *The Pearl* also should not be considered the former because it is "too complex and rich in meaning" (68).

The Pearl's epigraph does not make a conclusive determination any easier. Evoking the spirit of an oral tradition, the speaker reports that the story of Kino, Juana, and their baby Coyotito is famous throughout the town. Everyone, it seems, not only knows the story, but retains and freely shapes their own version of it. The speaker shares, "And, as with all retold tales that are in people's hearts, there are only good and bad things and black and white things and good and evil things and no in-between everywhere" (1). In other words, even before it begins, the story is the town's tale, with meanings for everyone who has made it their own. As much as this clarifies its great value, it also implicitly calls attention to the limitations of the oral tradition. As told by the townspeople, the story inevitably appears in the form of either a parable or allegory, a short tale with profound and immediate lessons. The speaker closes the epigraph by adding, "If this story is a parable, perhaps everyone takes his own meaning from it and reads his own life into it. In any case, they say in town that . . ." (1). This final sentence is noncommittal about the nature of the tale's form. It points out that the story's events may fit well into the form of a parable or allegory. Yet, it also informs readers that the version they have is merely one account, and in the case of Steinbeck's narrator, a version that pushes beyond the more common and simplified verbalized form.

Accounts of the genesis and development of *The Pearl* shed greater light on its presentation. Steinbeck first heard a similar story of an Indian boy and a pearl in the spring of 1940, but he did not begin composing the novella until November 1944. During this four-year interval, the writer experienced significant life changes. Following a divorce in 1942, he remarried in 1943 and then became a father in August of 1944. He also served as a U.S. war correspondent in 1943, an opportunity that placed Steinbeck close to the Allied invasion of Italy at the Salerno beachhead and left him in a state of exhaustion upon his return home (Simmonds 175). Alienated by war, Steinbeck ventured to Mexico in 1945 to research what became *The Pearl*, and while there, as Susan Shillinglaw notes, he embraced what he believed to be a less materialistic culture more amenable to his vision of an ideal world (162). Given the difficulties of the prior years, this change of pace provided great relief, although Steinbeck also faced a new career challenge. Unlike his prior work, he had to imagine *The Pearl* in a compressed, screenplay form for a film to be produced and released in 1947. The situation was unique because the novella would be released simultaneously with the film, so he sought to develop a similar story in two separate mediums. In the process, he realized that the words he chose had to "convey a disciplined tone . . . completely removed from anything Mexican, American, or Spanish, native or educated" (Wagner-Martin 95). This constraint, arguably more than anything else, shaped the development of a novella that resonates as deeply personal while also suggesting elements of a parable or allegory. In the course of time, it also fueled a separate debate among critics about whether *The Pearl* should be judged as evidence of a "significant realistic novelist or merely a didactic preacher" (Meyer 161). Altogether, the novella, verbally tight though not as exhaustively detailed as Steinbeck's lengthier novels, compresses the complexities of what Steinbeck intuited or experienced while not fully falling into the mode of parable or allegory, creating a distinct tension that nourishes and sustains its lasting impact.

Songs, Poisons, and Poverty

The opening paragraphs of *The Pearl* isolate the tension between culture and individuality. Kino awakens and listens to the sounds that surround the brush house where he lives with his wife Juana and young child Coyotito. Highlighting the noises of roosters, pigs, birds and the waves outside, the narrator notes that they function as part of Kino's daily music. When Kino closes his eyes and focuses on what he hears, the narrator adds, "Perhaps he alone did this and perhaps all of his people did it. His people had once been great makers of songs so that everything they saw or thought or did or heard became a song. That was very long ago. The songs remained; Kino knew them, but no new songs were added" (3–4). The narrator acknowledges a cultural tradition that stems from many generations prior to Kino's life and provides the comforting consistency of songs, which convey the value of an ongoing culture that shapes Kino's identity. Yet, the presence of the songs does not diminish Kino's individuality or render him a stereotype. Immediately following this passage, the narrator adds, "That does not mean that there were no personal songs" (4). This early scene pivotally delineates Kino as a person of his culture and also as an individual, and simultaneously unites the two parts of Kino's personality through the songs of his culture and the songs that he perceives and shapes on his own. The first song mentioned is the Song of the Family, a combination of the sounds of the most important people in Kino's life. Kino begins the day by hearing Juana begin her morning rituals and routines while Coyotito sleeps. As he steps outside, he recognizes the sounds of other animals and neighboring families in the distance, which coalesce to form something similar to, though not exactly the same as, the Song of the Family. Again, Steinbeck stresses the commonalities between

Kino's family life and those of his neighbors without generalizing an entire community. Kino pauses and listens before walking back into his house for breakfast. At this point, the story depicts a man waking up and beginning an average morning. Untroubled, he steps into a daily routine unaware of the coming conflict.

The semblance of normality and the everyday comfort of the Song of the Family dissipates with the introduction of poison, a central motif in *The Pearl*. When Kino walks inside, the narrator notes that his breakfast consists of a corncake with pulque, "the only breakfast he had ever known outside of feast days and one incredible fiesta on cookies that had nearly killed him" (6). Though the first major family crisis involves poisonous venom when a scorpion stings Coyotito, this initial reference is also important because it foreshadows the material divide that will later threaten Kino and his family. Calling attention to the impact of sugar on a person unaccustomed to its impact, the narrator hints at a wealth gap that will later resurface. For Kino, the break from his cultural tradition in the overconsumption of cookies precipitates either a great sickness, if the narrator's comments are taken in jest, or near death, if they are read sincerely. Although there is no additional information about the fiesta, Steinbeck introduces an unsettling idea. By aligning a common baked good associated with Western Culture as a potentially poisonous product, he suggests that the cultural and material divide between separate groups of people can abruptly become life-threatening.

This situation sets the stage for a greater conflict once a scorpion stings Coyotito, when the Song of the Family becomes the Song of Evil. Juana responds quickly, sucking away the venom, but there is an air of uncertainty as other villagers arrive at the scene. The venom, known to make adults sick, has the capacity to kill infants, so Juana cries out for the help of a doctor. Immediately, Steinbeck's narrator switches from Kino's perspective to the viewpoint of the entire village. He writes, "A wonderful thing, a memorable thing, to want the doctor. To get him would be a remarkable thing. The doctor never came to the cluster of brush houses. Why should he, when he had more than he could do to take care of the rich people who lived in the stone and plaster houses of the town" (8–9). At this point, Kino's family's narrative becomes representative of something greater, indicating the great divide between need and access by highlighting the unlikelihood of a family like Kino and Juana's receiving help from a community in which physicians regularly work. As the villagers know, their chances are slim. By switching to a broader, collective point of view, Steinbeck briefly undercuts the drama of a family emergency to convey the inequities of the situation. Jolted away from Juana's urgency, readers uncomfortably see what she cannot through the perspective of the villagers.

Steinbeck enlarges the scope of this situation when Juana insists that they seek the doctor's assistance. By continuing to focus on the onlookers who follow Kino, Juana, and Coyotito towards the doctor's house, he builds towards to a crucial moment in *The Pearl*. The crowd expands as they cross the threshold from village to town. Steinbeck spotlights the knowledge of those trailing and participating in the unfolding situation. In particular, he notes the wisdom of four beggars who sit on the steps of the church, giving voice to their knowledge and keen social awareness. Not only are the beggars able to read the facial expressions of common people in town, but they can also intuit the doctor's character based on his disposition and decisions. The beggars know him to be ignorant, cruel, and materialistic based on their prior observations. In presenting the beggars' point of view just before a key moment in the text, Steinbeck asserts the value of the incisive observations of those presumably "locked in wordlessness" (Covici xxii). He suggests material and educational boundaries as false and limiting constructs that even a community's poorest can understand. This heightens the drama of the situation, given that a child's life is at stake, and places ethnicity and class divisions at the forefront of *The Pearl*'s concerns just as Kino and Juana arrive at the doctor's door.

The Doctor's Denial
Given *The Pearl*'s focus on the plight of Kino, the doctor appears less often in critical discussions even though he plays a sinister role in the unfolding of the story. As the novella's wealthiest and most

powerful figure, he wields great influence, although he remains fully separated from Kino's life until Coyotito's emergency. Switching from the beggars' point of view to the doctor's background, Steinbeck details the great divide between the doctor and the villagers. Socially, the doctor is a member of a race of people who, for a period of four hundred years, have exercised power and authority over those of Kino's ethnicity. For Kino, he is, therefore, unapproachable. Not unlike uninsured Americans in need of medical treatment in the present day, the fearful and upset Kino seeks his help only in great need. Steinbeck writes, "Rage and terror went together. He could kill the doctor more easily than he could talk to him" (11). The social separation between the two becomes fully apparent when Kino first knocks outside the doctor's door. A servant of Kino's race arrives and refuses to speak with him in their language, heightening the tension as he leaves to inform the doctor that Kino waits outside.

The ethnic divide between Kino and the doctor proves to be merely an introduction to the decadence within the house, which Steinbeck portrays as part of the doctor's own sickness. In sharp contrast to the brush houses of the village, the doctor lives ensconced in material wealth that drives his lifestyle and disposition. Steinbeck reinforces this idea by identifying some of the doctor's possessions before offering a description of the doctor. He describes the doctor resting in "his high bed," adorned in "red watered silk that had come from Paris," and drinking from a "silver chocolate pot and a tiny cup of eggshell china" (12). Nearby, cigarettes sit near a small Oriental gong and religious pictures. The contrast between the description of the doctor sitting in bed and Kino's everyday morning routine in the village that opens *The Pearl* is stark. In place of the comforting Song of the Family, expensive objects and a commissioned picture of his dead wife clutter and clot the room, framing the doctor as isolated with little else but desire for more. The narrator dispels the idea that the doctor may be mourning the loss of his wife by noting that he longs for a time when he was able to keep a mistress in Paris and eat out at restaurants. Steinbeck writes, "The doctor had once for a short time been a part of the great world and his whole subsequent life was memory and longing for France" (12). He suffers from an absence of purpose and desires things that provide little comfort. Insensitive to the plights of others and selfish without a greater sense of purpose or community, the doctor maintains a social separation from the villagers. Paradoxically, he is the socially sickest person in the story, immune to understanding what Kino's request for help means to the villager's family and community. Walled away and shielded by a servant who prevents interactions with the lesser others from occurring, the doctor occupies a position offering help only to the degree that will serve his material interests.

Though it occurs early in *The Pearl*, the confrontation between Kino and the absent doctor via a servant points to one of the novella's stronger critiques: the danger of placing too much power and trust in the hands of private authorities as it relates to human health. In Kino's case, the doctor has a choice to deny care based solely on the patient's ethnicity and background. From his vantage point, the problem is a lack of funding and more systemic in nature. Yet, in the social setting that Steinbeck presents, there is no way for the doctor to fully know the consequences of his prejudices because he lives so deeply divided from the villagers. He assumes their interests are not similar to his own because they are lesser people and do not accrue enough material wealth to pay for his services. Consequently, he denies access to Kino, who learns firsthand that he and the villagers cannot gain help from the doctor even in the most pressing emergency situations. By emphasizing the contrast between the manners in which Kino and the doctor live, *The Pearl* criticizes the silent ways that ethnicity and social status determine the extent of an emergency. The choice that the doctor makes not to help Kino initially sparks a downward spiral for Kino because he comes face-to-face with the fact that his ethnicity and lack of material wealth separate his son from adequate care. In the comfort of his room, the doctor questions why he should help a group of people he considers little more than animals, while outside the gate Kino is left without the possibility of service.

The Appearance of the Pearl and the Doctor's Return

The doctor reappears later in the novella with the discovery of an extraordinary pearl. Before Kino's luck changes, Juana treats Coyotito's sting with brown seaweed, "which was as good a remedy as any and probably better than the doctor could have done" (16). The trajectory of Coyotito's improving health prospects follow the narrative events closely, as Steinbeck focuses on the unpredictability of health and the human body, and the ways in which financial incentives sway the chances of receiving effective treatment. While composing *The Pearl*, Steinbeck was sensitive to the darker realities lurking beneath the surface of daily life. During his stint as a journalist during the Second World War, he routinely felt frustrated by the fact that what he observed would be censored and never reach his audience as he hoped it might (Lewis 40). Powerful financial interests obscured the truth, a major theme that he develops in *The Pearl*. At length, Steinbeck emphasizes the formation of the pearl that Kino finds, stressing the fact that pearls are natural accidents that become tokens in which humans arbitrarily bestow great value.

During the search for a pearl, Kino is desperate for a way to help his son, so to imagine his plight as a soon-to-be, rag-to-riches parable undermines the gravity of the situation and its lasting impact. Having been shamed at the doctor's door, he goes to sea as a last resort. The blind hope of procuring a pearl represents his final chance, and even though the quest is a familiar one, it does not deter the notion that he feels indebted to the obligation of locating a token that will merit service for a health-related emergency. Put another way, Kino does not return to the village from the doctor's house as the same person because he learns that he has to play by a different set of cultural rules. On the heels of the trauma, stress, and frustration he undergoes at the doctor's doorstep, Kino will remain blinded by the absurdity of chance until the end of *The Pearl*. The doctor's denial of his request for help prompts him to see things differently, which Steinbeck clarifies when Kino hoists the pearl from the sea. At the exact moment that he realizes its value and relishes his great fortune, Kino looks at Coyotito and observes "that the swelling was going out of the baby's shoulder, the poison was receding from its body" (20). As soon as this occurs, Coyotito's health status is set aside in favor of Kino's great celebration of finally locating the means to alter their circumstances.

The doctor reappears in the next chapter, but not before Steinbeck details the impact of the pearl's discovery on the town. The news spreads like a virus, and it immediately alters Kino's status from an everyday villager to a person of great notoriety. Crucially, Steinbeck describes how the pearl alters the vantage points of other people in town. A priest, for example, ponders whether he has baptized Coyotito or not, and a shopkeeper thinks of men's clothes that he has not sold. Then, the news reaches the doctor, who sits "with a woman whose illness was age, though neither she nor the doctor would admit it" (21). In the same instance of avoiding the truth to maintain a good business relationship with this woman, he begins to imagine what he might do with Kino's wealth and quickly claims Coyotito as his patient. Ironically, this moment indicates that the one thing that Kino lacked now disqualifies his son from receiving adequate care. Steinbeck writes, "The poison sacs of the town began to manufacture venom, and the town swelled and puffed with the pressure of it" (23). Although he indicts everyone who greedily desires the pearl, no one is more purposefully impacted than the doctor, who exercises great authority over the people's beliefs about their health.

Facilitated by the news of the pearl, the first meeting between Kino and the doctor details how wealth furthers the divide between need and care. Notably, it is the only instance in *The Pearl* in which someone of Kino's ethnicity and social status merits a visit from the doctor, who comes to Kino's house and enters freely. Steinbeck isolates the function of inequality as it relates to deceit in their interactions. When the doctor arrives, Kino stands at the door, "filling it, and hatred raged and flamed in the back of his eyes, and fear too, for the hundreds of years of subjugation were cut deep in him" (29). As much as the history of oppression factors into this moment, Kino also appears unwell. The joy associated with finding the pearl is nowhere to be found, as he senses that the doctor's appearance is one of many potential predatory figures hoping to capitalize from the pearl. Still, because the situation involves the health of his son, he allows him to see Coyotito; then, Kino cannot be fully confident of the doctor's ill will when the latter claims that the scorpion's poison remains within Coyotito and could resurface and cause harm. Kino suspects that the doctor exploits his lack of knowledge, but the risk of ignoring his advice is too great. He reflects, "He was trapped as his people were always trapped, and would be until … they could be sure that the things in the books were really in the books" (30). The divide between what Kino and the doctor knows, combined with wanting to make sure Coyotito's health continues to improve, convinces the father to allow the doctor to treat his son.

The doctor administers medicine to Coyotito that will make him sicker and guarantee that he must return within a short amount of time. After he leaves, Kino hears the music of evil as he watches Coyotito's condition become worse. Steinbeck then focuses on the doctor at home, as he awaits the exact moment he needs to return to the house and treat Coyotito again. Even if Kino cannot fully know the truth, this scene solidifies Steinbeck's critique. In a story that features more direct attacks on Kino and his family from others who openly desire the riches of the pearl, the doctor represents the novella's major calculating predator. Neighboring villagers suspect his motives and watch as he returns to the house to help solve symptoms of an illness that he engineered. Unlike the robbers that creep towards Kino's brush house or the men that later trail him, the doctor waltzes back to the household in a heroic fashion filled with ill will. As Juana, "with haunted eyes," suspiciously watches him work, the doctor exclaims, "'It is lucky that I know about the poison of the scorpion, otherwise— . . . '" (34). Taking advantage of his knowledge, he reverses what appears to be a poison that he administered to Coyotito. Unlike the other predatory figures in *The Pearl*, the doctor commits an unseen crime, claims credit for solving the problem, and then denies having knowledge of the pearl, fully aware that the great amount he charges will be paid from what the pearl fetches from the marketplace.

During the interlude following the doctor's first visit and his return, just as the news of Coyotito's declining condition following the doctor's treatment spreads among the villagers, Steinbeck writes, "sickness is second only to hunger as the enemy of poor people" (33). Partially as a means to combat the fear of his powerlessness in the face of sickness, Kino dreams that his son will not have to live in the way of his mother and father. As Stephen K. George suggests, these aspirations align with the American Dream and appeal to an American audience. George writes that the "average Western reader cannot help but applaud Kino's desires to gain knowledge (albeit vicariously) in order to defend himself against such predators as a doctor who would administer poison to a baby in order to profit from the pearl himself" (95–96). From the rejection he first feels at the doctor's doorstep to the suspicion that the doctor poses a threat to the family, Kino epitomizes someone threatened by poverty and then wealth.

The remaining portion of *The Pearl* details the great lengths that Kino pursues to guard what the pearl promises, though underpinning his cascading hopes remains the hunger for his son to have the basic forms of social assurance that the doctor denied him. To this extent, *The Pearl* presents not a parable of a man's rise and fall in pursuit of wealth, but rather a complicated story of someone whose motivation emerges from a desire for honest and fair treatment from a powerful medical official. Having experienced denial, Kino, like others living in poverty, finds himself in a stressful position of worry, distrust, and desperation, and these feelings impact his subsequent decisions. Though his wife and older brother warn him about the dangers of holding onto the pearl, he eschews their advice until the end, when Coyotito dies at the hands of men pursuing the pearl. The great tragedy and irony of Kino's attempt to retain the pearl for the benefit of his son is unmistakable with Coyotito's loss. At a great loss, he hurls the pearl back into the sea at the story's end. As horrific and cautionary as the conclusion appears on its own, it cannot be divorced from the mindset that prompts Kino's resistance to releasing the pearl. Lack and inequality fostered his desire, and the assurance of safety and his son's well-being motivated Kino to protect the pearl at all costs. The urgency to protect Coyotito and his family stems directly from his traumatic interaction with the corrupt doctor, which precipitates his descent.

Speaking directly to medical predicaments that appear nearly a century later, *The Pearl* protests the ways in which financial status rather than need determines treatment and care. Through Kino's plight, it also illustrates the detrimental impact of the inaccessibility of care based on race, social status, and class on one person's identity. Working against the concept of parable, the novella details problems that still tax the poor in the short-term and long-term, and that inevitably plague for-profit health-care industries in the absence of oversight and regulation. John Steinbeck asserts that so long as wealth influences the level and types of medical care, society's most susceptible bear the costliness of degradation and greed.

Works Cited

Allegretti, Joseph. "John Steinbeck and the Morality of Roles: Lessons for Business Ethics." *The Moral Philosophy of John Steinbeck*. Edited by Stephen K. George, Scarecrow P, 2005, pp. 21–32.

Astro, Richard. "*The Pearl: A Parable of the Human Condition.*" *Readings on* The Pearl. Edited by Jill Karson. Greenhaven P, 1999, pp. 62–66.

Covici, Pascal, Jr. "Introduction." *The Portable Steinbeck*. Edited by Pascal Covici, Jr. Penguin,1976, pp. xi-xxix.

Gannett, Lewis. "John Steinbeck: Novelist at Work." *The Atlantic Monthly*. vol. 176, no. 6, Dec. 1944, pp. 55–60.

George, Stephen K. "A Taoist Interpretation of John Steinbeck's *The Pearl.*" *The Steinbeck Review*, vol. 1, no. 1, 2004, pp. 90–105. *JSTOR*, www.jstor.org/stable/41581951.

Lisca, Peter. "The Allegory of *The Pearl.*" *Readings on* The Pearl. Edited by Jill Karson. Greenhaven P, 1999, pp. 68–73.

Metzger, Charles R. "*The Pearl*: A Parable of Hope." *Readings on* The Pearl. Edited by Jill Karson. Greenhaven P, 1999, pp. 41–47.

Meyer, Michael J. "Precious Bane: Mining the Fool's Gold of *The Pearl. The Short Novels of John Steinbeck*". Edited by Jackson Benson. Duke U P, 1990, pp. 161–72.

Shillinglaw, Susan. *Carol and John Steinbeck: Portrait of a Marriage*. U of Nevada P, 2013.

Simmonds, Roy S. "Steinbeck's *The Pearl*: Legend, Film, Novel." *The Short Novels of John Steinbeck*. Edited by Jackson Benson. Duke U P, 1990, pp. 173–84.

Steinbeck, John. *The Pearl*. 1947. Penguin, 2002.

Wagner-Martin, Linda. *John Steinbeck: A Literary Life*. Palgrave Macmillan, 2017.

"The Detachment of God": A Theopoetic Reading of Steinbeck's *The Pearl*_____

Kelly C. MacPhail

John Steinbeck's *The Pearl* questions religion's explanations for God's role in the tragic events that so frequently cloud human lives. Read as a theodicy—a theological justification for the problem of evil—*The Pearl* offers only pessimistic answers, but at the same time it complicates common assumptions about theological responses to the human situation. Although *The Pearl* at first appears to be a simple tale, it is meant as a parable that has several layers of application to the complex ultimate questions of human life. Through play with parable, allegory, intertextual references, and symbolism, Steinbeck reveals the evil that too often characterizes human interactions and offers the possibility of a non-teleological theodicy that finds ultimate meaning in the wholeness represented by the family.

The word "parable" derives from the same Greek root as the word for a parabola and literally means to throw something beside, or parallel to, something else. A story might concern itself with one simple set of events and characters with the task of delivering an obscured parallel lesson. The Biblical parables of Jesus, for example, include stories about the Prodigal Son, the Seed and the Sower, and the Good Samaritan, they respectively teach specific theological messages about forgiveness, the Kingdom of God, and community. *The Pearl*'s basic story derives from a traditional Mexican folktale that Steinbeck heard and understood as a parable that he recorded in its entirety in *The Sea of Cortez*. The original story as rendered by Steinbeck recounts:

> An Indian boy by accident found a pearl of great size, an unbelievable pearl. He knew its value was so great that he need never work again. In his one pearl he had the ability to be drunk as long as he wished, to marry any one of a number of girls, and to make many more

a little happy too. In his great pearl lay salvation, for he could in advance purchase masses sufficient to pop him out of Purgatory like a squeezed watermelon seed. (102)

The boy, like Kino, discovers the collusion of the manipulative pearl buyers and suffers beatings from men trying to steal the pearl. He becomes angry at this treatment, returns to the shore where he hid the pearl, and "he cursed it and threw it as far as he could into the channel. He was a free man again with his soul in danger and his food and shelter insecure. And he laughed a great deal about it" (102–3). Steinbeck was drawn to the story and decided to turn it into a novella by adding several characters and focusing on the tribulations of a family unit as opposed to one boy.

In the same passage of *The Sea of Cortez,* Steinbeck argues that while the story sounds true, "it is so much like a parable that it almost can't be" because the boy is too "heroic," "wise," and "reasonable" (103). Steinbeck grappled with how best to present the kernel of the story anew. For this reason, when readers open Steinbeck's novella, they are first met by a somewhat peculiar introductory statement on its own page and contained within quotation marks. Although Steinbeck penned this passage himself, it has the appearance of an epigraph or perhaps an "all persons fictitious" disclaimer. The statement's content, which ascribes some ambiguous level of veracity and realism to the narrative, is likewise questionable. It specifies that this story includes Kino, Juana, and Coyotito, which the original does not. It also begins, "In the town they tell the story of the great pearl," and it ends, "In any case, they say in the town that . . .," concluding with an ellipsis that suggests the novella commences from that point (i). Clearly, Steinbeck is attempting to maintain the parable qualities of the story while overcoming the problems that he felt detracted from its realism.

Steinbeck's symbol of the pearl presumes a special theopoetic history within allegory from religious and literary texts. Most immediate is Christ's parable "The Pearl of Great Price" from the Gospel of Matthew 13:45–46: "Again, the kingdom of heaven is like unto a merchant man, seeking goodly pearls: Who, when he had found one pearl of great price, went and sold all that he had, and bought it" (King James Bible). A student of religion, Steinbeck was also aware of the early third century Gnostic *Acts of Thomas*, which includes a still older section called "The Song of the Pearl" or "Song of the Soul." In it, a boy is sent to retrieve a precious pearl from a serpent in Egypt but once there forgets his mission until a letter reminds him of his task, which he then completes. The parable affirms Gnostic beliefs that the world is illusory and that humans must obtain knowledge to unshackle the divinity that lies hidden within them. There is a further link to the pious late fourteenth century dream poem, *The Pearl*, authored by the anonymous Pearl Poet. In this text, a man grieves the loss of his "perle," possibly his deceased daughter whom he later identifies in his dream vision with an adult woman who comes to him from heaven wearing a gown of pearls and telling him of the path to salvation. Nathaniel Hawthorne's *The Scarlet Letter* likewise uses the symbol specifically to refer to a baby when Hester names her daughter "Pearl" to emphasize that the baby was "of great price—purchased with all she had—her mother's only treasure!" (92). Certainly, the ending of Steinbeck's narrative—in which Kino and Juana's baby son, Coyotito, is killed by a bullet— mirrors the trauma of losing a child and so parallels the medieval tale to a certain degree. Yet, there is no indication that Steinbeck's grieving parents find a hopeful vision of future salvation akin to the *Pearl* father.

Steinbeck's attempt to blend elements of both an extended parable and realism has led to some difficulties of interpretation. Warren French repeatedly dismissed the novella in three different books he authored on Steinbeck. In 1961, he snubs *The Pearl* as "defective," "suitable fare in 1945 for a woman's magazine," "not just a disappointment but a betrayal" (137), and "paste" (142), with an ending that is "widely admired as symbolizing a rejection of materialism" but which "may be interpreted not only as noble renunciation, but also as defeatism" (139). In 1975, French further regrets that *The Pearl* is so often read by students because he sees this as a disservice both to Steinbeck, "who wrote much better, controlled works," and "to fiction itself by failing to suggest the tough-minded complexity of the greatest examples of the art" (130). For French, the original Mexican folktale is a perfect parable because its meaning is self-contained, much like, he claims, Hemingway's *The Old Man and the Sea* (1952). French grew even more dismissive by 1994, when he argues, "Steinbeck was not listening closely to his sources, was missing their point—as he had often claimed readers had his—and was attempting to exploit their folklore in an alien context" (106–7). French here approaches charging Steinbeck with cultural appropriation, an improper transplantation of the Mexican and Indian folktale into the concerns of white middle-class American suburbia.

Other critics read allegorical and spiritual resonances that vary widely. Harry Morris posits tensions between Steinbeck's allegory and realism. For example, the title changed from the obviously allegorical *The Pearl of La Paz,* indicating both the Mexican setting and the idea of the pearl of peace, to *The Pearl of the World* for its publication in *Women's Home Companion* to the final title of *The Pearl* when it was published in book form to coincide with the RKO movie version (150). John H. Timmerman examines Steinbeck's interest in Carl Jung and sees in *The Pearl* the process of self-discovery that "parallels the Jungian confrontation with the shadow of the unconscious, an ultimate act of reading one's own life" ("The Shadow" 143). A contrasting Jungian view is offered by Michael Meyer, who takes issue with Timmerman's dualism and instead focuses on the relevance to Steinbeck of "Jung's study of moral dilemmas as integral parts of all human existence" (133). Following Eastern religions, Stephen K. George offers a Taoist reading based on ideas of "anti-materialism, anti-intellectualism, acceptance of what is, and becoming one with the Tao" (94) and concludes that Kino is, indeed, following a path to enlightenment, albeit in a paradoxical sense. For Richard Astro, conversely, the parable is a secular but straightforward lesson of "the destructive nature of material wealth," which brings "tragedy and disappointment," and the larger lesson of "the agony involved in man's recognition of the vanity of human wishes" (28).

However, there are risks to reading *The Pearl* as a simple allegory. Jay Parini notes that while we can agree that "Kino is Everyman, and his journey is the classic hero's journey in search of fortune," Steinbeck's characters, in fact, have "distinctive personalities and cannot be simply regarded as stock figures from the classical repertoire of peasant types" (319). Parini further maintains there are details that offer possible parallels between the novella and Steinbeck's own life. Kino's little hut is akin to the shed where Steinbeck wrote *The Pearl*: this was a dark, unheated woodshed behind his house wherein he used a kerosene lantern for both heat and light (283–4). Parini notes that the novella is "clearly a story about the price of success, and about the inevitable consequences of trying too hard to rise above one's position in life. Part of Steinbeck must have sympathized deeply with Kino" (319). Furthermore, if one were, indeed, to risk a biographical reading of *The Pearl,* it is notable that Steinbeck began writing it when he returned to Monterey in October 1944 with his wife, Gwyn, and his son, Thomas, who was born not long before on August 2. This context offers another parallel in that Steinbeck replaces the boy in the original parable with a man with a wife and baby son who was much like himself and who no doubt experienced many similar hopes and fears for his young family.

Ultimately, can *The Pearl* successfully deliver credible characters and plausible situations while at the same time offering unambiguous allegory? What of the titular pearl itself? Is it good, evil, indifferent? Is Kino's final action of throwing it back whence it came an action of hope, a declaration of regret, or a ritualistic sacrifice? Unlike the pearls in the earlier parables, Steinbeck's pearl does not represent just one thing, and what it does represent seems ultimately to be contradictory. Indeed, the narrator anticipates this reaction in the epigraphic heading by explaining that tales that are often told take on meanings that are good and bad, black and white, and good and evil without any "in-between anywhere," while the reading to which he seems to ascribe is that "perhaps everyone takes his own meaning from it and reads his own life into it" (i). At first, it seems to Kino that the pearl does represent something simple, which soon becomes obvious as a misreading. The pearl is hope and the means to freedom. As the pearl is frequently described as the moon, it is something that provides light (even if only reflected light) in the darkness. He and Juana will be married in the church; they will have new clothes; they will buy things they previously thought impossible, such as the rifle Kino covets. Most importantly, the pearl represents the education that Coyotito will have and the amazing benefits of having a son who can read and write. As Steinbeck's narrative voice explains, "it is said that humans are never satisfied, that you give them one thing and they want something more. And this is said in disparagement, whereas it is one of the greatest talents the species has and one that has made it superior to animals that are satisfied with what they have" (25). Certainly, this commentary rests on a developed sense of irony. Either these particular traits of human nature are negatives that ought to be disparaged, or they are positives that make humans strive to compete at a level far above other non-human animals. Conversely, the narrator's dark hint is that humans might indeed be happier if they remained satisfied with what they have, even if their desires are as innocent as Kino's.

Quickly though, and due to the same motivations, the pearl brings suffering and death upon Kino's family as a result of human greed and violence. Morris relates this once again to the problems for the narrative's symbolism that stem from the parable adaptation: unlike the boy's "primitive" desires in the original folktale, Kino's desires are more "sophisticated," ending with his desire for a rifle, an "impossibility" (155). For Morris, this "pearl-rifle fusion" poses a particular complication that means the pearl, the book's central symbol, cannot be read as "clearly good or evil, black or white" (156). Conversely, Juana is much quicker to characterize the pearl as "a sin" that "has brought evil" and to urge her husband to destroy it or return it to the sea (38, 56–7). Kino, undeterred, is convinced that the pearl will do great things for his family, most importantly that Coyotito will "break out of the pot that holds us in" and that by selling the pearl "the evil will be gone, and only the good remain" (39), as if he has any control. Eventually, the pearl becomes entwined with Kino's innermost being; when his brother urges him to give up the pearl because of its evil and danger, Kino replies with striking finality, "This pearl has become my soul. . . . If I give it up I shall lose my soul" (67). However, he soon comes to agree with Juana when they flee for their lives, for "the music of the pearl had become sinister in his ears and it was interwoven with the music of evil" (71). This impression becomes fully realized at the end of the tale, when Kino looks at the pearl for the final time and sees that "Evil faces peered from it into his eyes . . . And the pearl was ugly; it was gray, like a malignant growth. And Kino heard the music of the pearl, distorted and insane" (89). This entity that at first appears desirable but ultimately leads to terrible suffering presents a further parallel to Adam and Eve in the Garden of Eden. Kino and Juana are poor but happy, yet even in this innocent state there are serpents to tempt and scorpions to sting. Until the pearl, there are only the usual troubles of survival, but, like Adam and Eve eating from the Forbidden Tree, Kino now sees differently and is full of hope for immense changes to his situation.

In reality, the only change to his situation is to make him a target for human enemies, an attention that ends in suffering and death. In *The Pearl*, Steinbeck invokes several theopoetic metaphors for suffering, including light and dark, mountains and sea, and the destroyed ancestral boat. Indeed, this state of human affairs is best revealed in Steinbeck's animal imagery, including the deadly scorpion, various fish, a puppy, different birds, amphibians, domesticated and wild mammals, insects, and several crustaceans, including, of course, oysters. Specific animal symbols that reveal how humans mistreat one another can be seen in the animals near the town: the great fishes that "slaughter" smaller fish and the hawks that silently hunt mice (32–3), for example, undoubtedly stand in for figures like the priest, doctor, and pearl buyers who take advantage of the poor fishermen and their families. Peter Lisca sees here Steinbeck's continuing ecological attention, which "serve[s] not to suggest that nature is evil, but to remind man of his continuity with nature, and to reveal the predatory drive which, beneath his civilized mask, he shares with other living creatures" (229). Undoubtedly, there is a failing here on the part of the pearl buyers and their controller. Even as predatory animals, later described as wolves and vultures (50), they overreach by trying to cheat Kino so fully and to such a high degree. While it is clear that the multiple buyers are in fact in collusion with one another and have been cheating the Native fishermen for their entire lives (53–4), could they not now pay more to Kino like the man in Christ's parable? They go too far by refusing to negotiate and preferring to murder Kino and his family to take the pearl as opposed to any compromise, which, as a matter of economic certainty, would have seen them turn a great profit nonetheless. They play a zero sum game for the pearl and trust their ability to cheat the unaware. As emblematic of their cheating, the first buyer is described as practicing literal legerdemain behind his desk, making a coin appear and disappear as if by magic by mechanically rolling it over his knuckles (48).

A part of what the pearl therefore represents is a challenge to generations of assumptions about how individuals fit into their prescribed social roles. Perhaps the most telling symbol is Kino's perspective of the ants that mirrors "the detachment of God" (3), given God's distant perspective of suffering human beings. Steinbeck returns to similar ant images three times (3, 70, 80), compounding the notion of God as transcendent and uninvolved in human affairs. Despite the narrator's aside that pearls are accidents and that "the finding of one was luck, a little pat on the back by God or the gods or both" (16), God or the gods do not benevolently fate Kino to find the pearl nor is there any divine intercession to protect Kino or save Coyotito's innocent life.

Consequently, the pearl turns out to be a source of empty hope. Pearls, as the narrative voice explains, are nothing more than the accidental products of irritants inside oysters (16). Despite their rarity, pearls have value only because of human aesthetic tastes. Oddly, whether French was aware of it or not, his final judgment of *The Pearl* as mere "paste" in his 1961 book on Steinbeck (142) was also the judgment rendered by one of the cheating pearl buyers in the novella, who lies and insists to Kino that "Better pearls are made of paste" (51). For both French and the pearl buyer, "paste" indicates something fake and of low value. Paste in this context was a wet mix of various materials (including lead, silica, and colored pigments) that hardened into a glasslike solid that could be cut to look convincingly like precious stones but which had no significant value.

Steinbeck referencing the pearl as paste may also offer an intertextual reference to one of the most well-known symbols in American literature, Herman Melville's *Moby-Dick* (1851). Robert DeMott has argued for intimate connections between *Moby-Dick* and Steinbeck's *East of Eden* (1952), and it is likely that the rich symbolism of *The Pearl* likewise reveals Melville's influence. In one of the clearest hints at the symbolic nature of the white whale, Captain Ahab argues:

> All visible objects, man, are but as pasteboard masks. But in each event—in the living act, the undoubted deed—there, some unknown but still reasoning thing puts forth the mouldings of its features from behind the unreasoning mask. If man will strike, strike through the mask! . . . That inscrutable thing is chiefly what I hate; and be the white whale agent, or be the white whale principal, I will wreak that hate upon him. (178)

Pasteboard here refers to sheets of paper pasted together, somewhat like papier-mâché. For Ahab, the creature appears real and outrageously powerful, but perhaps it is fake or a façade or mask covering something or perhaps covering nothing. It is inscrutable as a symbol, and that is chiefly what Ahab hates about Moby-Dick, the white whale. Kino's white pearl, likewise, symbolizes many things but is ultimately inscrutable.

The complexity of the pearl as a symbol may stem from Steinbeck's adherence to non-teleological thought and the influence of his intellectual collaboration and friendship with the California-based marine biologist Edward F. Ricketts. In 1940, the two men collected and studied marine specimens from the Sea of Cortez (the Gulf of California) and published their account in 1941 as *The Sea of Cortez: A Leisurely Journal of Travel and Research*, wherein Steinbeck first recorded the original Mexican parable. Distinct from most scientific treatises, the book includes aspects of fiction, travel narrative, ecology, and philosophy. After Ricketts' death, Steinbeck republished the book's narrative sections as *The Log from the Sea of Cortez*, omitted the specimen catalogues, and added a eulogy for Ricketts. Particularly well known is the entry for Easter Sunday, referred to as the "Easter Sunday Sermon" (*The Log* 109–125), which is a revised version of Ricketts' "Essay on Non-teleological Thinking" that examines the gaps inherent in the assumptions and scopes of knowledge of both science and religion. Ricketts' idea was that most Western thought was teleological, a word that derives from "telos," the Greek for "end," "goal," or "purpose," and, therefore, analyzes systems, including evolution and ecology, with the assumption that the process is inherently working towards a goal. Ricketts' non-teleological philosophy, by contrast, concerns itself with a more accurate description of what is and of what exists in its present state or context. Therefore, a non-teleological study is separate from concerns of cause and effect and certainly apart from notions of an end, goal, or purpose of an entity within its ecosystem. For example, the chapter applies non-teleological thinking not only to animals and diseases but also to the conditions of human society, including a specific description of the harsh conditions of the Great Depression. Whereas teleological thinking is represented by those like Henry Ford who blamed the unemployed and insisted they just had to roll up their sleeves and show initiative, non-teleological thinking sought not a cause and effect explanation of the individual's initiative or lack thereof but rather a description of "what is" in terms of wider conditions that focused on the economy and society as an accretion of units (110).

Undoubtedly, Steinbeck's non-teleological thinking predominates *The Pearl*. Charles Metzger particularly emphasizes how Steinbeck's additions to the original parable derive from his description of the Native Americans' way of life in *The Log from the Sea of Cortez* as being in "relationship with their environment" in a way that was "so intimate as to approach a condition of unconscious, or nonverbal identification" that suggests "their nonteleological—one might even say, in their primitively existential—way of knowing" (99). Metzger further claims that Kino represents Steinbeck's understanding of

Native ways of thought as non-teleological specifically surrounding concepts of language, time, and an absence of what Steinbeck called "causal thinking warped by hope" (100). Indeed, Kino's thoughts are musical primarily because they are nonverbal. He experiences fear when he first verbalizes his hopes for what the pearl will bring him and his family; prior to the pearl, Kino's is a non-teleological epistemology that fits him into nature as a part of it and not opposed to it or ruling over it. Hence, as Metzger concludes, Kino's problem is hope: at the novella's beginning, Kino "is living, incredibly to us, without aspirations, without plans, i.e., without hope" (104) while chapter 3 of *The Pearl* ends with a contrary description of Kino and Juana that "they began this day with hope" (40). Most readers will see this as a positive, but, to non-teleological thinking, it is a negative. Indeed, Kino has begun to think in teleological ways because of what is nothing more than the accidental discovery of the great pearl, which itself is nothing more than an oyster's natural response to an accidental irritant. Kino fights and does not cease because of this warped hope that he believes will change his conditions. He is beaten, beats his wife, loses his house and canoe, flees for his life, kills four men, and loses the life of his baby son. Ironically, a rifle is the only material good with which Kino comes home, and it is of course the same one that tragically killed his baby son. He returns to his village community only when he is finally able to renounce his hope, symbolized by throwing back the pearl.

The text's theological argument aligns itself with one type of traditional theodicy, an attempt to offer a theological justification for the role of God in a world that endures the ongoing problem of evil. In short, if a good, loving, and all-powerful God exists, why would such an entity allow humans to suffer so terribly, both from moral evils like murder and violence and from natural evils like disease and natural disasters? In *The Pearl,* the greatest evils come from other people and not from what Kino sees as divine fate. Human greed is the evil that intervenes in the lives of Kino and his family as he finds himself cheated by the doctor, priest, and buyers and attacked by the hunter and his trackers. Kino finds loyalty and happiness only with his family as the plot moves toward Coyotito's meaningless death.

In facing these trials, it is notable that Kino and Juana represent a particular type of Latin American religious syncretism, meaning that their spirituality blends the traditional organized religion of Catholicism with traditional Native American beliefs that are here revealed in ritual songs (84). Steinbeck described these songs as "ancient Indian music long preceding the Conquest. And I think they are beautiful" (*Steinbeck: A Life* 281). As such, these songs spur Kino to action by enshrining the goodness of family against the evils of men who seek to do the family harm.

Invoking these spiritual songs and drawing upon further parallels to the Garden of Eden is yet another representative of the Song of Evil and of "the enemy, or any foe of the family" (5). This initial dark figure is of course the scorpion that stings Coyotito early in the narrative. Kino, the protective father, approaches a near-bestial attitude in his fury at the scorpion after it stings: "snarling, Kino had it, had it in his fingers, rubbing it into a paste in his hands" (5–6). Certainly, from a non-teleological stance, the animal is simply following its natural inclinations for self-preservation and is not an enemy or an evil presence, but from Kino's perspective, it is exactly an enemy. Hence, the scorpion becomes the opposite and yet the twin of the pearl and must be rendered by Kino into yet another paste that covers its precise symbolic meaning.

Of the various spiritual songs that are heard over the five days that comprise this narrative, it is the Song of the Family that remains, and its message is the only comforting theodicy that is offered. Although the narrator says earlier that Kino "had lost one world and not gained another" (53), he is still able to hold onto this one meaningful song. Various evils, like the scorpion and the violent men, have been overcome, and the death of Coyotito will of course have lasting consequences. In the last scene, Kino and Juana return to the town and walk to the water's edge in misery. Kino takes strength from the Song of the Family, which even now is "as fierce as a cry. He was immune and terrible, and his song had become a battle cry" (89). At the seashore, Kino first offers to Juana to toss the pearl back into the water, but she insists that he throw it. Lisca emphasizes this as Kino's admission that Juana was right about the pearl's evil and that Juana's choice to have Kino throw it instead is an act by which "she gives dignity and pride once more to her husband, whose position it is to do such final things. And all this is understood by Kino as he accepts again his rightful role and throws the pearl into the sea" (227). Although this power structure is an outdated notion, this couple and their village do appear entrenched in socially constructed norms based upon gender, class, and ethnicity that are keenly felt and enforced throughout the story.

Ultimately, Kino and Juana are intimately reunited. Earlier, although Juana fears the pearl, she rejoices with Kino "because they were in some way one thing and one purpose" (40). The couple's renewed relationship is seen in the physical relation of their bodies. Previously, Juana takes the lead and holds the baby when they go to the doctor, and Kino leads when he goes to sell the pearl and when they flee for the mountains; they stand side by side after they are turned away from the doctor's, and they return to La Paz walking side by side after Coyotito has been killed with Juana still carrying his body wrapped in her shawl. After Kino puts an end to the power of the pearl by throwing it far out into the water, they again stand "side by side watching the place for a long time"; finally, "the music of the pearl drifted to a whisper and disappeared" (90). Now, they stand united once again by the bonds of the Song of the Family. Its message does not offer a theological explanation for their suffering, nor does it explain the apparent detachment of God, but it does make manifest the ancient spiritual meaning that lies behind the musical resonance of the Song of the Family: "an aching chord that caught the throat, saying this is safety, this is warmth, this is the *Whole*" (3).

Works Cited

Astro, Richard. "Imitations of a Wasteland." *Modern Critical Views: John Steinbeck*. Edited by Harold Bloom, Chelsea House, 1987, pp. 19–34.

DeMott, Robert. "'Working at the Impossible': *Moby-Dick*'s Presence in *East of Eden*." *Steinbeck and the Environment: Interdisciplinary Approaches*. Edited by Susan F. Beegel, et al. U of Alabama P, 1997, pp. 211–28.

French, Warren. *John Steinbeck*. Twayne, 1961.

_____. *John Steinbeck*. 2nd ed. Twayne, 1975.

_____. *John Steinbeck's Fiction Revisited*. Twayne, 1994.

George, Stephen K. "A Taoist Interpretation of John Steinbeck's *The Pearl*." *Steinbeck Review*, vol. 1, no. 1, 2004, pp. 90–105. *JSTOR*, www.jstor.org/stable/41581951.

Hawthorne, Nathaniel, *The Scarlet Letter.* 1850. Vintage, 2014.

The King James Bible. kingjamesbibleonline.org.

Lisca, Peter. *The Wide World of John Steinbeck.* Rutgers U P, 1958.

Melville, Herman. *Moby-Dick.* 1851. Penguin, 1992.

Metzger, Charles R. "Steinbeck's *The Pearl* as a Nonteleological Parable of Hope." *Research Studies*, vol. 46, 1978, pp. 98–105.

Meyer, Michael J. "Wavering Shadows: A New Jungian Perspective in Steinbeck's *The Pearl.*" *The Steinbeck Review*, vol. 1, no. 1, 2004, pp. 132–45. *JSTOR*, www.jstor.org/stable/41581954.

Morris, Harry. "*The Pearl:* Realism and Allegory." *Steinbeck: A Collection of Critical Essays.* Edited by Robert Murray Davis, Prentice-Hall, 1972, pp. 149–62.

Parini, Jay. *John Steinbeck: A Biography.* Henry Holt, 1995.

Steinbeck, John. *Steinbeck: A Life in Letters.* Edited by Elaine Steinbeck and Robert Wallsten, Viking, 1975.

_____. *The Pearl.* 1947. Penguin, 1992.

Steinbeck, John, and Edward F. Ricketts. *The Log from the Sea of Cortez.* 1951. Penguin, 1995.

_____. *The Sea of Cortez: A Leisurely Journal of Travel and Research.* Viking, 1941.

Timmerman, John H. "The Shadow and the Pearl: Jungian Patterns in *The Pearl.*" *The Short Novels of John Steinbeck.* Edited by Jackson J. Benson, Duke U P, 1990, pp. 143–61.

Surrendering: Steinbeck's *The Pearl* as an Artistic Failure

John J. Han

Corporate and Individual Greed

Many readers of *The Pearl* (1947) see it as a morality story about the danger of greed: Kino's deprived, yet peaceful world turns into a world of violence through his excessive desire for wealth, and he regains his innocence only after he throws the pearl back into the sea.[1] The popularity of *The Pearl* in secondary English classes, as well as among the reading public, seems to derive from this so-called moral vision. Since its publication, however, the novella has always received mixed reviews. Some early critics of *The Pearl* accepted the story with enthusiasm. For instance, Tetsumaro Hayashi considers the pearl a symbol of moral degeneration; for him, Kino's act of renouncing the pearl is a way to restore his salvation and inner peace. According to Hayashi, Kino's journey "teaches him the way to bring himself from bondage to freedom, from fear to fearlessness, and from Death to Rebirth. He restores himself by means of his total self-negation" (52). Likewise, Harry Morris reads *The Pearl* as a story of Kino's moral victory:

> Kino is not defeated. . . . He has proved that he cannot be cheated nor destroyed. But his real triumph, his real gain, the heights to which he has risen rather than the depths to which he has slipped back is the immense knowledge that he has gained about good and evil. This knowledge is the tool that he needs to help him on the final journey, the inescapable journey that everyman must take. (160)

However, unlike Steinbeck's sociologically oriented stories from the 1930s, *The Pearl* seems to illustrate his moral confusion. While writing his novella, Steinbeck noted that the story was a parable, and thus was open to interpretations: "If this story is a parable, perhaps everyone takes his own meaning from it and reads his own life into it" (*Pearl* 3). The story is, indeed, a parable that has the theme of good versus evil, and it uses mostly cardboard characters. Although Steinbeck allows his readers to adopt their own interpretations, it is not difficult to understand his purpose of retelling of the Native American tale from La Paz, Mexico: the evil pearl disrupts the peace of traditionalist, rural lifestyle, and Kino achieves a moral victory by courageously giving it back to the sea where it supposedly belongs. Many readers, including well-known critics, agree with this feel-good interpretation.

However, the plot of the story makes it difficult to see Kino as someone who wins a moral victory. Steinbeck convincingly describes corporate and individual greed in *The Grapes of Wrath* and ideological greed in *In Dubious Battle*; in *Of Mice and Men*, he also skillfully shows how the simple dreams of working-class people are shattered by society. The theme of greed in *The Pearl*, however, seems misplaced. Early in the story, Steinbeck demonstrates that Kino has the right to pursue happiness and well-being for him and his family, and that, through hard work, earns a pearl of great price. In the rest of the story, Steinbeck makes Kino succumb to societal pressure to remain in his lowly station in life. Although poor and uneducated, Kino is not a man without senses. He acutely perceives and expresses his anger against the social injustices against his race. Instead of helping him fight for his rights, however, Steinbeck makes him surrender to the societal forces for supposed peace. In its failure to portray Kino as a victim of society who deserves a better life, *The Pearl* fails as a work of art. In addition to an analysis of the defective plot of *The Pearl*, Erich Fromm's *Escape from Freedom* (1941) and John McWhorter's *Losing the Race: Self-Sabotage in Black America* (2001) will help shed light on Kino's plight as we assess the artistic merit of Steinbeck's story.

The Source Text of Steinbeck's *The Pearl*
In his January 1, 1945, letter to Elizabeth Otis, Steinbeck hinted at his novella in progress as a parable: "It's a strange piece of work, full of curious methods and figures. A folk tale I hope. A black-white story like a parable. But we'll see" (qtd. in Benson 564). Until

the acceptance of the manuscript by Viking Press, Steinbeck was not entirely confident about *The Pearl*. In a May 3, 1945, letter to Otis, he expresses his relief that his story would see the light of day: "Naturally I am very glad and frankly relieved that you like *The Pearl*. It was so full of experiments and I had no idea whether they would come off at all. Also the thing seemed doomed never to get there. It was all ominous" (*Steinbeck: A Life* 568).

As his letter to Otis indicates, Steinbeck conceived *The Pearl* as a "parable"—a didactic, allegorical story. In 1944, Steinbeck outlined the plot of *The Pearl* in Mexico, where he conducted research on Spanish folklore that served as the basis of his novella (Benson 542–43). *The Log from the Sea of Cortez* (1951)—the narrative portion Steinbeck extracted from *Sea of Cortez*, which he and Ed Rickett had co-published in 1941—briefly introduces the background of *The Pearl*. The setting of the source text is La Paz, the capital of Baja California Sur and a coveted area known for producing expensive pearl oysters. The *Log* offers a summary of the story, which is cited below. In discussing the artistic merit of *The Pearl*, it is essential to compare Steinbeck's story with its source text:

> [A]s in all concentrations of natural wealth, the terrors of greed were let loose on the city again and again. An event which happened at La Paz in recent years is typical of such places. An Indian boy by accident found a pearl of great size, an unbelievable pearl. He knew its value was so great that he need never work again. In his one pearl he had the ability to be drunk as long as he wishes, to marry any one of a number of girls, and to make many more a little happy too. In his great pearl lay salvation, for he could in advance purchase masses sufficient to pop him out of Purgatory like a squeezed watermelon seed. In addition he could shift a number of dead relatives a little near Paradise. He went to La Paz with his pearl in his hand and his future clear into eternity in his heart. He took his pearl to a broker and was offered so little that he grew angry, for he knew he was cheated. Then he carried his pearl to another broker and was offered the same amount. After a few more visits he came to know that the brokers were only the many hands of one head and that he could not sell his pearl for more. He took it to the beach and hid it under a stone, and that night he was clubbed into unconsciousness, and his clothing was

searched. The next night he slept at the house of a friend, and his friend and he were injured and bound and the whole house searched. Then he went inland to lose his pursuers and he was waylaid and tortured. But he was very angry now and he knew what he must do. Hurt as he was crept back to La Paz in the night and he skulked like a hunted fox to the beach and took out his pearl from under the stone. Then he cursed it and threw it as far as he could into the channel. He was a free man again with his soul in danger and his food and shelter insecure. And he laughed a great deal about it. (*Log* 119–20)

This Mexican Indian story is different from *The Pearl* in several ways. First, the main character is an immature boy, not a married man with a baby. Second, the boy accidentally finds a pearl of great price, whereas Kino and his wife work hard to obtain their pearl. Third, the boy in folklore uses the pearl mostly to indulge himself, whereas Kino intends to use the pearl for good purposes: to marry Juana in the church, to pay for their son's schooling, to buy some decent clothes for his family, to buy a new harpoon for his fishing, and to buy a rifle supposedly for self-protection. Fourth, the Indian boy throws away the pearl after realizing the danger of his greed, whereas Kino renounces the pearl under pressure from his wife, Juana. Fifth and finally, the boy laughs when he throws the pearl away, whereas Kino looks horrified—and probably glum—when he renounces his pearl. These differences are significant in assessing the artistic merit of *The Pearl*. As in the case of Jesus' parables in the Bible, stories of good and evil can be an excellent tool for conveying moral teachings. The source text of *The Pearl* has all the essential ingredients of a parable: character development is convincing, the plot has perfect causality, and the moral lesson makes sense. The problem with Steinbeck's story is that it is not clear exactly what is good and what is evil. All parables' endings are moral, yet a well-written parable's ending is agreeably convincing. Unfortunately, it is hard to find moral causality in *The Pearl* as we shall see later. There is no textual evidence that Kino makes a moral decision about the pearl when he throws it away. Of course, any fictional story, even a parable, is open to various interpretations, but *The Pearl* fails to clarify Steinbeck's supposed moral teachings in the first place, thereby confusing his readers.

In Response to Warm Responses to *The Pearl*

As with many other novels and novellas by Steinbeck, *The Pearl* has received mixed critical comments. Jackson J. Benson diagnoses the hostility of some critics of *The Pearl* as a display of bewildering snobbery of academics (647–48). Benson himself considers *The Pearl* and *Cannery Row* "artistic successes" (646). Paul McCarthy also praises *The Pearl*: "In this finely crafted work, the unreal mood of a parable is beautifully sustained" (109).

More recently, Robert McParland offers a highly positive critique of Steinbeck's short novel. In an otherwise excellent book on Steinbeck, *Citizen Steinbeck: Giving Voice to the People* (2016), McParland gives unqualified praise to *The Pearl*. First, he maintains that taking the pearl out of the sea was an anti-ecological act: "The story may reflect an ecological position as well: the pearl belongs to the sea and has been extracted from it. Taken from its natural setting it is transferred into an economic sphere where it is highly valued for its material worth. Kino and his people have always been closely aligned with the land, the sea, and earth's creatures and this material discovery disrupts the alignment" (155). One might respond to this comment with the question: how is catching a pearl different from catching fish for livelihood? Ecocriticism is a valuable approach to literature, but how much undisturbed nature should remain is largely a matter of opinion. One could argue that harvesting a pearl in the sea is not different from harvesting corn in the field or excavating gold from a mountain. They are economic activities that sustain or enrich human life for a fisher, a farmer, and a miner, respectively.

In his analysis of *The Pearl*, McParland also sees Kino as someone who fell victim to greed and then recovered his innocence by giving up his pearl:

> Kino perceives the pearl with hope. "So lovely it was, so soft, and its own music came from it—the music of promise and delight, its guarantee of the future, of comfort, of security…. It closed the door on hunger." However, "the circling of wolves and the hovering of

vultures" soon begin. The pearl buyers try to swindle Kino with their appraisal that the gem is worthless. Tension arises between Kino and his wife, Juana. Jealousy and avarice bring "darkness…closing in on his family." His boat is wrecked, his house burned. Trackers seek to eliminate his family, to take away his "treasure." Kino resolves to plot their deaths and to kill them and is transformed from loving father and husband into potentially an evil killer. Tragedy awaits him with the realization that his son Coyotito is far more precious a pearl in his life than the gem he has pulled from the ocean. (156)

First, the pearl offered Kino hope for a better life for him and his family. It is hard to blame him for wanting to provide better for his family with legitimately earned wealth. Kino should not take the blame for the presence of "wolves" and "vultures," either. It was not his fault to obtain the pearl and hope for a better future. What McParland calls "[j]ealousy and avarice" come from the neighbors. Unlike the original Native American version, *The Pearl* does not show that Kino became a man of vanity when he obtained the pearl. More than anything, he wanted to use it for his child's education which would bring his family liberation from ignorance: "My son will read and open the books, and my son will write and will know writing. And my son will make numbers, and these things will make us free because he will know—he will know and through him we will know. . . . This is what the pearl will do" (*Pearl* 31).[2] Regarding violence that follows Kino's acquisition of the pearl, he did not start it; rather, he was provoked. If Steinbeck portrayed Kino as a wayward man, *The Pearl* could have been a more plausible story.

Not surprisingly, *The Pearl* as a feel-good story about greed is a popular text in high school English classes. The novella is almost always taught as a text that warns against an excessive desire for material wealth. A teacher's guide to the story identifies greed as a main theme of the story: "This novel illustrates the destructive nature of greed as Kino's desire for wealth and status through the pearl causes him to be violent towards his wife and ultimately results in Coyotito's death" (Griffith). Another resource finds the theme of money, possessions, and greed in *The Pearl*. Steinbeck's story concerns "the quest for money and the desire for things of the material world, as well as references to the steps which people will take to attain those things" and the lesson from this moral story is that "money can buy happiness" ("*The Pearl* by John Steinbeck").

The positive critical reception of *The Pearl* seems to affect the way the story is interpreted outside the English-speaking world as well. In "Steinbeck's Worldview toward the Effects of Materialism in the Mexican Colonial Era as Reflected in *The Pearl*," a B.A. thesis written at a university in Indonesia, Moh Imawan Helmi exemplifies the misreading of Steinbeck's story:

> It was too late when he found that the only child he was fighting for was gone. Moreover, his death was caused by his own fault. At this point he began to realize that the pearl had directed him into horrible things. . . . Kino realizes that what Juana said, that the pearl is evil, is true. Kino's resignation was shown by handing the pearl to Juana. He realizes that his most precious treasure is not a pearl but the family he already has, Coyotito and Juana but now there is only Juana. The act of handing the pearl to Juana is his redemption attempt and as a sign of apology. He regrets why she [*sic*] did not surrender the pearl's fate to Juana while Coyotito is still alive. (64)

It is unclear whether Helmi intended to use it, but the choice of the word *resignation* is interesting. Kino decides to hand over the pearl to his wife, but he is resigned to the reality that does not allow him upward mobility. Helmi's argument that his son's death was "caused by [Kino's] own fault" is also debatable. Kino never provoked anyone with the pearl he earned; he had only good intentions with the pearl of great price.

Even before entering the doctor's house at the beginning of the story, Kino is enraged as he considers the European settlers' inhumane treatment of the indigenous people like him:

> Kino hesitated a moment. This doctor was not of his people. This doctor was of a race which for nearly four hundred years had beaten and starved and robbed and despised Kino's race, and frightened it too, so that the indigene came humbly to the door. And as always when he came near to one of this race, Kino felt weak and afraid and angry at the same time. Rage and terror went together. He could

kill the doctor more easily than he could talk to him, for all of the doctor's race spoke to all of Kino's race as though they were simple animals. And as Kino raised his right hand to the iron ring knocker in the gate, rage swelled in him, and the pounding music of the enemy beat in his ears, and his lips drew tight against his teeth—but with his left hand he reached to take off his hat. The iron ring pounded against the gate. (15)

This passage shows that Kino is fully aware of racial discrimination against native people and that he has the potential to act on his anger, but he meekly renounces his pearl—a gem he earned—at the end of the story.

Steinbeck's Moral Confusion in *The Pearl*: Insights from Social Psychology

The problematic ending of *The Pearl* can be explained by borrowing insights from social psychology, as expounded in Erich Fromm's *Escape from Freedom* and John McWhorter's *Losing the Race*. Social psychology analyzes the ways in which an individual's thoughts, emotions, and behaviors are affected by his or her interactions with other people. As Fromm's title *Escape from Freedom* implies, human beings have two paradoxical desires: a desire to escape to freedom and a desire to escape from freedom. Accepting certain aspects of Freudian psychology but diverging from it as well, Fromm examines how medieval society offered limited individual freedom yet a sense of security to people through social stratification. The publication of Fromm's book coincides with the rise of Fascism and Nazism. Two key questions the author asks are what freedom means for modern humanity and why people in modern times voluntarily renounce their freedom in return for protection. He views human history as a long struggle to overcome the natural and socio-political oppressions: "One tie after another was severed. Man had overthrown the domination of nature and made himself her master; he had overthrown the domination of the Church and the domination of the absolute state" (4). The struggle was to usher in the ideals of economic liberalism, political democracy, religious autonomy, and individualism in personal life (3–4). The goal of achieving all of those ideals seemed to be within reach when modern humans, except for a handful, voluntarily submitted to "an authority over which they had no control" (4).

The fact that Kino, a man of righteous anger and determination to improve his—and his family's—lot, surrenders his pearl can be explained by his fear of being left out of his community. Fromm explains modern humanity's fear of social alienation as follows:

> This separation from a world, which in comparison with one's own individual existence is overwhelmingly strong and powerful, and often threatening and dangerous, creates a feeling of powerlessness and anxiety. As long as one was an integral part of that world, unaware of the possibilities and responsibilities of individual action, one did not need to be afraid of it. When one has become an individual, one stands alone and faces the world in all its perilous and overpowering aspects. (29)

In *The Pearl*, Steinbeck unwittingly extols a medieval way of life for poor people like Kino, who relinquishes his well-earned pearl under social threats. After the night when an intruder bloodies Kino in chapter three, Juana tells him that the pearl is "evil," and thus they should renounce it (43). Although Juana is a woman of wisdom, she cannot evade her narrow world—the world in which people like her are fearful of attempting anything new for them. In response to her plea to throw the pearl away, Kino says, "This is our one chance. Our son must go to school. He must break out of the pot that holds us in" (44). Unfortunately, he does not follow through with his determination as more tragedies strike, and the Kinos are resigned to live in perpetual poverty. In a way, European colonizers, whom they hate but cannot resist, have nurtured their sense of defeatism.

In *The Pearl*, Steinbeck oversimplifies morality by adopting a false dichotomy of good and evil. The two songs at the beginning of the story—the Song of the Family and the Song of Evil, respectively—assume two clearly drawn moral lines as in the book of Genesis. Kino is tempted by evil music as Adam is tempted by the serpent: "Evil faces peered from it into his eyes, and he saw the light of burning. And in the surface of the pearl he saw the frantic eyes of the man in the pool. And in the surface of the pearl he saw Coyotito lying in the little cave with the top of his head shot away. And the pearl was ugly; it was gray, like a malignant growth. And Kino heard the music of the pearl, distorted and insane" (94).

In a way, Steinbeck compares the pearl to the forbidden fruit Adam and Eve ate. The biblical fruit clearly symbolizes sin, but the pearl is morally neutral unless one forces it to mean something sinister; as stated before, the pearl is under the water for a fisher to harvest. As the Bible says, the root of all kinds of evil is not money but the love of money (1 Timothy 6:10). Material possessions in themselves are neither good nor bad. Though Catholic monks, as well as their Anglican counterparts, take the monastic vows of poverty, the Bible does not praise poverty itself. Rather, many of its passages teach believers to work hard, earn money, and use it wisely. Kino intends to use the pearl for good purposes, but under pressure from society, he throws it away. Even after he loses his beloved son, he clings to the traditional way of life, thereby shackling his and his wife's lives. Having renounced the pearl, the couple will live as before with little money for their medical needs, little respect from the priest, and no room for upward mobility. They may live again in harmony with nature but at the expense of material well-being. Would the couple live happily ever after? The story does not guarantee other than that they will live as before—deprived, exploited, and feeling angry about white oppression but having no backbone to stand up for their rights. Kino has experienced the unkindness of people—not only pearl dealers but also his own people, who tried to rob him of his own possession. How can he regain his trust of people in La Paz? To borrow William Blake's terminology, it is hard to fully recover "innocence" once "experience" is gained; human development involves the realization that the innocent world of the "lamb" gives way to the fearsome world of the "Tyger."[3]

In his Nobel Prize speech, delivered in December 1962, Steinbeck voiced his moral vision as follows:

This is not new. The ancient commission of the writer has not changed. He is charged with exposing our many grievous faults and failures, with dredging up to the light our dark and dangerous dreams for the purpose of improvement.

Furthermore, the writer is delegated to declare and to celebrate man's proven capacity for greatness of heart and spirit—for gallantry in defeat—for courage, compassion and love. In the endless war against weakness and despair, these are the bright rally-flags of hope and of emulation. I hold that a writer who does not passionately believe in the perfectibility of man, has no dedication nor any membership in literature. (173)

The speech reaffirms his commitment to social justice, which is fully displayed in his fiction of the 1930s. Unfortunately, the ending of *The Pearl* does not seem to exemplify "gallantry in defeat," which Steinbeck brilliantly exemplifies in his 1938 short story "Flight."

In a way, the defeatism in *The Pearl* is in line with the cases of self-sabotage John McWhorter, a linguist at the University of California at Berkeley, observes among African Americans. In *Losing the Race*, McWhorter maintains that blacks' self-defeating behaviors are worse than white racism. According to him, blacks in America today lag behind whites not because of racism or discrimination but due to three reasons: anti-intellectualism, separatism, and victimhood. In other words, blacks sabotage themselves, thereby perpetuating their inferior status in society: "[B]lack America is currently caught in certain ideological holding patterns that are today much, much more serious barriers to black well-being than is white racism, and constitute nothing less than a continuous, self-sustaining act of self-sabotage" (x). When applied to the Native Mexican setting in La Paz, one can see how Kino and Juana defeat themselves, thereby perpetuating their victimhood; they fail to take action to regain their power.

Specifically, what could Kino and his family have done to avoid self-sabotage? When their safety was threatened, they could have moved elsewhere and started a new life. As a man of little knowledge about the outside world, however, Kino does not know how to. He is afraid of leaving the familiarity behind, so he—again, to borrow Fromm's phrase—"escapes from freedom." In this regard, *The Pearl* is a deterministic, fatalistic story.

Kino renounces the pearl under advice from his wife, who supposedly represents wisdom. Nevertheless, Juana does not seem to be always wise. At the beginning of the story, she insists that Kino go to the town doctor, although Kino knows that the doctor will not come to a brush house to treat their baby. At the end of the story, she forces Kino to give up the pearl—even after losing their precious child. On his part, Kino submits himself to his quietly demanding wife.

The main weakness of *The Pearl* is not that Steinbeck unwittingly supports a medieval view of society per se; based on one's ideological perspective, a medieval view can serve as a viable option for society. Kino remembers the priest repeatedly saying that every human being must stay in his or her station in life: "[E]ach one must remain faithful to his post and must not go running about, else the castle is in danger from the assaults of Hell" (Steinbeck, *Pearl* 51). The statement reflects the medieval social hierarchy that envisions royalty at the top and peasants, who encompass freemen, serfs, and slaves, at the bottom. The problem with *The Pearl* lies in the fact that Steinbeck makes the reading audience question whether or not he fundamentally sides with the medieval concept of social stratification. If he does, *The Pearl* seems to be in conflict with the social ethic of most of his work. If not, *The Pearl* does not consistently offer his sympathies for the poor and dispossessed.

Failing as a Work of Art

The Pearl represents one of Steinbeck's later works of fiction that seems to have lost its claim of moral vision. Not surprisingly, some of the early critics voiced their disappointments in the story. For instance, Warren French called *The Pearl* a "turgid, overinflated" story that is "not just a disappointment but a betrayal" for those who admire *The Grapes of Wrath* and *Cannery Row* (137). It is tempting to dismiss such a negative comment as uninformed, but it is also true that *The Pearl* lacks a clear moral vision. In a 1945 letter to Jack and Max Wagner, Steinbeck writes, "[*The Pearl*]'s really in its last stages.

It's a brutal story but with flashes of beauty I think" (*Steinbeck: A Life* 262). Indeed, it contains both brutality and "flashes of beauty." The problem is that the beauty in *The Pearl* is sporadic and does not contribute to a consistent moral vision.

For *The Pearl* to be truly successful, Steinbeck could have presented Kino as someone who heroically confronts an adversarial situation even if that meant death. Like the main character of Hemingway's *The Old Man and the Sea*, who returns home with only a skeleton of a shark, Kino could have fought to the end. Instead, he meekly renounces his manhood in *The Pearl*. Steinbeck could also have made Kino identical to the main character of the source text so that he has legitimate reason to turn from a misguided way of life by throwing the pearl away.

Yet another possibility would be for Steinbeck to embrace openly a medieval view of society in *The Pearl*. Literary history is replete with authors who changed their political perspectives over their careers. After all, writers and poets are not philosophers per se, and there is no shame in changing their political views. In his early years, William Wordsworth was an ardent supporter of the French Revolution, but later he adopted a more conservative political stance. The problem is that, in *The Pearl*, Steinbeck shows his sympathy for the poor and downtrodden before he prevents them from escaping the evil cycle of poverty and despair. He empowered the powerless in *The Grapes of Wrath*, *Of Mice and Men*, and other sociologically oriented stories in the 1930s. In *The Pearl*, he still retains his sympathy for the powerless but does not encourage them to fight for a better life whether they win or not. That is where Steinbeck's novella fails as a work of art.

Notes

1. The parable of the pearl of great price in the New Testament (Matthew 13:45–46) concerns the kingdom of heaven, which is priceless. It is unclear whether Steinbeck had Scripture in mind when he titled his story *The Pearl*.

2. The importance of literacy as a tool for successful life is a major theme in African American writing. Frederick Douglass's slave

---

narrative and Malcolm X's autobiography are two of the many African American prose works that emphasize the importance of education.

3. Blake's lyrical poems "The Lamb" and "The Tyger" represent innocence and experience, respectively. When the narrator of "The Lamb," a young boy, sees a lamb, it reminds him of the one who "calls himself a Lamb" (Blake, *Songs of Innocence* 18). In contrast, the narrator of "The Tyger" expresses both amazement and fear when he observes a tiger: "Tyger Tyger, burning bright, / In the forests of the night; / What immortal hand or eye, / Could frame thy fearful symmetry?" (Blake, *Songs of Experience* 56).

Works Cited

Blake, William. "The Lamb." *Songs of Innocence*. 1789. *Major British Poets of the Romantic Period*. Edited by William Heath, Macmillan, 1973, pp. 18–23.

_____. "The Tyger." *Songs of Experience*. 1794. *Major British Poets of the Romantic Period*. Edited by William Heath, Macmillan, 1973, pp. 53–60.

French, Warren. *John Steinbeck*. Twayne, 1961.

Fromm, Erich. *Escape from Freedom*. Rinehart, 1941.

Griffith, Chris. "How to Teach *The Pearl*." Prestwick House. n.d. www. prestwickhouse.com/blog/post/2016/09/how-to-teach-the-pearl.

Hayashi, Tetsumaro. "*The Pearl*: A Novel of Disengagement." *Readings on The Pearl*, edited by Jill Karson, Greenhaven P, 1999, pp. 48–52.

Helmi, Moh Imawan. "Steinbeck's Worldview toward the Effects of Materialism in the Mexican Colonial Era as Reflected in *The Pearl*." B.A. thesis. Yogyakarta State U, Indonesia, 17 Jan. 2018.

McCarthy, Paul. *John Steinbeck*. Frederick Ungar, 1980.

McParland, Robert. *Citizen Steinbeck: Giving Voice to the People*. Rowman & Littlefield, 2016.

McWhorter, John. *Losing the Race: Self-Sabotage in Black America*. Harper Perennial, 2001.

Morris, Harry. "*The Pearl*: Realism and Allegory." *Steinbeck: A Collection of Critical Essays*. Edited by Robert Murray Davis, Prentice-Hall, 1972, pp. 149–62.

"*The Pearl* by John Steinbeck: Unit Overview." Winston-Salem/Forsyth County School. www.wsfcs.k12.nc.us/cms/lib/NC01001395/Centricity/Domain/8655/ThePearlUnitLitGuide.pdf.

Steinbeck, John. *The Log from the Sea of Cortez*. 1951. Penguin, 1977.

_____. "Nobel Prize Acceptance Speech." *America and Americans and Selected Nonfiction*. Penguin, 2002, pp. 172–74.

_____. *The Pearl*. 1947. Penguin, 1994.

_____. *Steinbeck: A Life in Letters*. Edited by Elaine Steinbeck and Robert Wallsten. Viking, 1975.

Who Stole Kino's Cheese? Socioeconomic Determinism in *The Pearl*_____

Arun Khevariya

Is Man Really the Maker of His Destiny? The Debate Over Free Will and Determinism

The concept of determinism has received the attention of philosophers, thinkers, and social scientists from the advent of Christian thought. This philosophical concept could be found in early discussions such as Malthus' theory of population and the over-fecundity of nature (1798), Lyell's *The Principles of Geology* (1833), Darwin's *The Origin of Species* (1859), Spencer's *System of Synthetic Philosophy* (1860), Marx's theory of class struggle in *Das Capital* (1867), and Nietzsche's concept of the Superman in *Thus Spoke Zarathustra* (1883–92). American literature from the mid-nineteenth century onward witnessed a stream of determinism flowing through its major fictional works. Distinguished writers such as Hamlin Garland, Frank Norris, Stephan Crane, Theodore Dreiser, Jack London, William Faulkner, Ernest Hemingway, and John Steinbeck exhibited the influence of this philosophical concept in their writings.

The term "determinism" was made popular by Sir William Hamilton in his 1846 edition of Thomas Reid's works, to denote the doctrine of the necessitarian philosophers who believed that the life of a man is governed by the law of cause and effect. These philosophers believed that events in human life are so interconnected that each action of one person directly brings about a specific result, and as such, the second result would be impossible without the original act. To Perry D. Westbrook, determinism is "The doctrine that all occurrences in the universe are governed by inexorable laws of cause and effect. Since human activities, whether of the body or the mind, are subject to these same laws as part of the universal order, determinism is more narrowly used to denote absence of freedom in our volitions and choices" (ix).

This assertion candidly utters the role of cause and effect in human affairs. To another eminent philosopher, William James, determinism "professes that those parts of the universe already laid down absolutely appoint and decree what the other parts shall be. The future has no ambiguous possibilities hidden in its womb. . . . The whole is in each and every part, and welds it with the rest into an absolute unity, an iron block, in which there can be no equivocation or shadow of turning" (qtd. in Westbrook 216). Determinism thus shows the absence of freedom in our choices. Various psychological factors and external conditions influence and affect the behavior of a person and virtually compel him to act in a sort of mechanical way.

Determinism stands in sharp opposition to indeterminism. An indeterminist supports the belief that human will is not entirely subject to forces beyond an individual's control. To William James, in indeterminism:

> the parts have a certain amount of loose play on one another, so that the laying down one of them does not necessarily determine what the other shall be. It admits that possibilities may be in excess of actualities, and that things not yet revealed to our knowledge may really in themselves be ambiguous of two alternative futures which we conceive, both may now be possible. . . . Indeterminism thus denies the world to one unbending unit of fact. (qtd. in Westbrook x)

American Transcendentalism also lays stress upon freedom of the will, but to a limited extent. As Theodore Parker states: "Man has moral faculties that lead him to justice and right, and by his own nature can find out what is right and just, and can know it and be certain of it.. . . the transcendental system of morals is to be founded on human nature and absolute justice. . . . the will of man is free; not absolutely free as God's but partially free, and capable of progress to yet higher degrees of freedom" (132).

Ralph Waldo Emerson, perhaps the greatest thinker of American Transcendentalism, preached the doctrine of self-reliant freedom and moral perfection. He expressed scorn for those who thought that circumstances could overpower the individual, and says in his seminal essay, "The Transcendentalist," "You think me the child of my circumstances," he declared, "I make my circumstances" (334). A person, he says in "Self-Reliance," should "carry himself in the presence of all opposition as if everything were titular and ephemeral but he" (51).

As time went by, Emerson became less vociferous in his hopes for humanity. He began reflecting whether it was as easy as he had once thought for a person to build his own world. He started musing on the trials and tribulations of life and people. The perversities and struggle of man in the affairs of life gradually led him to temper his optimism with a harder, tougher view of the world with an acknowledgement of the limits and bounds that circumstances place on individual autonomy.

Although Emerson possessed strong conviction in the power of the individual to perform miracles, he became more and more impressed with the power of circumstances to block and frustrate his wishes and designs. There was, he declared in *The Conduct of Life*, "a stupendous antagonism" between the power of individual and the power of circumstances ("Fate" 256). Freedom and necessity were locked in endless battle. Also in "Fate," he admits frankly: "Once we thought positive power was all. Now we learn that negative power, or circumstance, is half. Nature is the tyrannous circumstance" (250).

Emerson felt that human beings were crushed by tyrannical circumstances and calamities of life, such as famine, typhus, frost, war, earthquake, etc. Although Emerson believed in the ultimate beneficent tendency at work in creation, yet he also thought that the individual work was often sacrificed to the continuous improving processes of the universe. In a passage, he exclaimed that Nature

> is no sentimentalist, does not cosset or pamper us. We must see that the world is rough and surly, and will not mind drowning a man or a woman, beauty swallows your ship like a grain of dust. The cold, inconsiderate of persons, tingles your blood, benumb your feet, freezes a man like an apple. The diseases, the elements, fortune, gravity, lightning, respect no persons. The way of providence is a little rude. . . . Providence has a wild, rough incalculable road to its end, and it is of no use to try to whitewash its huge, mixed

instrumentalities, or to dress up that terrific benefactor in a clean shirt and white neck cloth of a student in divinity. (244)

Philosophic naturalism also believes that man has freedom of choice. Its followers admit the existence of two kinds of laws—the physical and the social. They believe that the former are permanent while the latter are not. No doubt they are mostly the man-made laws, and hence by creating and imposing social laws, man contributes importantly "to the formation of his environment" (Winn 528).

The deterministic philosophy that comes in sharp opposition to indeterminism is naturalism. It explains that mankind is subject to the same law as the rest of the organic and inorganic universe. Denis Diderot asserts that naturalists do not have faith in the existence of God, but they believe in the material substance. According to Paul-Henri Thiry (Baron) d'Holbach, eighteenth-century naturalism was "a philosophical system that saw man living solely in a world of perceived phenomena, a kind of cosmic machine which determined his life as it did nature—in short, a universe devoid of transcendental, metaphysical or divine force" (Furst 2). With the inductive sciences still in their infancy, naturalism had yet to achieve its maturity.

In the nineteenth century, science expanded in many spheres such as geology, chemistry, physics, astronomy, anthropology, and biology. But it was the discoveries of the inductive and biological sciences that influenced the philosophy and literature of that time. In 1859, Charles Darwin published his *Origin of Species by Means of Natural Selection* and in 1871 *The Descent of Man*. The theory of evolution as propagated in these books brought about radical changes in social and literary circles. Darwin's concept that man is descended from the lower animals and that in animal life there is a continuous struggle for existence, which leads to the survival of the fittest by a process of natural selection. This thinking attracted the attention of thinkers, scientists, social scientists, litterateurs, etc. Darwin supported the idea that man is only slightly above the animal level. Lilian R. Furst and Peter N. Skrine assert Darwin's influence on naturalism: "[T]o the naturalist man is an animal whose course is determined by his heredity, by the effect of his environment and by the pressures of the moment. This terribly depressing conception robs man of all free will, all responsibility for his actions, which are merely the inescapable result of physical forces and conditions totally beyond his control" (17–18).

All naturalists have firm belief in determinism. In *The American Novel and its Tradition,* Richard Chase says, "Naturalistic doctrine assumes that fate is something imposed on the individual from the outside. The protagonist of a naturalistic novel is therefore at the mercy of circumstances rather than of himself, indeed he often seems to have no self" (199). Naturalists believe that man is only a part in the vast machine of universe, so it is futile and irrelevant to change the order of things. Emile Zola, one of the most prominent novelists of nineteenth century, also emphasizes the deterministic order of the world. He affirms that man is not able to direct his thoughts by free will. His thoughts, choices and actions are the results of his own heredity, environment, and biochemistry. Zola voices emphatically that man's body, passions, and mind are subject to an absolute determinism that finds the human race trapped in deterministic order. Thomas Malthus is another thinker who invigorates naturalistic thoughts. He observes a constant struggle in this world caused by circumstances. He feels nature as the biggest deterministic force and admits the inevitability of the law of nature: "No improved form of government, no plans of emigration, no benevolent institutions, and no degree or direction of national industry can prevent the continual action of a great check to population in some form or other; it follows that we must submit to it as an inevitable law of nature" (20).

Another contributor to the belief in determinism is Sigmund Freud. He is "devoted to the belief that mental phenomena are just as much subject to inflexible laws of causation as physical phenomena, and, in fact, that the causation in the two cases is virtually the same" (Wilson 92). According to him, whether we are neurotic or normal, we choose, and will, and behave, not in freedom but as a result of scientifically demonstrable laws of causality. Our conscious will is determined by unconscious desires over which we have no direct control and our "psychological freedom is an illusion" (Waller 38). He negates the role of chance and thinks that it plays no role in the mental world because "psychical processes are never isolated or accident phenomena, but are as precisely related to preceding ones as are successive physical events" (47). In the psychological world, nothing happens by accident. It is Freud's "claim that we live, body and soul, in a deterministic world" (Wilson 101). Both normal and neurotic have their unconscious causality in the matter of will.

Along with these elements, the influence of social and economic power is also responsible for determining the lives of human beings. Man has to struggle for the achievement of his goals in this predatory world, but he cannot achieve his cherished ambitions without the help from society and outer forces. It is extremely ironic that sometimes these socioeconomic forces act as a villain and, instead of rendering proper help; they debar the man of his birthrights and individualistic freedom.

The Bleeding Souls: Socioeconomic Determinism and Steinbeck

Is man really a social animal? Several of Steinbeck's novels expose one basic problem—the relation of the individual to society. These novels expose various socioeconomic evils that confine a person within their own boundaries and do not support the birthright of individualistic freedom. Expressing social consciousness through these novels, Steinbeck brings to light the mad exploitation of farm laborers, the dealings of political power, and distorted attitudes of society towards the poor and helpless. It is through these novels that Steinbeck investigates the socioeconomic factors that determine the destiny of man.

Socioeconomic determinism is the result of economic mismanagement, maldistribution of resources, and lack of empathy towards the downtrodden members of society. The economic scenario of twentieth-century America was greatly affected due to the Great Depression. The American economy of the 1920s and 1930s wrought havoc to a large segment of society with industrial workers, farm laborers, and poor people suffering on account of the economic mismanagement. The Great Depression was "Characterized by business bankruptcies, bank closings, factory shutdowns, farm foreclosures, low prices, hunger and huge unemployment" (Hurwitz 303). The first people affected were, of course, those with the fewest resources.

The resulting economic instability created a deep rift between the rich and the poor. The rich amassed wealth at the cost of blood and toil of the poor. The attitude of the business community revealed a philosophy that was devoid of charity and compassion, and the wealthy contributed little to the welfare of the poor. Then, in the mid-1930s, the dust bowl phenomenon arose as the result of severe draught and ecological mismanagement of the previous decades. Spreading across half of the eastern continent, dust storms were not only a great threat to the American economy, but also to the health and life of the people. Fertile soil was now poisonous dust, and this greatly affected the agricultural sector and those who worked in it. As a result, large numbers of farmers from the Plains moved in search of livable lands. But they were destined to get no relief from their misery.

The wheel of misfortune ran its course. The dust bowl caused large migrations of laborers and farm workers during the economic crisis of Depression years. The influx of thousands of new families toward the west coast created chaotic situations and near-financial ruin in California. For mere survival, these new migrant workers took on various odd jobs in the fields. But this situation made them defenseless and vulnerable to exploitation. As the poor and needy were unable to receive state relief for a long time, they had to accept whatsoever wage they were offered in the fields. California's growers received this oversupply of laborers with greedy eyes, and they took advantage of the situation to satisfy their economic desires. Even in 1936, the Associated Farmers of California, Inc. officially replied that they met "Okies with hatred" (Stein 45). The social, economic, moral, and ethical standard of American society witnessed severe imbalance in the era of the Great Depression. The vicious cycle of greed and exploitation continued, and there seemed no relief for the poor and needy. Society was divided into groups of haves and have-nots.

Steinbeck's empathic mind was sensitive to the problems of those poor and needy who could not rely upon anyone for help and support. He felt the pain of those who could do nothing except allow the exploitive farmers and landowners to snatch their share of the economic pie. He heard the cries of those victims of social injustice and economic mismanagement. The growing misery among the poor inspired him to raise his voice against the exploitation and oppression. That is why his writings are filled with "indignation at injustice, with contempt for false piety, with scorn for the cunning and self-righteousness of an economic system that encourages exploitation, greed and brutality" (Gray 09).

The Real Culprit

The Pearl exemplifies the role of socioeconomic forces in the lives of persons like Kino, its chief protagonist. This novella shows that Kino works under the compulsion of these forces. Various socioeconomic factors change, modify, shape and even distort his actions and achievements. First published in *Woman's Home Companion* of December 1945, under the title *"The Pearl* of the World,"* the novel then appeared in book form, as *The Pearl*, in 1947. Based on the exploiter-exploited world of La Paz, Mexico, the novel depicts the cruelty and avarice of economic forces that determine the actions of an individual. The source of the novella is an oral story that Steinbeck recalls in *The Log from the Sea of Cortez*:

> An event, which happened at La Paz in recent years, is typical of such places. An Indian boy by accident found a pearl of great size, an unbelievable pearl. He knew its value was so great that he need never work again. . . . He went to La Paz with this Pearl in his hand and his future clear into eternity in his heart. He took his pearl to a broker and was offered so little that he grew angry, for he knows he was cheated. Then he carried his pearl to another broker and was offered the same amount. After a few more visits he came to know that the brokers were only the many hands of one head and that he could not sell his pearl for more. He took it to the beach and hid it under a stone, and that night he was clubbed into unconsciousness and his clothing was searched. The next night he slept at the house of

a friend and his friend and he were injured and bound and the whole house searched. Then he went inland to lose his pursuers and he was waylaid and tortured. (102–103)

Instead of providing the boy happiness, however, the pearl brings calamities due to sheer role of economic greed of people. Like the Indian boy of the story, Kino, the chief protagonist of *The Pearl,* also faces the same predicament. Because Steinbeck has no faith in economic institutions to reward laborers, Kino's pearl only brings misfortune. This exposes Steinbeck's belief that money is the new god of the modern world.

The novella begins with a brief discussion of setting; Kino lives in a brush house near the beach with his wife, Juana, and infant son, Coyotito. One morning, a scorpion enters the hut and stings the baby. His wife, Juana, sucks out the poison, but she insists on seeing the doctor. Kino knows that the doctor will not come to his hut, so he goes to the doctor's house accompanied by his neighbors. The doctor's servant ascertains that the family is impoverished, so he tells Kino that the doctor is out. After great humiliation, Kino returns to the beach and goes out in a canoe to find something worthwhile for paying the doctor's fee. During his search, Kino finds a pearl of great size, and this discovery begins to act on Kino almost immediately.

Kino dreams of a better lifestyle and the possibilities of a more secure future after getting the pearl. He previously has been revealed as being quiet, sensitive, strong, and courageous. On the first night, now in possession of the valuable pearl, his transformation begins as he starts making plans and desiring possessions. In his little world he desires a church marriage, new clothes, a harpoon, and a rifle— and he dreams of sending Coyotito to school: "My son will read and open books, and my son will write and will know writing. And my son will make numbers, and these things will make us free because he will know—he will know and through him we will know" (31). But along with what Kino wants, fortunes bring temptation and enmity.

The news of Kino's good fortune spreads quickly among the townspeople, and as a result, almost everyone in the town either becomes his enemy or his supplicant (with requests based on their own vested interests). The doctor eventually comes and administers medicine to the baby, thereby exploiting the situation for his economic benefit. With the threat of theft, the safekeeping of the pearl almost immediately troubles Kino now, however, so he buries the pearl in the dirt floor. One night a thief approaches the house, and Kino bruises his own forehead while defending his precious possession.

Kino does not wish to keep the pearl. He has an ardent desire to give his family a bright future by selling it, though he now understands that such a wondrous pearl has some strings attached. Juana, however, considers the thing evil and advises her husband to get rid of it. Kino ignores her, still believing it has the power of great transformation for his family. The possession of "the great pearl makes Kino a man apart. . . . [H]e can no longer be sure which of his friends and neighbors he can now trust" (Simmonds 10). He becomes very cautious, calculating, and fearless in order to retain the precious possession. The transformation, thus, is not economic and positive, but social and negative.

Fighting a Man Is a Battle, but Fighting a System Is War

Kino, hoping for a brighter future, moves towards La Paz to sell the pearl. But no buyer is willing to pay him more than a thousand pesos for it. They recognize his disadvantage as seller, and their power as economic forces to make a purchase. Kino fights bravely when the existence of his family is at stake, and refuses to be a puppet in the hands of pearl buyers. But the socioeconomic forces are, as they always have been, his enemy. This truth "comes into sharp focus only when Kino refuses to be handled as a thing by the pearl buyers," when Kino demands true value for the pearl, "the town reveals itself by arranging to bring violence and murder to the family" (Levant 191). Kino refuses to sell the pearl for such a small price, and instead aims to bring it to the capital. In the morning he is attacked once again, and Kino kills his unknown assailant. He has now become a murderer to save the pearl, and he tries to escape from that town in the night. He, Juana, and Coyotito walk all night. On the way he sees three approaching figures. He tells Juana to keep the baby quiet as the figures pass by, but instead they stop to rest by the pool. Soon after, Coyotito cries, and one of the figures fires his rifle. The deadly bullet kills Coyotito. Infuriated, Kino murders all three people, then returns to the country road with Juana to rid himself of the pearl that has now become a burden and a curse. As James Gray says: "Possession of this rare object so poisoned the existence of the fisherman . . . that he cursed it and threw it back into the sea" (29).

Despite Kino's best efforts, the inevitable takes place. The weakness of his economic circumstances, the monetary greed of the pearl buyers, and the challenges of safekeeping the pearl finally defeat him. Like the Indian boy of the original story, Kino returns the pearl to the sea and returns "himself to his previous, uncompetitive position in the social . . . [s]ystem" (Lisca *John Steinbeck* 125–26). Lester Jay Marks rightly remarks in this matter: "Kino, in his primitive simplicity, is the good; the civilized world, glittering with deceitful wealth and power, is the bad. But unlike most parables, this one does not end with good triumphing over evil. . . . His bitter experiences finally lead him to throw the pearl back into the sea" (107). The economic forces and capitalistic system make Kino's defeat ultimately unavoidable (portraying the determinism of the century's culture). Monetary need inspires the need for the possession of an economic "good" such as the pearl, but there is no economic good, Steinbeck ultimately asserts, for only those in power can exploit the situation. Kino can never have such power. In his portrayal of the doctor and the pearl dealers, Steinbeck has depicted the greed and avarice of a social system too firmly in place to allow any social climbing. As one critic states, "The scorpion that stings Coyotito is less inhuman than the doctor who makes the child sick in order to gain a fee" (Levant 193). His treatment is more dangerous than the scorpion's sting: a "white powder" that could have killed Coyotito had the subsequent antidote not been given. He is free to go to any extreme for the sake of money, with no sympathy for the poor. Martha Heasley Cox observes: "[H]e tends their sick only when assured of ample recompense, feigning the need for his services when none exists, and practicing subterfuge rather than the healing art to attain ill-gotten wealth" (119). Steinbeck recognizes that the capitalist system is designed to exploit those who can be taken advantage of.

Like the doctor, the pearl dealers also want to exploit Kino. They are the sharks in the ocean of capitalism, always ready to devour small fishlike Kino. In the economic circle of life, the haves will always necessarily take advantage of the have-nots: "Like the 'owners' of *In Dubious Battle* and *The Grapes of Wrath*, they are but part of a system" (Lisca *The Wide World* 229). Kino's brother Juan Tomas knows the power and pressures of this greedy economic system that crushes the poor under its heavy weight. That is why when Kino insults the agents who tell him that the pearl is of no great value, Juan Tomas says to him, "[Y]ou have defied not the pearl buyers, but the whole structure, the whole way of life, and I am afraid for you" (*The Pearl* 59). Ultimately his opinion proves prescient. Once Kino challenges the system, no escape is possible for him from his miserable circumstances. Furthermore, he himself is corrupted: "[T]he ultimate turn is that Kino is forced to kill in the end to keep the actual pearl" (Levant 193). The grinding mill of a society built on economic avarice crushes the goodness out of him. His actions thus are determined by the social structure and the economic pressures. Once he finds the pearl, Kino faces a future with only two options to retain the pearl or not to retain it. Once the decision to retain the pearl is taken, Kino is bound to face the challenges, and it is the socioeconomic forces that rob him of his cheese.

Works Cited

Chase, Richard. *The American Novel and Its Tradition*. G. Bell and Sons, 1958.

Cox, Martha Heasley. "Steinbeck's *The Pearl* (1947)." *A Study Guide to Steinbeck: A Handbook to His Major Works*. Edited by Tetsumaro Hayashi, Scarecrow P, 1974.

Emerson, Ralph Waldo. "Fate." *The Journals and Notebooks of Ralph Waldo Emerson*, edited by Roger M. Crowther, McGraw-Hill, 1947. pp. 250–66.

_____. "Self-Reliance." *The Complete Works of Ralph Waldo Emerson, with a Biographical Introduction and Notes by Edward Waldo Emerson,* vol. 2. 1841. Houghton-Mifflin, 1904.

_____. "The Transcendentalist." *The Complete Works of Ralph Waldo Emerson, with a Biographical Introduction and Notes by Edward Waldo Emerson,* vol. 1. 1841. Houghton-Mifflin, 1904.

Furst, Lilian R., and Peter N. Skrine. *Naturalism.* Methuen & Co., 1971.

Gray, James. *John Steinbeck.* U of Minnesota P, 1971.

Hurwitz, Howard L. *An Encyclopedic Dictionary of American History.* Washington Square P, 1970.

Levant, Howard. *The Novels of John Steinbeck: A Critical Study.* U of Missouri P, 1974.

Lisca, Peter. *John Steinbeck: Nature and Myth.* Thomas Y. Crowell, 1978.

_____. *The Wide World of John Steinbeck.* Rutgers U P, 1958.

Malthus, Thomas R. *An Essay on Population.* Bradbury, 1960.

Marks, Lester Jay. *Thematic Design in the Novels of John Steinbeck.* Mouton, 1969.

Parker, Theodore. "Transcendentalism." *The Development of American Philosophy.* Edited by Rutmarge and Boven. Maxwell, 1948.

Simmonds, Roy S. *Steinbeck's Literary Achievement.* Ball State U P, 1976.

Stein, Walter J. *California and the Dust Bowl Migration.* Greenwood P, 1973.

Steinbeck, John. *The Log from the Sea of Cortez.* Viking, 1941.

_____. *The Pearl.* 1947. Pan Books London, 1984.

Waller, Edmund. *New Age Man.* City House, 1982.

Westbrook, Perry D. *Free Will and Determinism in American Literature.* Associated U P, 1979.

Wilson, Jerome. *Modern Psychology.* Simmons, 1991.

Winn, Ralph B. "Philosophic Naturalism." *Twentieth Century Philosophy.* Edited by Dagobert D Runes, Philosophical Library, 1947.

The Portrayal of "Poverty People" in John Steinbeck's *The Pearl* and *Tortilla Flat*_____

Emily P. Hamburger

Students of literature should consider, when encountering the death of a young child or children in fiction, what those figures may represent beyond the confines of the story they inhabit. A child could, for example, represent a parent's own private wishes for him or herself. A family of children could substitute for the hopes nurtured from older generations on to younger ones. A child in a story that is resilient may symbolize the grit of his community as a whole. Finally, the death of a young child, and how that death is experienced by other characters in a story, could be representative of the precariousness of a desired future for a particular demographic group. In John Steinbeck's literature, these scenarios arise frequently.

This study will show that children in John Steinbeck's literature can be read as representations of many of these concepts, and that a child that is resilient may also be a victim of forces beyond his or her control. How parents bring up their children in literature reveals a great deal more than simply domestic details of a story. In Steinbeck's folkloric novel, *The Pearl*, the narrator explains that "sickness is second only to hunger as the enemy of poor people" (34). This chapter will examine the story of the "poor people" protagonists in *The Pearl* as well as a related narrative Steinbeck published ten years prior, the novel *Tortilla Flat*. Both fictional texts involve Latinx families enduring desperate circumstances and attempting to save a baby's life. Further, both texts potently describe the sudden deaths of those babies. Caring for a suffering child is among the duties that matter most to Steinbeck's characters, regardless of his novels' settings, origins, or other broader themes. With *The Pearl* in particular, Steinbeck drew from a Mexican folktale to retell a story that could be applied in his time, in his own words and style. Similarly, we may look to *The Pearl* as well as *Tortilla Flat* to garner lessons about modern American society.

In *The Pearl*, exposition reveals that the rage and suspicion felt by the father character as he takes several steps to try and obtain help for his baby, is rooted in a four hundred year-long racial conflict between Spanish settlers in Mexico and the indigenous community to which he belongs: "he was trapped as his people were always trapped" (30, 46). The racial and class dynamics in *Tortilla Flat* are not as explicitly addressed; however, the overarching themes of lack of education or resources for the unemployed Latinx parents living in California during the Great Depression bear strong resemblance to those in *The Pearl*. The parenting choices and the portrayals of the vulnerable children in these two texts communicate much about Steinbeck's concern for the disadvantaged poor in the 1930s and 1940s.

These two novels are some of the only in Steinbeck's canon that place Latinx characters, communities, and dwelling places in the limelight. Although Latinx characters do appear in other Steinbeck novels of this period (see *To A God Unknown, The Red Pony*), their roles are less central therein. "Paisanos" are described in *Tortilla Flat* as "a mixture of Spanish, Indian, Mexican and assorted Caucasian bloods" (11). The novel is meant to be a comedy involving paisanos, and the text addresses hardships experienced by this specific demographic. The light, comedic tone is ruptured, however, by the appearance of a young man who is tending to his dying baby. Ten years passed between Steinbeck's publishing of *Tortilla Flat* and *The Pearl*, yet there is a plot similarity deserving of critique in the desperate plights of these two young babies and their guardians.

Before *The Pearl* was published, Steinbeck had already won the Pulitzer Prize and made a name for himself, enjoying the far-reaching commercial and critical success of novels such as *Of Mice and Men* (1937), *Tortilla Flat*, and *The Grapes of Wrath* (1939) (DeMott xvii). As Steinbeck's personal fortune grew, late in the 1930s, he shifted his interest and intellectual energies toward the lives of the dispossessed, the starving, and the indigent. His written projects began to give a powerful voice to the homeless and the dying on his native North American West Coast, specifically in California and Mexico. In analyzing these two texts, it is notable that infants living in poverty in Steinbeck's fiction lack medical care commonly expected to be provided in modern times and civilized societies. As will be discussed further, the parents in *The Pearl* and the father in *Tortilla Flat* do not earn enough income to access basic medical care. The families are without education and are not in positions to access government relief.

The Pearl's protagonist, Kino, as a parent and husband displays several competing and contradictory traits. He is capable of nurturing, as he intimately lays his palm on his baby's head (83). He is prone to anger and violence, even directing physical violence toward Juana, Coyotito's mother; he strikes her "in the face with his clenched fist" (59). He is protective and aspirational on behalf of his son Coyotito, "in the pearl he saw Coyotito sitting at a little desk in a school" (25). Although Kino and Juana are not married in the eyes of the church, in the story they are considered to be husband and wife by the other characters and described as such throughout the text. They have given their innocent child the diminutive name meaning little or dear coyote, which evokes Kino's fierce and fearless ambitions for his son.

Kino is attuned to the music of nature, of history, and of forces guiding (or misguiding) his family: "Perhaps he alone did this and perhaps all of his people did it. His people had once been great makers of songs so that everything they saw or thought or did or heard became a song" (2). This is an example of Steinbeck assigning intuitive strengths to characters of low education or sophistication. Said another way, reading Steinbeck's style here, it is because Kino is a fisherman who lives in a grass hut by the beach that he is possessed of the ability to hear the music of nature. His son is named after a wild, carnivorous animal. Despite Kino's receptiveness to spiritual forces and his own instincts throughout his day-to-day life, his physical drives often involve aggression and violence.

As with Kino's sensitivity to spiritual forces, his dynamic with Juana often appears to be somewhat organic and telepathic: "They had spoken once, but there is not need for speech if it is only a habit anyway. Kino sighed with satisfaction—and that was conversation"

---

(4). Much of their intentions, feelings, and concerns are expressed through their eyes and communicated across their faces, rather than through lengthy discussion. Again, the primitive lifestyle Kino and Juana inhabit lends itself to an unsophisticated, natural, and breeze-like communicative style. However, Kino's attempt to prevent the scorpion from stinging Coyotito is different from Juana's, and both parents fail to prevent the sting from occurring. The approach Kino takes involves standing "perfectly still" and leaping his hand "to catch it" (5). His instinct once the sting occurs is to pummel the scorpion into the ground while "snarling" (6). This tendency toward reactive violence after failing at something is a recurrent behavior of Kino's throughout *The Pearl*.

When Juana takes the bold step of commanding Kino to go "get the doctor," Kino responds that "the doctor would not come" (7). Their simple life by the beach up until then has not required complicated and expensive actions such as hiring a white doctor. The conflict existing between the financially comfortable doctor and Kino's impecunious family is one rooted in centuries of European imperialism, racism, exploitation, and rampant economic disparities in the village of La Paz, Mexico. Kino is described as having brown skin (4, 83). The doctor, on the other hand, is referred to as being "of a race which for nearly four hundred years had beaten and starved and robbed and despised Kino's race" (9). To the doctor, Kino's family are "little Indians" (11). Nonetheless, Kino and Juana attempt to have Coyotito seen and treated by this doctor because they are desperate to protect their baby from death in the wake of the scorpion bite. "Through an open door," the uneducated Kino had once watched children sit at desks and receive an education (25). Through a shut gate, Kino is denied access to the doctor; turned away, Kino "without warning" strikes the doctor's gate "a crushing blow with his fist" (12). When Kino dives for and recovers a pearl the size of a seagull's egg, with which he believes he can buy medical treatment for Coyotito, he "put back his head and howled" (20). It takes minimal time for the white doctor to pay a visit to the "little Indian" family and try to manipulate them and the baby with a dose of white powder and ominous medical warnings once he learns a great pearl is in their possession.

Kino's sensitivity toward natural forces and omens is activated in a fleetingly positive sense once he and Juana bring the pearl to their hut: "the music of the pearl had merged with the music of the family so that one beautified the other" (24). Kino's capacity to listen to the "music" of the environmental forces around him is not articulated in any character's dialogue. The music he hears is beneath and behind his actions and his words, but it is never spoken of outright. With his actions, he is neither musical nor spiritual, but blunt and often hostile. He shares none of his intuitive, anguished spiritual essence with the outside world. He says little, even to Juana and Coyotito, about his sentiments. However, his determination to provide for and protect them is evident in what he does.

It is necessary to closely examine the aspirations Kino expresses once he and Juana possess the pearl, because they are not, in fact, closely correlated with Coyotito's scorpion bite. This is a moral dilemma in the text to consider. Kino's desires take on a life of their own, having so little to do with the initial motivation with which he dove for the pearl. First, he envisions and articulates a desire for a church wedding (24). Although this is connected to the family bond motivating Kino and Juana, this vision ignores the medical urgency facing Coyotito the day this discovery occurs. Further desires are expressed in quick succession: Kino envisions new clothes for himself and his family, with Coyotito to be wearing "a blue sailor suit from the United States and a little yachting cap" (24). This want that Kino visualizes for Coyotito is ironic in that Kino's feelings toward the town doctor are so deeply hostile: his resentment toward the race that he feels has oppressed him for four hundred years, the same race as the doctor, is not recalled when he desires his son to be dressed up like a child in attire "from the United States." It is as if Kino forgets these resentments temporarily when contemplating what he will do when he has "become a rich man" (24). Steinbeck may be commenting on the corrupting power of wealth; however, it is not a simple point that Steinbeck is making. First, there is the mysteriousness surrounding the pearl's power, which is not simply the power of wealth, but appears to be more mystical and magical in the fate it brings to *The Pearl*'s protagonists. Second, there is the hostility already bubbling over within Kino—Kino's resentment. Regardless of whether he finds the pearl or not, he is a violent man who reacts emotionally and forcefully to slights, disappointments, and threats.

Violence comes to the surface with the next items on Kino's hypothetical list of desires: a harpoon and a rifle (25). He also kicks and strikes Juana in the face when she attempts to toss the pearl back into the sea, as the evil, mysterious forces of the pearl seem to encompass his life (59). Kino cannot prevent violence from befalling the innocent Coyotito as the story reaches its climax while he and his family are being hunted for the pearl; after Kino kills three of the men attempting to steal it from him. But despite his flaws and internal contradictions, Kino demonstrates deep love and affection for Juana and Coyotito when they are being pursued in the wilderness east of La Paz: "his hand . . . found the baby, and for a moment his palm lay on Coyotito's head. And then Kino raised his hand and touched Juana's cheek" (83). Here we see a fallible, frustrated yet determined figure that Steinbeck's narrative is going to push to the precipice of survival.

Kino's ambitions for Coyotito to blossom in life, before the baby's violent death, include more than owning a sailor suit from the United States. The promise that education is the best means by which to overcome prior deprivations, and by which to be taken seriously in society, is a common theme Steinbeck often employs in his underdog-laden literature. Not all Steinbeck's "poverty people" (8) desire or seek a way out of their circumstances, but briefly, in *The Pearl*, Kino does, and recognizes education as the means of escape. Specifically, Kino intends for Coyotito to go to school: "he must break out of the pot that holds us in" (39). The pot that Kino refers to is discussed again in the context of the doctor of the different race, and the doctor's refusal to initially treat Coyotito because Kino's family *are* so-called "poverty people." The economic disparity felt between the doctor and Kino's family is described in relation to "hundreds of years of subjugation" by the Europeans (specifically Spanish) in Mexico (16, 30).

This is how Steinbeck uses the parenting of children to reveal deeper themes in the text. Kino's belief, in efforts to aid Coyotito, is that he himself is unschooled and ignorant to medical methods, and that he must put his trust in the white doctor because the doctor has training: "He was trapped as his people were always trapped . . . He could not take a chance" (30). This is why Kino is so adamant that, in addition to purchasing medical care, he must purchase an education for Coyotito; as he says himself, he wants to break the cycle of "his certain ignorance" (30). The dilemma Steinbeck expertly introduces in this scene (which is ostensibly about parenting) is the suspicion Kino and his family have toward the doctor. But Kino is not educated enough to know whether the doctor is scheming, manipulating Coyotito's symptoms in order to be paid and to brag to the town that he saved the baby whose father found the Pearl of the World. Juana, ironically, is capable of treating Coyotito just as well as the doctor. Unfortunately, both Kino in his ambitions and Juana in her concern, defer to the doctor and give him the last word. The power the doctor's rank carries is enough to counteract the newfound wealth Kino and Juana find themselves with. Steinbeck may be implying here that innate wisdom and intuition are as valuable if not more sacred than commodified fixes and professional opinions that are bought with money. The money wins out, however, and Steinbeck's underdogs are resolved in their choice to defer to the doctor. The reader is left wondering whether the doctor is lying.

It is Juana who seems to instinctively make choices based in logic, though, like her husband, she is not always able to undo stronger forces at work in their lives. She is ultimately not able to keep Coyotito from harm. Juana, from the first, is as alert (if not more so) than Kino to the reality of their daily responsibilities: "Juana's eyes were open too. Kino could never remember seeing them closed when he awakened" (1). Juana sucks the venom out of Coyotito's arm, she demands that Kino fetch the doctor, and she makes "a flat damp poultice . . . this she applied to the baby's swollen shoulder, which was as good a remedy as any and probably better than the doctor could have done" (15). But because commodified Western medicine has a price—and a steep one at that—it gives the impression that it is more valuable. Thus it coerces Kino to take part in the scheme where previously he could not. Capitalism takes advantage of the poor in this way; once it includes them at the bottom of the economic system, it drains their money as soon as they can make it.

In addition to these practical and medically oriented steps, Juana also takes spiritual steps in her crisis. She repeats an "ancient magic" to guard against evil, in addition to reciting the Hail Mary (5). Her insistence that Coyotito is worthy of being seen by a doctor is described by the narrator as "a wonderful thing, a memorable thing" (7). Her desperation mounts when the doctor refuses to see them, and at that point her focus shifts slightly. She is no longer reciting Hail Mary or ancient magic; instead, she prays not directly "for the recovery of the baby" but instead that they "might find a pearl" (15). She thus abandons her intuition and spirituality in favor of the economic gods. Still, Juana never abandons her maternal instinct; the night of the scorpion sting she "did not put the baby in his box . . . but cradled him in her arms" (36–37). This is another example of how parenting scenes can illustrate Steinbeck's broader literary intent.

The pearl is a wish Juana has never had the audacity to pray for until now. There is no limit to her supplication to forces beyond herself to preserve the extension of herself—her baby. Steinbeck is deftly able to demonstrate maternal strength, grit, and force of will in his fiction. In his literature, parental love is as supernaturally profound as any great pearl's preciousness. But is it strong enough? If it is not, then what destructive forces overwhelm it? Consistently in Steinbeck's work, as in *The Pearl,* characters falsely believe that economics—the evil that has damned them in the first place—also can save them. Here, we are directed to another of the novel's essential yet shrouded themes. By examining the parenting choices of the characters, we can also learn about the treatment of women characters by Steinbeck, the strengths of his female characters, and the limits his female characters may run up against.

Though Juana is the one who prays for the pearl's discovery, it is also Juana who attempts to dispose of it when misfortune first befalls her and Kino. However, she is met with violence as Kino strikes her and kicks her by the seaside and prevents her from returning the pearl to the ocean. In the end, however, once Coyotito has been killed in the violence that ensues because of the pearl, Juana defers to Kino in his moment of release, and he is the one to toss the cursed pearl out to sea. Juana's deference to Kino is not entirely consistent throughout the text. However, it seems to arise at critical moments like the final release of the pearl. Kino demonstrates some affection and admiration toward Juana throughout, and their connection is intuitive and mutually comforting. That Juana walks by Kino's side and not behind when they return to La Paz is an important acknowledgment on Steinbeck's part of how she is sharing the burden, the responsibility and grief equally with Kino (88). It is important to note that this equality is also explicitly mentioned when the pearl is released: "they saw the little splash in the distance, and they stood *side by side*" (emphasis added) (90).

Among the differences between *Tortilla Flat* and *The Pearl*, is the detail that the baby in *Tortilla Flat* is nameless. Could it be that the absence of a name communicates significance in some way? Meaning can be perceived even in moments of silence, much like the academic approach outlined in Steedman's *Dust: The Archive and Cultural History* that speaks of reading for what is *"not there"* (emphasis in original): "An absence speaks [and] we give his namelessness meaning, make it matter" (151). The child thus becomes an "everyman" in its universality. The sudden deaths of the infants portrayed in both texts may correspond with how Steinbeck is conveying an uncertainty about the fate of indigent Latinx peoples during the 1930s and 1940s. That the child in *Tortilla Flat* is never named matters in illustrating the anonymous, deprived lives some groups encounter in societies that ignore their basic needs of care, employment, nutrition, and medicine.

Coyotito is not only named, but also the first-born child to Kino and Juana in *The Pearl*. Although they are "poverty people" and he sleeps in a hanging box, he is lovingly cared for by both of his parents (8). One cannot help but wonder, however, if the scorpion sting was a result of the parents' indigent lifestyle in a grass hut with a dirt floor near the sea. Would a scorpion have easily invaded the comforts of a nursery in town? The doctor's home in La Paz probably did not allow as many opportunities for ingress and egress for pests. La Paz is described as having secret gardens, cool water, and caged birds and of course walls, while Kino's hut is made of grass and vulnerable to arson and the invasion of such predators as the scorpion (8). Regardless of whether the exposure to the dangers of nature stems from where Kino and Juana live, Coyotito is, on the whole, a resilient figure in the text.

Coyotito is the same "despised" race of Kino. Therefore, the doctor has no desire to interact with them: "they *never* have any money" (emphasis added) (9, 11). His mother is able to suck the poison from him, and when the doctor gives him a mysterious white powder to drink, he overcomes whatever poison he may have been given by the doctor and returns to relative health. In fact, it is ambiguous whether Coyotito needed a doctor's involvement at all, but this is an intentional ambiguity Steinbeck employs; it adds to the complex mystery of the pearl, and the people who want it. Steinbeck notes, in this way, that Juana's remedy lacked any "authority because it was simple and didn't cost anything" (15). One could argue the parents get carried away not only in their seeking of medical treatment for Coyotito, but also in their seeking of the pearl and the lengths they go to keep, conceal, and sell it. It is not the scorpion who ultimately kills Coyotito; it is instead a gunshot from the thieves chasing Kino—thieves also inspired by the evils of a capitalist economic system that Kino and Juana agree to take part in once they trade their innate wisdom for monetary gains. And all the prayers and ancient magic that Juana attempts to conjure can no longer protect her baby.

Steinbeck aligns the pearl's evil with imperialism by explaining that the source of the pearl—the "bed where the frilly pearl oysters lay"—was "the bed that had raised the King of Spain to be a great power in Europe" (16). In essence, when the pearl becomes a source of unchecked ambition for Kino and Juana, it poisons their lives the way the imperialist Europeans poisoned the lives of Kino's ancestors and the scorpion poisoned Coyotito. Kino is helpless when he comes up against the forces of classism at the doctor's, exploitation by the pearl traders, and violence of the thieves who kill Coyotito. These menacing forces are not as present in *Tortilla Flat* where the harsh realities of poverty are not overtly linked to conflicts between people of European origins and those of Latinx heritage.

Steinbeck wrote that he considered the paisano people depicted in *Tortilla Flat* as "delightful" and his goal with this novel was to share with the world a "little known" people whom he came to know while he lived in Monterey as a young adult (qtd. in Gannett xiii). Tortilla Flat is the name of the neighborhood in which the characters all live. Some of the characters are veterans of World War I, some work on the docks, and others continue to seek employment and wealth around Monterey—with limited success. All love wine and drink it by the jug. Throughout the novel, a band of friends supports and betrays each other multiple times, and the tone of the text is predominantly silly and at times ridiculous.

The youth with the dying baby appears in town, holding him (the child's mother has gone off somewhere unknown), and he encounters the main cast of characters. He introduces himself saying, "'It is my baby. . . . I am a corporal, and he is my baby. He is sick now; but when he grows up, he is going to be a general'" (176). The response of the paisanos, once the father and son are brought into their house, is brisk and attentive. The presence of a sick baby galvanizes everyone to assist immediately: "the friends arose with alacrity" (177). That the father is a corporal does not spur any discussion of service to his country entitling him to services from his country.

As has been discussed, this child has no name, neither does his father. In fact, many other children in a neighboring bungalow in *Tortilla Flat* appear without names, and they survive, in part, by eating beans off of their floor. The men in *Tortilla Flat* tell the youth they will immediately solicit milk from a friend who has a goat (177–78). The presence of the infant draws out the charity of the characters and showcases the novel's theme of surviving by dint of friendship and mutual support. However, the absence of the child's mother may be a commentary on the instability and brokenness of the families Steinbeck is portraying.

Some discussion of fetching a doctor ensues, the baby is placed to rest in an apple box (resting babies in boxes is a common occurrence among Steinbeck's indigent characters), then suddenly, "the baby stiffened and the struggle ended. The mouth dropped open, and the baby was dead" (183). Despite the communal approach to tending to the baby, this event highlights how existence for the paisanos and the nameless baby is extremely fragile. In a story that is intended to be mostly comedic, the death of the nameless baby is abrupt, troubling, and made more poignant when juxtaposed with the father's shattered aspiration to raise him to be a general. As the baby dies, so does that dream.

Despite the rapid response displayed once the paisanos encounter the dying child, they simply do not have the resources or medical knowledge to save the baby. Their good intentions fail. Although fetching a doctor is discussed, they do not take concrete steps to find a doctor who can save the baby, and similarly to *The Pearl*, it is possible no doctor would have willingly aided them at all. This infant's death calls attention to the desperate straits and anonymous suffering of the paisanos during the Great Depression. Not only can the paisanos not find steady work, health care, nutrition, or accommodations (the baby dies in an apple box), in Steinbeck's created world of *Tortilla Flat*, their future is uncertain and ill-omened.

On the other hand, the collaborative effort made to save the child could be interpreted as involving a message of hope; that those in the immediate vicinity of the baby, who simply by being adults are in a position to assist and protect children, lend a hand to someone else in their community demonstrates Steinbeck's use of the so-called phalanx theory. The phalanx theory is the concept (based on the word for a type of shield-like military formation) in which a mob or any gathering of similarly-situated characters come together and close ranks for a collective purpose wherein the group seeks to obtain greater strength than that strength possessed by the individuals comprising it (French 199). In this story, the phalanx would be the characters the father seeks help from; the fate of the young baby is left not only to his biological father, but also to those in the neighborhood. This urgent, communal, and unconventional portrayal of caregiving is a potent concept also in Steinbeck's *The Grapes of Wrath*, when not only do suffering children become "the children of all," but an after-effect of birthing—a mother's ability to nurse—becomes a resource that can help a dying community beyond just the nourishing of a single infant (264, 619).

Close reading of Steinbeck's nonfiction in the late 1930s leads one to wonder whether a medical profession could have satisfied the Nobel Prize winner. His concern for children's health care is present throughout the series of articles he wrote in the *San Francisco News* in October of 1936 (*Harvest Gypsies*). Hundreds of thousands of farm families from the middle western region of the country became homeless due to the drying out of their land in the Dust Bowl, and many journeyed to California during the Great Depression in search of work (Banach 47). In his news articles, Steinbeck describes one family living in a tent with flies buzzing around children and a baby. "Two weeks ago there was another child, a four year old boy. For a few weeks they had noticed that he was kind of lackadaisical, that his eyes had been feverish. They had given him the best place in the bed. . . . But one night he went into convulsions and died" (28). He writes in his sixth article, "there is no prenatal care. . . . [T]he presence of a doctor is a rare exception" (50). In *The Pearl*, "sickness is second only to hunger as the enemy of poor people" (34). Certainly, the health and well-being of the downtrodden was a significant concern for Steinbeck.

Steinbeck appears in this way to be an advocate for prenatal care and for access to health care in general. Although the rhetoric was not to arise in American political discourse for several decades after the publication of *The Pearl*, one wonders whether Coyotito or the baby in *Tortilla Flat* would have fared better and lived longer had prenatal care existed. The higher-order communities—the white communities—in both texts do nothing to aid the Latinx children. Only when the doctor in *The Pearl* hears Kino may become rich with a pearl does he involve himself in Coyotito's case—a clear indictment against capitalism. And the reader is left wondering whether his involvement did not put Coyotito at more risk, as Juana's sucking out the poison and Coyotito's apparent recovery afterwards make the doctor's contribution ambiguous at best and sinister at the worst. Thus a cloud hangs over Juana and Kino for the majority of the text in which they do not know whether Coyotito will recover. They defer to the doctor's schooling and professional experience because they have none of their own.

Discrimination appears throughout *The Pearl* and is accentuated when the doctor refers to Kino and his family as "little Indians" (11). That Juana even proposes bringing Coyotito to a doctor evokes befuddlement in her community: "a wonderful thing, a memorable thing, to want the doctor" (7). It is impossible to read *Tortilla Flat*, *The Grapes of Wrath*, or *The Pearl* and ignore how alleviating the suffering of children is the impetus for so many of the adult characters' actions. Juana's competence in caring for Coyotito is contrasted with the costly and suspicious attention later given by the doctor: "She gathered some brown seaweed and made a flat damp poultice of it . . . probably better than the doctor could have done" (15). The *Pearl* is explicit in illustrating the necessity of parents to act for the good of their young. However, any semblance of a phalanx evaporates when Kino and Juana take possession of the pearl.

The fates of the babies described in this study are aligned with the fates of their families. They are symbols of hope or the loss of hope. Additional review of Steinbeck's nonfiction may also prove enlightening in interpreting his literature. For example, in *The Log from the Sea of Cortez* he wrote that hope is "an evolved trait of the species that had protected him from extinction" (100). The crisis of infant mortality remains a reality today. Health care has become a commodity and is still a privilege the wealthy can access far faster and more fully than those living on the margins of society. Prices for medical care fluctuate depending on where you live, where you work, and who you are. Nearly a century after publication these poignant texts, and the families portrayed within them, can still teach readers about humanity with its many virtues, faults, and hopes.

Works Cited

Banach, Jennifer. "'Roar Like a Lion': The Historical and Cultural Contexts of the Works of John Steinbeck." *Critical Insights: John Steinbeck*. Edited by Don Noble, U of Alabama P, 2011, pp. 38–58.

DeMott, Robert. Introduction. *The Grapes of Wrath*. Penguin, 1992.

French, Warren G. "Steinbeck's 'Self-Characters' as 1930s Underdogs." *Critical Insights: John Steinbeck*. Edited by Don Noble, U of Alabama P, 2011, pp. 197–207.

Gannett, Lewis. Introduction. *The Portable Steinbeck*. Viking, 1966.

Steedman, Carolyn. *Dust: The Archive and Cultural History*. Rutgers U P, 2001.

Steinbeck, John. *The Log from the Sea of Cortez*. Penguin, 1951.

_____. *The Grapes of Wrath*. 1939. Penguin, 1992.

_____. *The Harvest Gypsies*. Heyday, 1988. Originally published in *The San Francisco News,* 5–12 Oct. 1936.

_____. *The Pearl*. 1947. Penguin, 1992.

_____. *The Red Pony*. 1937. Penguin, 1994.

_____. *To a God Unknown*. 1933. Penguin, 1995.

_____. *Tortilla Flat*. 1935. Penguin, 1995.

A Comparative Exploration of Devaluation of Women, Ownership, and Violence in John Steinbeck's *The Chrysanthemums* and *The Pearl*___

Elisabeth Bayley

What is the feminine equivalent of 'emasculating?' (Benson 276) In 1937, John Steinbeck published one of his most well-known short stories, "The Chrysanthemums." After struggling on and off with the writing of the tale, Steinbeck produced a succinctly structured and manicured account of a talented and knowledgeable woman living in a man's world. Although seldom compared with "The Chrysanthemums," Steinbeck's novella *The Pearl* first arrived in 1945 in serial form, and then was retitled in 1947 when it was released as it now appears. In *The Pearl,*[1] Steinbeck likewise has written a compact account of a woman's story when the power and access to her world is given to a man. This chapter will compare and contrast these two stories by looking at notions of value and ownership of the natural world, violence and disposability toward the female characters, and shaming of women in order to keep them silent.

Elisa's Struggle in "The Chrysanthemums"

"The Chrysanthemums" begins with the physical description of protagonist Elisa's surroundings, giving the feeling of entrapment and limited movement. She is in her fenced garden, on an isolated farm, in a valley heavy laden with fog that made the valley feel like a "closed pot" (9) and "closed off . . . from all the rest of the world" (9), with her husband, Henry, beyond the garden fence doing monetary business with other men. The story continues to tell of the description of Elisa's outward appearance that portrays a hard-working able gardener wearing appropriate gardening clothes and equipped with gardening tools. Her appearance serves to mirror her ability in the garden, while the physical circumstance of the fence and her husband engaging in monetary transactions beyond the fence mirror her limited mobility and access to the larger structure of the farm. Further, Elisa and Henry proceed to have a conversation that solidifies Elisa's limited access to the farm work and transactions of the farm as he recognizes her skill of having "planter's hands" (11). Elisa is a gifted horticulturalist but Henry does not give Elisa "permission" nor access to use this skill on the farm. The confinement of Elisa and her passion and skill for horticulture is the key focus as the story begins, considering it sets Elisa into a frustrated position of limitation and desire to use her horticultural skills on a larger scale.

Within this confined circumstance enters the infamous Tinker. The Tinker comes seeking money for fixing pots or sharpening scissors. He drives his dented, old wagon up the long driveway, with his mutt dog. However, Elisa does not need him to do any of that kind of work, because she is capable of mending her own pots and sharpening her own scissors. At first the Tinker is not able to get Elisa to do what he wants her to do, which is give him work, but then the Tinker soon changes his approach: he lies to Elisa with a feigned interest in her chrysanthemums, which is something that is incredibly important to her. We know it is a feigned interest because he lies to Elisa telling her about a woman up the road who wants, he claims, some chrysanthemums. He states:

> Look. I know a lady down the road a piece, has got the nicest garden you ever seen. Got nearly every kind of flower but no chrysantheums. Last time I was mending a copper-bottom washtub for her . . . she said to me, 'If you ever run acrost some nice chrysantheums I wish you'd try to get me a few seeds.' That's what she told me. (16)

In her excitement and with the possibility of her plants being transported outside the confines of the fenced garden, Elisa gives him a shoot in one of her pots. His willingness to pretend that her flowers are important and his ease in which he does it, shows that he has no interest whatsoever in her skills, nor in truly connecting with her as a person but only in getting what he values, her trust so that he can then get a paying job from her.

At this point we see the often-analyzed portion of the story. As Elisa describes how to care for the chrysanthemums, she begins to show passion because she actually really cares about her flowers and shows skill in horticulture. It is at this very moment of self-expression and expertise that "her hand went out toward his [the Tinker's] legs in the greasy black trousers. Her hesitant fingers almost touched the cloth. Then her hand dropped to the ground. She crouched low like a fawning dog" (18). As Elisa reaches toward the Tinker, the latter instantly withdraws, as he immediately switches his demeanor and returns right back to what he wants, money. He says, "It's nice, just like you say. Only when you don't have no dinner, it ain't" (18). His manipulative response in getting Elisa to do what he originally intended to get her to do, brings Elisa back to the reality that he is just there for his own gain. She realizes she was foolish to have expressed her care for the flowers and her skill with plants with this strange man. Elisa sees how the Tinker was quick to dismiss her reaching out for a moment of interconnection with him. After this rapid shift in his approach, "She stood up then, very straight, and her face was ashamed" (18).

As she feels ashamed for talking about her skills in gardening and further, her connection with the larger world, the reader is left to wonder, what is it about what she said that causes her shame? Or more acutely, considering what she said was not shameful, what is it about the Tinker's response that causes her shame? Why does she quickly find the Tinker a pot to mend, pay him, and watch him leave? According to Dr. Brené Brown, a shame researcher, "[S]hame is the fear of disconnection. We are psychologically, emotionally, cognitively, and spiritually hard-wired for connection, love, and belonging" (Brown 68). Therefore, we can understand shame as being afraid that one is fundamentally disconnected from others. It is in this instant that Elisa feels strongly a fear of disconnection. If the Tinker has the power to deem what is of value and Elisa is not recognized as something the Tinker values, then her natural fear of disconnect evokes shame, so much so that it leaves her "crouched like a fawning dog" (Steinbeck 18).

The notion of interconnection is something Steinbeck valued and explored in his work. In this earlier story of Steinbeck's, we can already see him writing about what happens to people when they devalue others and their skills, and shame them into a perceived notion of disconnection. According to Jackson J. Benson, in "The Chrysanthemums" Steinbeck "is not just telling us about the frustrations of a rancher's wife . . . he is also—and for him, more importantly—defining the nature of reality" (Benson 246). The reality of how interconnected the characters actually are, is Steinbeck's focus here.

Further, as William Souder notes, Steinbeck focuses on "the ecology of humans" or "social ecology," and his ecological philosophy is based on the phalanx theory. Souder notes that in this theory is the notion of the whole, in nature, is an entity unto its own self. Thus, when individuals decide to overemphasize notions of the particular, they are unable to recognize the concept of the whole, or the interconnection that is between all living things. When the Tinker over-emphasizes the particular, in this case the monetary gain, he then loses focus of the whole. Interconnection, in this story, is found in Elisa's ability to take part in horticulture. Through her gardening skill, she is able to recognize and establish an interconnection to the world around her. However, the Tinker is heavily focused on the particularity of money and getting what he wants. In this, he is unable to recognize the interconnection between Elisa, the flowers, and himself.

Elisa knows her own strength, but becomes ashamed of her expression of it because the Tinker does not value it. Before the Tinker leaves, she attempts to then enter into the fray as one who is able to compete in this disconnected world of competition and monetary individualism. She puts herself into the hypothetical ring by saying, "You might be surprised to have a rival some time. I can sharpen scissors, too. And I can beat the dents out of little pots. I could show you what a woman might do" (19). The Tinker does not note her skill or recognize what she is saying— that she actually did not even need for him to do the job. But he dismisses her by saying, "It would be a lonely life for a woman, ma'am, and a scarey [sic] life, too, with animals creeping under the wagon all night" (19). His quick dismissal of Elisa's skills and abilities is easy to do by playing into her fear. In other words, he plays on her emotions by telling her she would be scared versus listening to what she is saying. The irony does not strike him that it is people like him, people and men in particular, who manipulate, lie, use, and discard others, that she is actually in need to be afraid of.

Elisa proceeds to go into her house and bathe herself. How she bathes herself is described similarly to one who has been shamed and violated. She "scrubbed herself with a little block of pumice, legs and thighs, loins and chest and arms, until her skin was scratched and red. When she had dried herself, she stood in front of a mirror in her bedroom and looked at her body" (20). She seems to attempt to scrub off her shame, scratching her skin, to the point of turning it red. She examines her naked body in the mirror, as though she is looking for something. She puts on make-up, penciling in her eyebrows and rouging her lips. She goes out on the porch and "sat primly and stiffly down" (21). This echoes her earlier response of standing up very straight, ashamed. Then Steinbeck tells us, "She sat there, unmoving for a long time. Her eyes blinked rarely" (21) as if she is disassociating from all that has just happened. It is not until Henry sees her and notes for the rest of the story the continual shifting with which Elisa fluctuates between someone who is "strong" then all of a sudden "weak" again and then "strong" again, that we see how deeply Elisa has been affected by what just occurred with the Tinker.

The final action of the Tinker in the story is his disposing of the flowers on the side of the road. It is here that Elisa's last attempt to "be strong" falters. The Tinker is doing something to her, in this case, disposing of all that mattered to her, where her energy and expression and skill blossomed and was most cared for. To become the victim of another person's greed, violence, and de-valuing, may lead one to a disconnecting of the self from the world around them due to feelings of shame. In the end she "cries weakly—like an old woman" (23). Her expression of weakness and Steinbeck's symbolizing her as an old woman displays her as a person who is feeble and ineffectual. After all, what hope is there that things will ever be different for Elisa? If this is the way she will be treated, then of course she becomes like an old woman and weeps with the knowledge of how she will be possibly disposed of and treated throughout her life.

Elisa has no space to show her passion for her flowers, nor her skill in growing them, because she is perceived as disposable—just like her flowers. The value judgments of her and her flowers are placed on her from outside sources of power, mainly men, and create a devaluation of her and her skills. Thus, she is not able to take part in the socioeconomic world where value is essential. This lack of access creates a disconnection for Elisa to the world outside of her garden fence. It leaves Elisa isolated and frustrated as she is unable to use her talent nor her knowledge to contribute on a larger scale to the socioeconomic world around her.

Kino Possesses *The Pearl;* What Does Juana Possess?

In *The Pearl,* although a very different story from "The Chrysanthemums," Steinbeck revisits some of the same ideas of value, shame, manipulation, and interconnection. The beginning of the story shows the relationship between the main characters, Juana and her husband, Kino. Kino awakens every morning to find Juana already awake and alert, a trait that shows her readiness to take action for the family. Kino awakens to find, "Juana's eyes were open too. Kino could never remember seeing them closed when he awakened. Her dark eyes made little reflected stars. She was looking at him as she was always looking at him when he awakened" (233). The story continues to note Kino's contentment in his life. At this point, a scorpion bites their son Coyotito. In great haste, they make their way to the doctor who does not help poor Indians such as themselves. They then go desperately to the sea to hunt down a pearl in order to pay the doctor. What Kino ends up finding is what is described as "The pearl of the world" (252).[2] While the language suggests it is the finest pearl Kino could possibly envision, it also suggests the pearl represents the entire world. The concept of something in nature possessing the entirety of the world is intriguing, because it also suggests that the person who owns the pearl likewise has in their palm the entirety of the world. However, it is important to note that the idea of the pearl containing a whole is one placed upon the pearl by the characters in the story, and the value given it determines the relationship the characters have with the pearl going forward.

Another important point is how the pearl is claimed to have both "The essence of pearl mixed with the essence of men" and as a result of this mixture, "a curious dark residue precipitated" (253). It is thus through the interpretation of men, the mixture of the essence of men and the pearl, that darkness is precipitated. Maybe it is not so much the notion of the two essences of humans and nature that provokes darkness, but it is when humans, placing monetary value and ownership on nature, that darkness enters. Perhaps it is when humans ascribe their "essence" to the pearl that darkness is created and blinds them to a true interconnected relationship with others and the world around them. The result of this false understanding of value placed upon the pearl, focuses people on the fear of losing possession of it and as a result, a fear of other people stealing it. Rather than focusing on the joys of possession, the pearl becomes a focal point for loss and theft.

If the pearl contains the world, and if the pearl is owned by Kino, and Kino possesses the essence of men and the pearl, what does Juana, Kino's wife, possess in the pearl? It does not take long for Juana to see that the pearl is something that is harmful for their family: "Now the tension which had been growing in Jauna boiled up to the surface and her lips were thin. 'This thing is evil,' she cried harshly. 'This pearl is like a sin! It will destroy us,' and her voice rose shrilly. 'Throw it away, Kino. Let us break it between stones'" (264). However, Kino neither listens to her nor believes her warnings. Several times she begs Kino to destroy the pearl because it is evil and, in the end, it will destroy their family (277). His responses to her are often dismissive and commanding, "'I will fight this thing. I will win over it. We will have our chance.' His fist pounded the sleeping mat. 'No one shall take our good fortune from us,' he said. His eyes softened then and he raised a gentle hand to Juana's shoulder. 'Believe me,' he said. 'I am a man.' And his face grew crafty" (277).

Juana's response: "Kino . . . I am afraid. A man can be killed. Let us throw the pearl back into the sea." But Kino is dismissive of her, and makes his final judgment: "'Hush,' he said fiercely. 'I am a man. Hush' and she was silent, for his voice was command" (278).

Kino claims his gender as the authority that gives him the power to win in fights over the pearl, to maintain its ownership, and to decide what is to be done with it. Steinbeck notes that his face grew "crafty" (277). This shift in his character into becoming crafty and commanding over Juana is solely a response to his newfound economic power as owner of the pearl. He hushes Juana out of his position of power as a man and refuses to listen to the possibility that he, like any other human, is indeed mortal.

At one point, Juana sneaks out of the house and attempts to throw the pearl back into the sea. When Kino realizes what she is trying to do, he follows her down to the sea; he beats her by hitting her face and kicking her stomach and leaves her there in her suffering. After he beats her, he repeats the same refrain "I am a man" (209). He says this as though it means he not only has permission to hurt anyone who stands between him and his pearl, but also that he will not be beaten himself—not by the pearl, or by his wife, or by the pearl buyers in town, or by the townspeople.

After Juana is beaten, she reflects on Kino's words:

> "I am a man," and that meant certain things to Juana. It meant that he was half insane and half god. It meant that Kino would drive his strength against a mountain and plunge his strength against the sea. Juana, in her woman's soul, knew that the mountain would stand while the man broke himself; that the sea would surge while the man drowned in it. (280)

Kino is understood to be half man and half god and that this division of identity is one that made him insane. His insanity is bound in the thought that his own strength can take on a mountain or the surge of the sea. Similar to a god, he believes he possesses a strength that can withstand anything nature may throw at him. Once again, we can see what happens when man in his hubris places himself above nature. Kino refuses to see himself as a human with natural limitations alongside all other things upon the earth. In the end, nature necessarily crushes him, and he walks, side by side with

---

Juana as she holds their dead child, back to the sea to throw the pearl into it.

The ownership of the pearl creates a great amount of fear in Kino, and thus changes his relationships with his family and fellow townspeople. The relationship within the town is what Souder points out as an example of the phalanx: "Before Kino and Juana and the other fishers had come to Kino's brush house, the nerves of the town were pulsing and vibrating with the news—Kino had found the Pearl of the World." The town is like its own animal, with a nervous system and with its own emotions.

However, greed and fear between Kino and the people in the town run deep when he gains ownership of the pearl. Kino becomes even more violent and willing to hurt and even kill others in order to protect his pearl. The change in Kino's contentment from the beginning of the story to his constant fear once he has found the pearl is pointed out in the story, as the people around him note: "From now on they would watch Kino and Juana very closely to see whether riches turned their heads, as riches turn all people's heads" (260). Kino is afraid and experiences a major shift in his identity and actions. He feels as though "he had lost one world and had not gained another" and because of this, he "was afraid" (275). As Kino loses himself in his new identity as the owner of The Pearl of the World, he finds that he is turning into that which he is fearing: a violent murderer who stalks in the night. His sense of interconnection with his neighbors, the town, and his family are all shifting as his identity is shifting. He begins to fear everyone: "And Juana, sitting by the fire hole, watched him with questioning eyes, and when he had buried his pearl she asked, 'Who do you fear?' Kino searched for a true answer, and at last he said, 'Everyone.' And he could feel a shell of hardness drawing over him" (263).

Ruptured Interconnection: A Comparative Analysis

There are three main ideas of comparative analyses that we will be looking at in these stories. The first is the notion of interconnection and how, when monetary value is given to certain objects in these two stories, the result is a severed notion of interconnection and yielding an abusive or destructive relationship. The result in behavior by both the Tinker and Kino are similar in that they both sever connections with others to attain and retain what they desire. In the Tinker's case, he is willing to dispose of the chrysanthemums, which is a symbol of being willing to "dispose" of or not connect with Elisa as she reaches out to share her skills. In the much more dramatic and violent case of Kino, he is willing to beat his wife, and to commit murder in order to keep the pearl. It is not that we are comparing throwing a flower on the road to abuse and murder; it is the motivations for the actions of both men that we are examining. When monetary value is placed above people or relationships with people, violence and disposability occur.

In "The Chrysanthemums," the relationship the Tinker has to the natural world, or in this case the natural world as represented by Elisa, shifts when he realizes he can take possession of it. Kino's relationship with the people around him shifts when he finds the pearl. In both instances, acquisition of the sought-after parts of nature creates a different relationship to nature, and by extension, their notion of interconnection with others. As a result, what happens to these two men impacts the women (who are part of the socially constructed dependency on the men for their identities, value, and voice).

The choice of the disposability of both nature and oppressed people is a notion that ecofeminism explores. Greta Gaard, in her introduction to ecofeminism writes that, "[E]cofeminism's basic premise is that the ideology which authorizes oppressions such as those based on race, class, gender, sexuality, physical abilities, and species is the same ideology which sanctions the oppression of nature" (1). The "authorization" of both Elisa's and Juana's oppression takes place because the men in the story deem themselves the masters of both nature and other humans. Similar to the aspects of nature in the stories, the women are likewise oppressed. Through this oppression an "atomistic" sense exists; as Gaard continues to note, there is a self/other distinction that occurs in this thinking (2). It leaves those who operate this way to see themselves as fundamentally different than the world around them.

The second area of comparison we can inspect is how each of the women is treated as a result of this rupture in interconnection. Both the Tinker and Kino change their approaches to the world when they have a need to get something or have attained what it is they desire. They lie, become crafty, manipulate, dispose of flowers and people, and in the case of Kino, become fearful. This forces a rift in their interconnection, and the women in the stories are the victims of the men's foolish and manipulating behaviors. Both Elisa and Juana are silenced regarding their expression of care, for Juana it is for her family, and for Elisa it is for her flowers. They learn that they are dependent on the men in their lives. They are treated with oppression and dismissed as disposable. They are not valued as part of an interconnected whole but are considered as simply pieces that can be ignored or thrown away. Juana notes this dependency after Kino beat her, "Juana had need of a man; she could not live without a man" (280). Likewise, Elisa notes her dependency by asking Henry about the fights, stating she does not want to go, and letting him know that wine is enough for her, that it will be plenty, that she will not seek any more than what she is offered (23).

A third area of consideration analyzes the idea of shaming the female characters. This shaming happens when the female characters express themselves, and then the male characters either dismiss or dispose of the value in what the women are offering. This dismissal leads to shaming the characters and, as a result, a form of (emotional) violence occurs. Both women are dependent on the men, and both men easily manipulate their relationships with the world around them in order to get what they want. There is a space in these men's worlds where they both take advantage of the women's vulnerability (Elisa and Juana).

The Tinker shames Elisa after she tells him her thoughts and feelings. He deftly manipulates her into feeling close to him. After he gets what he wants from her, her passion, he quickly shifts the focus of their conversation back to his own desires so that he can get a job and take some money from her. He ignores that she is able to fix pots and sharpen knives and dismisses her skills in horticulture.

Similarly, Juana knows what is best for her family, to throw the pearl back into the water. Kino physically assaults her in order to take back what he perceives to be his possession—his owned good. He leaves her struggling on the sand, physically and verbally shamed. As noted earlier, the power to make the choice and own the pearl belongs to Kino for no other reason than his gender being a man. Her right to speak to the situation and make choices regarding the pearl is commandeered by Kino. He makes sure she knows why she cannot contribute anything new to the conversation about the pearl. He basically tells her to be quiet, and silences her voice. He shames her for being a woman and lets her know that it is because of her gender that she does not have the right or access to decision making or to action in their lives.

This oppression, disregard, shaming, and taking advantage of the women's vulnerability results in the final deaths of the stories. For Elisa, it is the disposal of her flowers. For Juana, it is the death of their child, Coyotito. Weeping, therefore, is an understandable reaction. Both women are captive in the men's world that devalues women's lives and gives primacy to items of monetary value that the men around them desire.

Through an analysis of these two stories by Steinbeck, we can focus on the notion of value placed on material items in the natural world. We can locate how the male characters are privileged to assign what is of value and what is not. This privilege leads to a disconnection between the men and the world around them. As a result, those women dependent on them (as a result of the social constructs of gendered norms) are victims to their lying, abusive, murderous, and greedy behaviors. The women are thus left to contend with the illusionary perceptions of the men who believe themselves to be independent, atomistic, and in the case of Kino, believing himself to be half god. The fissure of disconnection in an interrelated world leaves the women unheard and disposed of. Steinbeck exposes the interworking of interconnections and oppression in these stories and leaves us to delve further into recognizing our own interconnected realities.

Notes

1. Other areas of comparing and contrasting that Michael Meyer writes about with regard to *The Pearl*, are located on pages 44–45 in his article "Diamond in the Rough: Steinbeck's Multifaceted Pearl."

2. As Kyoko Ariki notes, it is important to understand that the ownership of the pearl in this story would allow Kino and his family socio-economic access, and that Kino, "sees in it the possibility of escaping poverty and persecution" (51). In other words, the ownership of the pearl should not be analyzed merely as changing Kino's behavior but as the possibility of access to more financially stable life.

Works Cited

Ariki, Kyoko. "From 'Flight' to *The Pearl*: A Thematic Study." *John Steinbeck's Global Dimensions*. Eds. Kyoko Ariki, Luchen Li and Scott Pugh. The Scarecrow P, 2008, pp. 49–56.

Benson, Jackson J. *The True Adventures of John Steinbeck, Writer: A Biography*. Penguin, 1990.

Brown Brené. *Daring Greatly: How the Courage to Be Vulnerable Transforms the Way We Live, Love, Parent, and Lead*. Avery, 2015.

Gaard, Greta Claire. *Ecofeminism: Women, Animals, Nature*. Temple U P, 1993.

Meyer, Michael. "Diamond in the Rough: Steinbeck's Multifaceted Pearl." *The Steinbeck Review*, vol. 2, no. 2, 1 Oct. 2005, pp. 42–56. *JSTOR*, www.jstor.org/stable/41581982.

Souder, William. "John Steinbeck and the Environment: Complete Video." *John Steinbeck and the Environment: Complete Video: The Bill Lane Center for the American West*, 18 May 2017, https://west.stanford. edu/research/works/john-steinbeck-and-environment-complete-video.

Steinbeck, John. "The Chrysanthemums." *The Long Valley*. Viking P, 1970, pp. 9–23.

_____. *The Pearl. John Steinbeck: Novels 1942–1952*. Edited by Robert DeMott. The Library of America, 2001, pp. 229–304.

Culture, Identity, and Otherness: An Analysis of Kino's Songs in John Steinbeck's *The Pearl* and Pilate's Melody in Toni Morrison's *Song of Solomon*

Tammie Jenkins

The use of musical scores in motion picture offerings as well as small screen renderings is commonplace. Audiences are drawn into the plot of these audiovisual narratives through the pairing of rhythmic accompaniment and the characters' dialogue or action. In films and on television shows, music is often used to set the tone, drive the plot, or stress the climax of a given story. Unlike cinematic offerings, literary works rarely include musical or lyrical substructures in the narratives of their characters or in the storylines of their texts. The use of music in literary works seems an implausible approach to storytelling. Yet, writers such as W. E. B. DuBois (*The Souls of Black Folk*), Langston Hughes ("Weary Blues"), and F. Scott Fitzgerald (*The Great Gatsby*) entrench musical rhythms in the narratives of their novels and poems. DuBois's, Hughes's, and Fitzgerald's use of musicality provide readers with information about their characters' experiences and social realities in nuanced ways (Lux 207). Similarly, writers like John Steinbeck and Toni Morrison have integrated music or song into their works as part of their characters' discourses (e.g., internal, external) or as an element accentuating their novels' action (Caswell 65). This essay conducts a close reading of *The Pearl* and *Song of Solomon* using narratology to compare and contrast how Steinbeck and Morrison use music in their texts to represent the culture, identity, and otherness of their characters.

Set in La Paz, Mexico, during the 1900s, *The Pearl*, was published in 1947. In this novella, Steinbeck retells the myth of El Mechudo, a Yaqui Indian, who discovers a valuable pearl that transforms him from good to evil. Morrison's *Song of Solomon*, published in 1977, features the myth of the Flying Africans as a foundation for its narrative. Both novels are situated at a time in history when Indigenous Mexican Indians and African Americans were endeavoring to maintain their ancestral bonds while creating a self-defined identity (Herndon 54; Khaleghi 21). These familial and communal narratives portray the lived experiences of Indigenous Mexican Indians and African Americans through the composite characters of Kino and Pilate, specifically through their song titles or melody's lyrics. From this perspective, Kino's songs and Pilate's melody become stories of survival in which "traditions . . . are embedded in [the] music" (Braley 69) and by proxy the folklores that Steinbeck and Morrison include in their works. This enables Steinbeck and Morrison to use song or melodies in their narratives as vehicles for passing down generational wisdom (Finnegan 197; Vansina 442) "derived from word of mouth" (Okpewho 3) transmissions.

Centering on the characters of Kino and Pilate, respectively, *The Pearl* and *Song of Solomon*'s composition give readers insight into their personal, spiritual, and social lives. Utilizing relevant excerpts from *The Pearl* and *Song of Solomon*, I analyze Steinbeck's and Morrison's language use, word choices, and their attached meaning in Kino's songs and Pilate's melody. Additionally, I use intertextuality theory to conceptually interpret and discuss how the texts blend their narratives with musicality in ways that connect the culture, identity, and otherness of these characters with their songs or melodies.

Reciting Stories as Generational Tunes

For centuries, humans have endeavored to maintain a connection to their ancestors by passing on their wisdom in the form of folktales (Levin 61; Matory 36; Sanasam and Chaningkhombee 61). The Indigenous Mexican Indians utilized shamans and Africans used griots as storytellers who integrated music into their oral narrations during rituals, rites of passages, and to transfer cultural artifacts to future generations (Hamlet 27; Murphy 143). The task of transmitting these narratives was placed upon gifted narrators with the ability to retell these older stories with modernized interpretations. In many ways, these revitalized verbal texts empowered their audiences while ensuring the survival of their narratives across time and space. *The Pearl* highlights Kino's songs as summaries of previous events that enable Steinbeck to rewrite the history of not only Kino's ancestors but also the Indigenous Mexican Indian folklore that served as his inspiration. Steinbeck uses the Indigenous Mexican Indian folktale *El Mechudo and the Pearl of the Sea of Cortez* (Adcock and Metcalf). This is an old fisherman tale in which the character of El Mechudo meaning "the hairy one" participates in a pearl diving contest every year in La Paz. The winner of the competition has their pearl presented as an offering to Our Lady of Guadalupe. El Mechudo is a young, Yaqui Indian who has won this event for several years. On the day of the event, El Mechudo arrives late and is disqualified from participation; angered, he dives into the sea in search of a pearl that will rival that of the winner. During his dive, El Mechudo locates a large oyster with a pearl to match. El Mechudo makes multiple attempts to extract the pearl before resurfacing for air. After he describes what he had seen to his fellow divers, El Mechudo is advised to return to the sea in pursuit of the pearl. As time passes, El Mechudo's fellow divers begin to worry, and one by one they dive into the water to search for him. The divers do not resurface, but El Mechudo emerges from the water with a pearl in one hand and the oyster's shell attached to his other hand. The divers who had entered the sea to rescue El Mechudo have perished at the hands of El Mechudo with the exception of one. According to the lone survivor, El Mechudo had been overcome by greed and in a fit of rage mercilessly murdered his fellow divers. Today, locals believe that the specter of El Mechudo still haunts the spot where the pearl was discovered and that his spirit attacks those who dare to enter that area (Adcock and Metcalf).

In *The Pearl,* Steinbeck universalizes the El Mechudo narrative by appealing to the reader's sensibilities through the internal songs of Kino. This is represented by Kino lying on his mat, with his eyes closed listening to the sounds of the waves against the beach. Steinbeck uses this verbal image to inform readers that "in Kino's head there was a song now, clear and soft, and if he had been able to speak of it, he would have called it Song of the family" (6). Through its unspoken verses, Kino's song connects him to the folklore of his ancestors and community regarding the importance of kinship bonds as well as finding contentment in the simplicities of life. The word "Song" has a capital "S," which emphasizes the importance of Kino's tune to the plot of the story (6). The word "Song" also becomes a descriptor signifying Kino's internalized conversations as his life changes over the course of the novel (6). By providing readers with his subjective interpretation of the myth about *El Mechudo and the Pearl of the Sea of Cortez*, Steinbeck established "a dialogic relationship between the past and present" (R. Mitchell 54) through the lived experiences of Kino (Copeland and Thompson 3; Kissel-Ito 340). In addition, Steinbeck reinvents the legend of *El Mechudo* to include themes (e.g., family, evil, danger, the pearl) as represented by the songs that Kino alone hears. These motifs are presented in Steinbeck's description of the events serving as a prelude to Kino's protagonist journey (Abed 55; Pocock 172).

At the beginning of *The Pearl*, Kino is led by an internal song he calls "The Song of the Family," a tune that haunts him with its sound (8). This harmony is transformed when Kino spots a scorpion near his young son. Steinbeck explains that "in [Kino's] mind a new song had come, the Song of Evil, the music of the enemy, of any foe of the family, a savage, secret, dangerous melody, and underneath, the Song of the Family cried plaintively" (8). To show the emotions Kino experiences at that moment, Steinbeck uses "enemy" and "foe" not as synonyms, but as a menacing disruption of Kino's frailty, innocence, and inner peace (8). The words "savage" and "dangerous" portray the violent nature of the scorpion and the harmful effects of its sting (8). Steinbeck employs Kino's songs to show readers the internal monologues that Kino experiences throughout the text. Although Kino manages to kill the scorpion, the serenity that Kino had known was changed by the scorpion's act of violence against his son.

Unlike Steinbeck, Morrison employed a story from the African American folkloric tradition about the Flying Africans (Sanasam and

Chaningkhombee 63). This myth is based on an Igbo slave revolt near St. Simon's Island (also known as Igbo Landing), circa 1803. According to witnesses, a group of enslaved Africans overpowered their captors before jumping to their deaths in Dunbar Creek. Their deaths became synonymous with flight as African Americans began including narratives of freedom, independence, and empowerment in their retellings. Studying the ways that history is constructed in memorized oral narratives, Chiji Akoma ascertained that storytellers are responsible for transmitting verifiable truths to audiences. Akoma suggests that memories are "willed creations" (6) that enable a story to be retold from multiple points of view simultaneously. A mass suicide, the Igbo Landing narrative lends credence to the story of the flying Africans that seamlessly connects African Americans to their African roots. Morrison introduces the myth of the Flying Africans in *Song of Solomon* at the site of Mr. Robert Smith's attempted flight. In his announcement, Mr. Smith writes, "I will take off from Mercy and fly away on my own wings" (3) which is the first allusion to the flying African myth in the novel. It is here that Pilate stands before stepping forward singing with her eyes on Mr. Smith. Pilate rhythmically laments:

O Sugarman done fly away
Sugarman done gone
Sugarman cut across the sky
Sugarman gone home. (Morrison 5–6)

During her serenade, Pilate intermittently exchanges singing for humming as she prepares for Mr. Smith to "fly away" home (Morrison 6). Mr. Smith's suicide is where readers are introduced to Pilate Dead, as the "singing woman" (Morrison 5) standing in the crowd. Pilate sings what listeners perceive as a requiem for Mr. Smith; however, her melody carries more meaning than Pilate is privy. Pilate Dead is a secondary, but a strong female character in *Song of Solomon* who plays a pivotal role in guiding the action of the novel. Pilate becomes her family's matriarch and storyteller who has been singing the history of their ancestor all her life. Morrison uses this legend to create the Dead family history, which is retold by Pilate, who sings the life and death of her grandfather, Solomon. Later renditions of Pilate's melody transposes her ancestor Solomon with that of "Sugarman" and inadvertently Mr. Smith (Morrison 5). The folklore of the flying Africans is interwoven with the melody Pilate sings throughout the novel. Even though the readers never hear Kino's songs, his titles like Pilate's lyrics contain repetitious rhythmic patterns in which Steinbeck and Morrison use folklore to recreate an "amalgamated past" (Braley 67) in their novels.

Thinking Musicality . . . Speaking Lyrically

The history of folklore dates back to the dawn of humankind with oral narratives making the rounds before being committed to paper years later. Each society has stories that describe the origins of their civilizations while outlining the contributions of specific ancestors to their community's development. However, when mentioned in casual conversation, the term folklore elicits connotations involving an expert storyteller reciting fictionalized truths to a captive audience. Historically, elders or communal storytellers transmitted knowledge to their listeners via ballads, chants, songs, or verbalized speeches (Grayson 7). Coined in 1846, by William Thoms, the word "folklore" was used to capture the realistic truthfulness ingrained in oral stories handed down from one generation to the next. Over time, the folkloric tradition evolved into a literary genre in which verbally transferred narratives or songs were recorded in printed form. Exploring how knowledge is transmitted through storytelling, Mahboobeh Khaleghi found that such texts relied on the narrator's memory to situate past events in the present (15). Khaleghi concluded that this wisdom transcends time and space as succeeding generations interpret the narrative and recreate its meaning (15). These verbally conveyed folk products enable storytellers to share wisdom, rituals, and history with their listeners.

Stories such as those featured in *The Pearl* and *Song of Solomon* are part of a tradition in which didactic narratives are repeated with either embellished or deleted parts taken from the original text for a particular audience. *The Pearl* reinvents El Mechudo as the protagonist Kino, a free pearl diver of Yaqui Indian descent. Similar

---

to his distant ancestor, Kino finds an enormous pearl that changes his life. Although greed and rage invade El Mechudo's actions, Kino is driven by his desire to provide for his family. The folklore Steinbeck uses becomes a cautionary tale shrouded in the songs Kino hears, whereas *Song of Solomon* uses Pilate's melody to retell the story of the flying Africans through the actions of two characters, Solomon and Mr. Smith. Pilate verbalizes Solomon's voyage home in a haunting rendition as she recites a story of loss and rebirth in which the protagonist, Solomon, escapes his circumstances (i.e., slavery), but at great personal cost (i.e., abandoning his family). The folklore of the flying Africans was visited with Mr. Smith's attempt at flight. As a spectator, Pilate steps forward to share her melody with Mr. Smith who leaps to his death wearing blue silk wings. Like the Igbo slaves, Mr. Smith committed suicide by jumping to his death and spiritually flying away home.

The Pearl and *Song of Solomon* integrate folklore with song titles or melodies to create locations where the heard and written word coexist. Steinbeck uses music by giving Kino's non-lyrical tunes and the reader descriptions of events that contribute to the affixed adjectives such as family, enemy, danger, and family. The reader receives enough information to decipher the meaning buried in Kino's invisible tunes. While Morrison uses Pilate's melody to reimagine the Igbo slave revolt and mass suicide by connecting the stories of the Africans Who Could Fly with African American expressive culture (Hamlet 27; Levin 61). Likewise, Morrison uses Pilate's melody about Sugarman to establish a relationship between the Dead family and their long-forgotten ancestor. Referred to as Shalimar, Solomon was a descendant of the flying Africans who escaped slavery by flying back to Africa and leaving his progeny behind. Kino's and Pilate's soundtracks reflect the rural nature of their narratives and traditions that Steinbeck and Morrison mix with folklore to embody the ethno-history of their ancestors and their lives as descendants (Herndon 55; Sanasam and Chaningkhombee 61; Yasek 1064). By capturing the multiplicitous nature of the folklores they heard, Steinbeck and Morrison musically encode their alternative meanings into their novels (Abed 58; Pulitano 3).

Steinbeck uses song titles such as Song of the Family and Song of the Enemy to develop contrasts between the original narrative and his more inclusive retellings.

Music/song in *The Pearl* and *Song of Solomon* are folkloric tales that enable Kino and Pilate to "bear witness to the past" (Kukreja 28) while remaining grounded in the present. Kino and Pilate have been listening to or singing the stories of their ancestors all their lives. Steinbeck's worldview, like Morrison's, is natural with each enabling their characters to express their emotions through music. The songs Kino hears are unscripted stories of his ancestors as they endeavor to conform to the expectations of the larger society while maintaining their indigenous traditions. The inclusion of song/melodies in *The Pearl* and *Song of Solomon* offers readers an oral history of these characters complex intergenerational narratives that reflect the verbal nature of their family and communal traditions.

Everyone, Just Us, Only Me

The reliance on folklore has been an instrumental part of passing on narratives of a given community or family history. Steinbeck's and Morrison's decision to include such texts in their novels enable these stories to not only survive, but to offer insight into the culture, identity, and otherness represented by their characters. The songs or melodies that Kino and Pilate keep close to their hearts enable them to establish "hybrid" (Gilroy 162) retellings in which a shared history connects them to their ancestors and community (Greenwood 194). Steinbeck and Morrison use Kino's and Pilate's tunes to "defamiliarize" (O'Sullivan 34) the original folklores that contributed to the plot of their novels. In their respective text, Kino's and Pilate's tunes are presented as their "response to changes in [their] lives experiences" (Banks-Wallace 413) that Steinbeck and Morrison embellish to offer readers insight into Kino's and Pilate's culture, identity, and otherness.

Drawing on the Indigenous Mexican Indian and African American folklore in their printed works, Steinbeck and Morrison present readers with an ethnohistoric understanding of how kinship bonds and intergenerational knowledge are implanted in their characters' narratives, lived experiences, and social realities (Fletcher 172; Lux 207). Through Kino's internal songs, the reader learns that he is a spiritual man, but not necessarily a religious one. Kino is an honorable hard-working man who remembers the ways of his ancestors; however, Kino transforms into a man of violence when threats against his way of life arise. Steinbeck demonstrates Kino's culture, identity, and otherness by explaining the precipitating events that lead to the tune Kino hears. At the beginning of *The Pearl*, Kino lives a life of tranquility with his family, which is reflected in the Song of the Family. But when Kino's canoe is vandalized and his home destroyed by fire, Kino's song changes to a horrified rhythm. Steinbeck writes:

> In Kino's ears the Song of the Family was as fierce as a cry. He was immune and terrible, and his song became a battle cry. They trudge past the burned square where their house had been without even looking at it. They cleared the brush that edged the beach and picked their way down toward the water. And they did not look toward Kino's broken canoe. (94)

Kino's tune changes and its rhythm fluctuates in his mind as depicted by the phrase "fierce as a cry" (94). Hence, demonstrating Kino's dual role as protector and ancestral storyteller. Steinbeck has woven these intergenerational narratives into the unpenned lyrics of Kino's "battle cry" (94). The Song of the Family expressed Kino's innocence that has forcibly turned toward violence as "his song [becomes] a battle cry" (94). Kino's song changes as he gives into his instinctual behavior that are foretold by the song tiles that appear in the preceding narrative (Wagner-Martin xv). The changing harmony symbolizes Kino's disconnect from his ancestral history, which is visualized by his "broken canoe," (94) a family heirloom inherited from his grandfather. Kino's otherness is highlighted by his "immune" and "terrible" expression once he sees the devastation to his property that he ignores by not acknowledging his former possessions (e.g., hut; canoe) (94). The pearl that Kino found reflects his ancestral yearnings and his desire to return to his previous way of life as depicted in the Song of the Family. Steinbeck emphasizes this when

Kino throws the pearl back into the sea. This act signifies Kino's recommitment to his ancestral beliefs and practices. Once the pearl reenters the sea, Kino mentally "rewrites" (Vega-Gonzalez 7) these older songs in his present-day entrenched with the new wisdom he obtained during his protagonist journey (Hogue 122). While Kino's physical possession of the pearl stresses his lost connection to his culture and identity, his willingness to return the pearl to the sea reveals his otherness. This is represented in Steinbeck's portrayal of Kino's community as corrupted by greed against Kino's redemption story.

The same holds true for Pilate who, in spite of her self-imposed ostracism, maintains a link to her ancestral past and family history through the singing of Solomon's song. An omnipresent character, Pilate serves as a moral compass that drives the plot of the novel. Morrison demonstrates Pilate's culture, identity, and otherness as resiliency and the ability to survive, which Pilate's "act of singing reinforces" (Kirkham 5). Morrison writes, "The singing woman wore a knitted navy cap pulled far down over her forehead. She had wrapped herself up in an old quilt instead of a winter coat. Her head cocked to one side, her eyes fixed on Mr. Robert Smith, she sang in a powerful contralto" (5–6).

The "knitted navy cap," "old quilt," and her "powerful contralto" (Morrison 5–6) symbolizes Pilate's relationship to her community, isolation from her family, and her role as storyteller. Pilate's decision to wear a "knitted navy cap" and "old quilt" (Morrison 5) to keep warm exhibits her connection to her African roots and disconnect from other characters. Meanwhile, Pilate's "powerful contralto" (Morrison 6) singing register indicates her desire to not only be heard but also indicates her social status in her community and the larger society. Pilates singing sessions provide guidance to other characters in the novel such as Reba and Hagar. The lyrics Pilate shares with her daughter and granddaughter respectively have multiple layers of meaning expressed in the three-part harmony shared between them. Their harmony is presented to the readers as the ladies sing in their kitchen with the window open. One night,

"They were singing some melody that Pilate was leading. A phrase that the other two were taking up and building on. Her powerful contralto, Reba's piercing soprano in counterpoint, and the soft voice of the girl, Hagar, who must be about ten or eleven now" (Morrison 29).

By sharing her melody's lyrics Pilate "preserves a link" (Xiaoming 29) to her African tradition of storytelling by bridging her ancestry with her present-day realities through singing. The voices of Pilate, Reba and Hagar conduct a call and response in which Pilate is "leading" (Morrison 29) Reba and Hagar who are adding their interpretation to the melody. Morrison contrasts Pilate's vocal range against Reba's "piercing soprano" and Hagar's "soft voice" (Morrison 29) to show the "invisibility of that past" (LaCroix 29) and to signify the intergenerational separation of African Americans from their African roots (Rosenberg 197). Of the three Pilate has the strongest connection to her ancestral and family history, which Morrison reflects in the varying vocal ranges of Reba and Hagar. Initially, Pilate was presented as an unnamed character described as "the singing woman" (Morrison 5), but Morrison uses Pilate's melody to reclaim the myth of the flying Africans as part of her culture, identity, and otherness. Yet, through her singing we learn that like Kino, Pilate upholds her family and communal traditions.

Both Kino and Pilate are presented by Steinbeck and Morrison as communal people who share their lived experiences in their tunes. The folkloric tradition, specifically the tales of El Mechudo and the Flying Africans, provided both Steinbeck and Morrison with fertile literary soil on which to plant their narratives. Drawing on their memorized recollections, Steinbeck and Morrison retell these old narratives (i.e., El Mechudo, Flying Africans) with a twentieth-century twist. Through non-chronological storytelling and thematic narrations, Steinbeck and Morrison use music/song to transmit knowledge from one generation to the next. Relying on "historical distance," (Wood 86) Steinbeck and Morrison adapt the original folkloric tales in their novels. By using Kino's songs and Pilate's melody, Steinbeck and Morrison interrogate these older narratives as emergent discourses situated in the present while expanding the meaning to include other aspects of human existence.

Nostalgic Tempos, Past and Present

Music undeniably plays an instrumental role in shaping the lives of listeners. The rhythmic and lyrical transmission of emotions, ideas, and life lessons has been some of the many key components embedded in musical compositions (Kukreja 26). From the big screen to the printed page individuals have become adept at pairing harmonic tunes with textually verbalized situations. In *The Pearl* and *Song of Solomon*, Kino and Pilate take journeys to "reclaim ownership of [their] tradition[s]" (Braley 76) and ancestral stories (Hogue 126). *The Pearl* and *Song of Solomon* present narratives of culture, identity, and otherness as spaces of responsibility (Hooks 93; McMillan) in which Kino and Pilate "return to the past in order to move forward" (A. Mitchell 51). This essay conducted a close reading of *The Pearl* and *Song of Solomon* using narratology to compare and contrast how Steinbeck and Morrison use music in their novels to depict Kino's and Pilate's culture, identity, and otherness. Steinbeck uses Kino to retell the legend of the El Mechudo while Morrison employs Pilate's singing to reimagine the myth of the flying Africans.

Steinbeck and Morrison employ situated knowledge to establish a sense of belonging in which Kino's songs and Pilate's melody reconnect each with their ancestral past and family history (Jones 39). These authors juxtaposition of their characters with the folklore they represent as composite characters (i.e., Kino/El Mechudo; Pilate's song about Sugarman/Solomon) who use music/song to bring their ancestral past into their present (Fletcher 168; Lewis 91).

Works Cited

Abed, Sally. "From Feet to Wings: The Importance of Being Bare-footed in Toni Morrison's *Song of Solomon*." *UFLR,* vol. 24, 2014, pp. 55–72, Utah Foreign Language Review. www.epubs.utah.edu/index.php/uflr/article/view/1179.

Adcock, Richard, and Fred Metcalf. "The Legend of Mechudo." *Tales of Baja California*. U of California, Riverside. 2010. math.ucr.edu/ftm/bajaPages/Tales/Mechudo.html.

Akoma, Chiji. "The 'Trick' of Narrative History, Memory, and Performance in Toni Morrison's *Paradise*." *Oral Tradition*, vol. 15, no. 1, 2000, pp. 3–25. Penn. St. Univ. http://citeseerx.ist.psu.edu/viewdoc/download?doi=10.1.1.486.8403&rep=rep1&type=pdf.

Banks-Wallace, JoAnne. "Talk that Talk: Storytelling and Analysis Rooted in African Oral Tradition." *Qualitative Health Research*, vol. 12, no. 3, 2002, pp. 410–426. SAGE. journals.sagepub.com/doi/10.1177/104973202129119892.

Braley, Caleb R. "Red Blues: The Musical Confluence of African and Native American Identities in Toni Morrison's *Song of Solomon*." *UFLR*, 2011, pp. 67–82. Utah Foreign Language Review. epubs.utah.edu/index.php/uflr/issue/view/51.

Caswell, Roger. "A Musical Journey Through John Steinbeck's *The Pearl*: Emotion, Engagement, and Comprehension." *Journal of Adolescent and Adult Literacy*, vol. 49, no. 1, 2005, pp. 62–67. *JSTOR*, www.jstor.org/stable/40009270.

Copeland, Huey, and Krista Thompson. "Perpetual Returns: New World Slavery and the Matter of the Visual." *Representations*, vol. 113, no. 1, 2011, pp. 1–15. *JSTOR*, www.jstor.org/stable/10.1525/rep.2011.113.1.1.

Finnegan, Ruth. *Oral Literature in Africa*. Oxford U P, 1970.

Fletcher, Judith. "Signifying Circe in Toni Morrison's Song of Solomon." *Classical World*, vol. 99, no. 4, 2006, pp. 405–418. *JSTOR*, www.jstor.org/stable/4353064.

Gilroy, Paul. *The Black Atlantic: Modernity and Double Consciousness*. Harvard U P, 1993.

Grayson, Sandra M. *Symbolizing the Past: Reading* Sankofa, Daughters of the Dust, & Eve's Bayou *as Histories*. Lanham, U P of America, 2000.

Greenwood, Ashley. "Floating Roots: Diaspora and Palimpsest Identity in Danticat's *Breath, Eyes, Memory*." *Watermark*, no. 7, 2013, pp. 191–203.

Hamlet, Janice D. "Word! The African American Oral Tradition and its Rhetorical Impact on American Popular Culture." *Black History Bulletin*, vol. 74, no. 1, 2011, pp. 27–29. *JSTOR*, www.jstor.org/stable/24759732.

Herndon, Gerise. "Returns to Native Lands, Reclaiming the Other's Language: Kincaid and Danticat." *Journal of International Women's Studies*, vol. 3, no. 1, 2001, pp. 54–62. Cengage Learning. Questia. www.questia.com/library/journal/1G1-90442443/returns-to-native-lands-reclaiming-the-other-s-language.

Hogue, Bev. "Naming the Bones: Bodies of Knowledge in Contemporary Fiction." *Modern Fiction Studies*, vol. 52, no. 1, 2006, pp. 121–42. *JSTOR*, www.jstor.org/stable/26286925.

Hooks, Bell. *Yearning: Race, Gender, and Cultural Politic*s. South End P, 1999.

Jones, Carolyn M. "Southern Landscape as Psychic Landscape in Toni Morrison's Fiction." *Studies in the Literary Imagination*, vol. 31, no. 2, 1998, pp. 37–48. *EBSCOhost*. search.ebscohost.com/login.aspx?direct=true&site=eds-live&db=asn&AN=1664299.

Khaleghi, Mahboobeh. "From Ignorance to Knowledge: A Study of Toni Morrison's *Song of Solomon.*" *International Journal of Multicultural Literature*, vol. 2, no. 1, 2012, pp. 15–22. EBSCO. 140.234.252.185/c/literary-criticism/83413037/from-ignorance-knowledge-study-toni-morrisons-song-solomon.

Kirkham, Freda. "Women and Voices in *Song of Solomon.*" *Discoveries*, pp. 1–6. STUDYLIB. studylib.net/doc/8798548/women-and-voice-in-song-of-solomon.

Kukreja, Pooja. "Broadening Horizons: Toni Morrison's *Song of Solomon.*" *New Man International Journal of Multidisciplinary Studies*, vol. 2, no. 7, 2015, pp. 26–29, Newman Publications. www.newmanpublication.com/br/4%20New%20Man%20Publication-%20NMIJMS%20%20July%202015_www.newmanpublication.pdf.

LaCroix, David. "To Touch Solid Evidence: The Implicitly of Past and Present in Octavia Butler's *Kindred.*" *The Journal of the Midwest Modern Language Association*, vol. 40, no. 1, 2007, pp. 109–19. *JSTOR*, www.jstor.org/stable/20464214.

Lewis, Vashti Crutcher. "African Tradition in Toni Morrison's *Sula.*" *Phylon*, vol. 48, no. 1, 1987, pp. 91–97. *JSTOR*, www.jstor.org/stable/275004.

Lux, William R. "Black Power in the Caribbean." *Journal of Black Studies*, vol. 3, no. 2, 1972, pp. 207–25. *JSTOR*, www.jstor.org/stable/2783844.

Matory, J. Lorand. "Surpassing Survival: On the Urbanity of Traditional Religion in the Afro-Atlantic World." *The Black Scholar*, vol. 30, no. ¾, pp. 36–43. *JSTOR*, www.jstor.org/stable/41068897.

McMillan, Timothy. "Black Magic: Witchcraft, Race, and Resistance in Colonial England." *Journal of Black Studies*, vol. 25, no. 1, 1994, pp. 99–117. *JSTOR*, www.jstor.org/stable/2784416.

Mitchell, Angelyn. "Not Enough of the Past: Feminist Revisions of Slavery in Octavia Butler's *Kindred*." *MELUS*, vol. 26, no. 3, 2001, pp. 51–75. *JSTOR*, www.jstor.org/stable/3185557.

Mitchell, Roland W. "Cultural Aesthetics and Teacher Improvisation: An Epistemology of Providing Culturally Responsive Service by African American Professors." *Urban Education*, vol. 45, no. 5, 2010, pp. 604–29. SAGE. journals.sagepub.com/doi/10.1177/0042085909347839.

Morrison, Toni. *Song of Solomon*. 1977. Vintage, 2004.

Okpewho, Isidore. *African Oral Literature: Backgrounds, Characters, and Continuity*. Indiana U P, 1992.

O'Sullivan, James. "African Myth alongside Western Convention in Toni Morrison's *Song of Solomon*." *Durham English Review: An Undergraduate Journal*, vol. 1, no. 1, 2011, 34–47. Durham U. community.dur.ac.uk/durham.englishreview/index.php?option=com_content&view=article&id=9&Itemid=116.

Pocock, Judith. "Through a Glass Darkly: Topology in Toni Morrison's *Song of Solomon*." *Canadian Review of American Studies*, vol. 35, no. 3, 2005, pp. 281–98. *Project MUSE*, doi:10.1353/crv.2006.0018.

Pulitano, Elvira. "Landscape, Memory, and Survival in the Fiction of Edwidge Danticat." *Anthurium: A Caribbean Studies Journal*, vol. 6, no. 2, 2008, pp. 1–20. U of Miami. https://anthurium.miami.edu/articles/abstract/10.33596/anth.123/.

Rosenberg, Ruth. "And the Children May Know Their Names: Toni Morrison's *Song of Solomon*." *Literary Onomastics Studies*, vol. 8, no. 20, 1981, pp. 195–219. LOS. digitalcommons.brockport.edu/los/vol8/iss1/20.

Sanasam, Reena, and Soyam Chaningkhombee. "African Culture, Folklore, and Myth in Toni Morrison's *Song of Solomon*: Discovering Self-Identity." *The Echo*, vol. 2, no. 1, 2013, pp. 61–64. www.academia.edu/4140161/African_Culture_Folklore_and_Myth_in_Toni_Morrison_s_Song_of_Solomon_Discovering_Self_Identity.

Vansina, J. "Once Upon a Time Oral Tradition as History in Africa." *Daedulus*, vol. 100, no. 2, 1991, pp. 442–68. *JSTOR*, www.jstor.org/stable/20024011.

Vega-Gonzalez, Susana. "Memory and the Quest for Family History in *One Hundred Years of Solitude* and *Song of Solomon*." *Comparative Literature and Culture*, vol. 3, no. 1, 2001, pp. 1–9. *CLC*. doi.org/10.7771/1481-4374.1102.

Wagner-Martin, Linda. "Introduction," *The Pearl*. 1947. Viking, 1994, pp. vii–xxvii.

Wood, Sara. "Exorcising the Past: The Slave Narrative as Historical Fantasy." *Feminist Review*, no. 85, 2007, pp. 83–93. SAGE. journals.sagepub.com/doi/abs/10.1057/palgrave.fr.9400320.

Xiao-ming, Zhao. "Whitening, Revenge, and Root-Seeking Road for African Americans in *Song of Solomon*." *US-China Foreign Language*, no. 9, 2012, pp. 589–94.

Yasek, Lisa. "A Grim Fantasy: Remaking American History in Octavia Butler's *Kindred*." *Signs*, vol. 28, no. 4, 2003, pp. 1053–66.

RESOURCES

Chronology of John Steinbeck's Life _____

1902	John Ernst Steinbeck is born on February 27, 1902 to John Ernst II (who was owner of a feed and grain store, and a member of the Masons) and Olive Hamilton Steinbeck (who was a teacher and a member of the Order of the Eastern Star) in Salinas, California. He is their only son and the third of their four children.
1906	He is given his first pony, which he names Jill. This pony serves as an inspiration for his later series of stories, *The Red Pony* (1937).
1915-19	Attends Salinas High School until he graduates and goes to college. At the age of 16, Steinbeck decides to become a writer and begins composing poems and stories in his bedroom.
1919-25	Registers for classes at Stanford University, but after six years of sporadic attendance, he leaves the university without earning a degree. During his breaks, he takes jobs as: sales clerk, farm laborer, ranch hand, bench chemist, factory worker, and construction worker.
1926-28	Moves to Lake Tahoe, California, where he takes a position as a caretaker for a summer home.
1929	Writes and publishes his first novel, *Cup of Gold*, published by McBride.
1930	On January 14, 1930, Steinbeck marries Carol Henning. Later in the year, he becomes fast and long-time friends with Edward F. Ricketts.
1932	Writes *The Pastures of Heaven*, which is published by Brewer, Warren, and Putnam.

1933	Writes *To A God Unknown*, which is published by Ballou.
1934	Begins his interest in labor unions and economic disparities. He participates in interviewing labor union leaders and starts gathering information for future writings.
1935	Writes *Tortilla Flat*, his first popular novel, which is published by Covici-Friede. During this time, Steinbeck begins his long-time personal and professional relationship with his editor, Pascal Covici.
1936	Writes *In Dubious Battle*, which allows him to take his research into labor unions and uses it to tell the story of striking workers. This book is published by Covici-Friede.
1937	Writes play-novelette, *Of Mice and Men*, which is published by Covici-Friede. After its publication, he travels to Europe and Russia. Later in the year, he writes *The Red Pony* (a trilogy of related short stories). In November, *Of Mice and Men* has its Broadway debut and runs for 207 performances.
1938	Writes *Their Blood Is Strong*, a nonfiction account of the labor problem in California. This book is published by the Simon J. Lubin Society.
1938	In May, *Of Mice and Men* wins the New York Drama Critics Circle Award. In September, he writes a collection of short stories, *The Long Valley*, which includes his trilogy (*The Red Pony*). This collection is published by Covici, after he starts his own publishing firm as a solo venture.

1939	Steinbeck writes his most critically successful novel, *The Grapes of Wrath*, published by Viking. The novel garners both critical acclaim (by readers and reviewers) and denunciation (by politicians and farm owners) for its critical portrayal of the working conditions of migrant farm laborers in Oklahoma and California. Some readers accuse Steinbeck of preaching a socialist agenda and using boorish, unrefined language.
1939	In December, the film adaptation for *Of Mice and Men* is released.
1940	Shortly after the film release for *Of Mice and Men*, the film adaptation of *The Grapes of Wrath* is released.
1940	In spring, Steinbeck receives the National Book Award and the Pulitzer Prize for *The Grapes of Wrath*. After winning these two awards, Steinbeck writes and directs a documentary film about the economic and social conditions of laborers living in rural Mexico (*The Forgotten Village*). This proves influential on his writing of *The Pearl*.
1941	In the spring, he and Carol, his wife of nearly 11 years, separate. He moves to New York City where he becomes romantically involved with singer Gwyndolyn Conger. Later in the year he publishes *Sea of Cortez*, with Edward Ricketts (Viking).
1942	Carol successfully sues Steinbeck for divorce. In March, his novel *The Moon Is Down* is published by Viking. One month later, the novel is adapted for the stage and has its New York opening. While it does not specify Norway, the play receives the Norwegian King Haakon VII Freedom Cross for its realistic depiction of a small nation at war with two larger, invading nations.

1942	The film adaptation of *Tortilla Flat* is released. Soon after, *Bombs Away* is published by Viking.
1943	The film adaptation of *The Moon Is Down* is released. In March, Steinbeck marries Gwyn Conger in New Orleans. Mid-year, Steinbeck travels to both Europe and North Africa as a war correspondent for the *New York Herald Tribune*.
1944	On August 2, his first son, Thom, is born.
1945	On January 2, his novel, *Cannery Row*, is published by Viking.
1946	On June 12, his second son, John IV, is born.
1947	In February, his novel, *The Wayward Bus*, is published by Viking. During August–September, Steinbeck and photographer friend, Robert Capa, tour Russia and cover news events for the *New York Herald Tribune*. In November, Steinbeck's novella, *The Pearl,* is published by Viking.
1948	*A Russian Journal*, Steinbeck's account of his 1947 tour of Russia, is published by Viking. In May, his long-time friend, Ed Ricketts, is killed in a car accident. In August, he is divorced by Gwyn. Later this year, Steinbeck is selected for the American Academy of Arts and Letters.
1950	Writes his novella, *Burning Bright*. In October, the play adaptation of *Burning Bright* has its New York City opening. On December 28, Steinbeck marries Elaine Anderson Scott, his third wife.

1951	*The Log from the Sea of Cortez*, the narrative part of the *Sea of Cortez* (1941) is published by Viking. This book includes an homage to his friend, "About Ed Ricketts."
1952	In March, the film, *Viva Zapata!* is released. Steinbeck wrote the screenplay about the Mexican revolutionary Emiliano Zapata and his rise to power during the early years of the 1900s. The film is directed by Elia Kazan and stars Marlon Brando and Anthony Quinn (who wins an Academy Award for his performance).
1952	In September, Steinbeck's novel, *East of Eden*, is published by Viking.
1954	His novel, *Sweet Thursday*, a sequel to *Cannery Row*, is published by Viking.
1955	Moves to Sag Harbor, Long Island. In November, *Pipe Dream*, the play adaptation of his novella *Sweet Thursday*, premiers. This Richard Rogers and Oscar Hammerstein III musical is set in Monterey, California, and tells the story about a marine biologist and a prostitute. The production is a financial disaster.
1957	Steinbeck's novel, *The Short Reign of Pippin IV*, is published by Viking. The film adaptation of *The Wayward Bus* is released.
1958	*Once There Was a War*, a collection of his 1943 wartime dispatches, is published by Viking.
1959	From February through October, Steinbeck travels through England and Wales to research for a modern version of Malory's *Morte D'Arthur* (1485).

1960	Steinbeck and his dog, a poodle he named *"Charley,"* make a tour of the United States.
1961	His twelfth novel, *The Winter of Our Discontent*, is published by Viking.
1962	Steinbeck publishes his journal, *Travels with Charley*, with Viking. In October, Steinbeck is awarded the Nobel Prize for Literature, amidst much controversy and criticism.
1963	Steinbeck travels with American playwright Edward Albee through Scandinavia, Eastern Europe, and the Soviet Union.
1964	In September, Steinbeck is presented with United States Medal of Freedom by President Lyndon Johnson.
1966	*America and Americans*, his writings on life in modern America is published by Viking.
1966-67	Undertakes a one-year fact-finding tour of South Vietnam for *Newsday*. His columns are called "Letters to Alicia" and are provocative during this time of social, cultural, and political upheaval in the United States.
1968	Steinbeck dies of arteriosclerosis on December 20 in New York City.

Works Consulted

National Steinbeck Center. *Biography*. 24 May 2019. www.steinbeck.org/about-john/biography/.

Shillinglaw, Susan. *Biography in Depth: John Steinbeck*. The Martha Heasley Cox Center for Steinbeck Studies. 24 June 2019. www.sjsu.edu/steinbeck/biography/biography_biography_in_depth/index.html.

Works by John Steinbeck

Long Fiction

Cup of Gold: A Life of Sir Henry Morgan, Buccaneer, with Occasional Reference to History, 1929

The Pastures of Heaven, 1932

To a God Unknown, 1933

Tortilla Flat, 1935

In Dubious Battle, 1936

Of Mice and Men, 1937

The Red Pony, 1937, enlarged edition, 1945

The Grapes of Wrath, 1939

The Moon Is Down, 1942

Cannery Row, 1945

The Pearl, 1945 (serial), 1947 (book)

The Wayward Bus, 1947

Burning Bright: A Play in Story Form, 1950

East of Eden, 1952

Sweet Thursday, 1954

The Short Reign of Pippin IV: A Fabrication, 1957

The Winter of Our Discontent, 1961

Short Fiction

Saint Katy the Virgin, 1936

The Long Valley, 1938

Nonfiction/Letters/Journals

The Harvest Gypsies: On the Road to The Grapes of Wrath, 1936

Their Blood is Strong, 1938

The Forgotten Village, 1941

Sea of Cortez: A Leisurely Journal of Travel and Research, 1941 (with Edward F. Ricketts)

Bombs Away: The Story of a Bomber Team, 1942

A Russian Journal, 1948 (with Robert Capa)

The Log from the Sea of Cortez 1951(originally with Edward F. Ricketts, who was removed from this co-authoring against Steinbeck's wishes)

Once There Was A War, 1958

Travels with Charley: In Search of America, 1962

"Speech Accepting the Nobel Peace Prize for Literature," 1962

Letters to Alicia, 1965

America and Americans, 1966

Journal of a Novel: The East of Eden Letters, 1969 (published posthumously)

Steinbeck: A Life in Letters, 1975

Steinbeck and Covici: The Story of a Friendship, 1979

Working Days: The Journals of The Grapes of Wrath, 1989

America and Americans, and Selected Nonfiction, 2002

Screenplays

The Forgotten Village, 1941

Lifeboat, 1944

The Pearl, 1945

A Medal for Benny, 1945

La perla, 1947

The Red Pony, 1949

Burning Bright: A Play in Three Acts, 1951

Viva Zapata!, 1952

Drama

Of Mice and Men: A Play in Three Acts, 1937

The Moon Is Down: A Play in Two Parts, 1942

Burning Bright, 1951

Translation

The Acts of King Arthur and His Noble Knights, 1976 (An adaptation of
the legend of King Arthur, started in 1956, and unfinished at his
death. Published posthumously)

Bibliography

Ariki, Kyoko. "From 'Flight' to *The Pearl*: A Thematic Study." *John Steinbeck's Global Dimensions*. Edited by Kyoko Ariki, Luchen Li, & Scott Pugh. The Scarecrow P, 2008. pp. 49–56.

Astro, Richard. *John Steinbeck and Edward F. Ricketts: The Shaping of a Novelist*. U of Minnesota P, 1973.

_____. "Steinbeck's Post-War Trilogy: A Return to Nature and the Natural Man." *Twentieth Century Literature*, vol. 16, no. 2, 1970, pp. 109–22. *JSTOR*, www.jstor.org/stable/440865.

Astro, Richard, and Tetsumaro Hayashi, editors. *Steinbeck: The Man and His Work, Proceedings of the 1970 Steinbeck Conference Sponsored by Oregon State and Ball State Universities*. Oregon State U P, 1972.

Augenbraum, Harold. "Translating Steinbeck." *The Steinbeck Review*, vol. 14, no. 1, 2017, pp. 52–64. *JSTOR*, www.jstor.org/stable/10.5325/steinbeckreview.14.1.0052.

Baker, Carlos. *Ernest Hemingway: A Life Story*. Charles Scribner's Sons, 1969.

Bates, Barclay W., and Redlands California Association of Teachers of English. "*The Pearl* as Tragedy." *California English Journal*, vol. 6, no. 1, 1970, pp. 41–45. files.eric.ed.gov/fulltext/ED039246.pdf.

Beegel, Susan F., Susan Shillinglaw, and Wesley N. Tiffney, editors. *Steinbeck and the Environment: Interdisciplinary Approaches*. U of Alabama P, 1997.

Benson, Jackson J. *John Steinbeck, Writer*. Penguin, 1984.

_____. *Looking for Steinbeck's Ghost*. U of Oklahoma P, 1988.

_____. *The Short Novels of John Steinbeck: Critical Essays with a Checklist to Steinbeck Criticism*. Duke U P, 1990.

_____. *The True Adventures of John Steinbeck, Writer: A Biography*. Penguin, 1990.

Bertens, Hans. *Literary Theory: The Basics*. 2nd ed. Routledge, 2008.

Blaeser, Kimberly M. *Gerald Vizenor: Writing in the Oral Tradition*. U of Oklahoma P, 1996.

Bloom, Harold, editor. *Modern Critical Views: John Steinbeck*, Chelsea House, 1987.

"Briefly Noted." Review of *The Pearl. The New Yorker*, vol. 27, Dec. 1947, p. 59.

Buell, Lawrence. "Ecocriticism: Some Emerging Trends." *At the Intersections of Ecocriticism. Qui Parle: Critical Humanities and Social Sciences,* vol. 19, no. 2, 2011, pp. 87–115. *Project MUSE.* muse.jhu.edu/article/430997.

_____. *The Environmental Imagination: Thoreau, Nature Writing, and the Formation of American Culture.* Belknap P of Harvard U P, 1996.

Burkhead, Cynthia. *Student Companion to John Steinbeck.* Greenwood P, 2002.

Caswell, Roger. "A Musical Journey Through John Steinbeck's *The Pearl:* Emotion, Engagement, and Comprehension." *Journal of Adolescent and Adult Literacy,*" vol. 49, no. 1, 2005, pp. 62–67. *JSTOR,* www.jstor.org/stable/40009270.

"Counterfeit Jewel." Review of *The Pearl. Time,* 22 Dec. 1947, p. 92. Time. 22 Dec. 1947. content.time.com/time/magazine/article/0,9171,794022,00.html.

Covici, Pascal, Jr. "Introduction." *The Portable Steinbeck.* Edited by Pascal Covici, Jr. Penguin, 1976, pp. xi-xxix.

Center for Steinbeck Studies, and Project MUSE. *The Steinbeck Review.* Scarecrow P, 2004. *JSTOR,* www.jstor.org/journal/steinbeckreview.

Davis, Robert Murray, editor. *Steinbeck: A Collection of Critical Essays.* Prentice Hall, 1972.

DeMott, Robert J. *John Steinbeck: A Checklist of Books By and About.* Opuscula, 1987.

_____. *Steinbeck's Reading: A Catalogue of Books Owned and Borrowed.* Garland, 1984.

_____. *Steinbeck's Typewriter: Essays on His Art.* Whitston, 1996.

Ditsky, John. *John Steinbeck: Life, Work and Criticism.* York P, 1985.

Donkin, R. A. *Beyond Price: Pearls and Pearl-fishing: Origins to the Age of Discoveries.* American Philosophical Society, 1998.

Farrelly, John. "Fiction Parade." Review of *The Pearl. New Republic,* vol. 117, 22 Dec. 1947, p. 28.

Fensch, Thomas, editor. *Conversations with John Steinbeck.* U of Mississippi P, 1988.

Fontenrose, Joseph Eddy. *John Steinbeck: An Introduction and Interpretation.* Holt, Rinehart and Winston, 1963.

French, Warren. *John Steinbeck,* 2nd ed. Twayne, 1961.

_____. *John Steinbeck's Fiction Revisited.* Twayne, 1994.

Garrard, Greg. *Ecocriticism.* London: Routledge, 2004.

Geismar, Maxwell. "Fable Retold." Review of *The Pearl. Saturday Review,* vol. 30, 22 Nov. 1947, pp. 14–15. The UNZ Review, www.unz.com/print/SaturdayRev-1947nov22-00014a02/.

George, Stephen K. *The Moral Philosophy of John Steinbeck.* Scarecrow P, 2005.

_____. "A Taoist Interpretation of John Steinbeck's *The Pearl." The Steinbeck Review,* vol. 1, no. 1, 2004, pp. 90–105. *JSTOR,* www.jstor.org/stable/41581951.

George, Stephen K., and Barbara Heavilin. *John Steinbeck and his Contemporaries.* Scarecrow, 2007.

Gladstein, Mimi. "Fish Stories: Santiago and Kino in Text and Film." *The Steinbeck Review,* vol. 6, no. 2, 2009, pp. 10–21. *JSTOR,* www.jstor.org/stable/41582112.

Glotfelty, Cheryll, and Harold Fromm, editors. *The Ecocriticism Reader: Landmarks in Literary Ecology.* U of Georgia P, 1996.

Hamby, James A. "Steinbeck's *The Pearl*: Tradition and Innovation." *Western Review: A Journal of the Humanities,* vol. 7, no. 2, 1970, p. 65.

Hayashi, Tetsumaro, editor. *A New Study Guide to Steinbeck's Major Works, with Critical Explications.* Scarecrow P, 1993.

_____. "*The Pearl* as the Novel of Disengagement." *Steinbeck Quarterly,* vol. 7, nos. 3–4, 1974, pp. 84–88.

_____. *Study Guide to Steinbeck: A Handbook to His Major Work.* Scarecrow P, 1974.

_____. *Steinbeck's Literary Dimension: A Guide to Comparative Studies.* Scarecrow P, 1973.

Heise, Ursula K. "The Hitchhiker's Guide to Ecocriticism." *PMLA,* vol. 121, no. 2, 2006, pp. 503–16. *JSTOR,* www.jstor.org/stable/25486328.

Hogue, Bev. "Naming the Bones: Bodies of Knowledge in Contemporary Fiction." *Modern Fiction Studies,* vol. 52, no. 1, 2006, pp. 121–42. *Project MUSE.* doi:10.1353/mfs.2006.0029.

Hopkins, Candice. "Making Things Our Own: The Indigenous Aesthetic in Digital Storytelling." *Leonardo,* vol. 39, no. 4, 2006, pp. 341–44. *JSTOR,* www.jstor.org/stable/20206265.

Hughes, R. *S. John Steinbeck: A Study of the Short Fiction.* Twayne, 1989.

Kalb, Bernard. "Trade Winds." *Saturday Review,* vol. 36, 27 Feb. 1954, p. 8.

Karsten, Ernest E., Jr. "Thematic Structure in *The Pearl.*" *The English Journal,* vol. 54, no. 1, 1965, pp. 1–7. *JSTOR,* www.jstor.org/stable/810934.

Karson, Jill. ed. *Readings on* The Pearl. Greenhaven P, 1999.

Kiernan, Thomas. *The Intricate Music: A Biography of John Steinbeck.* Little, Brown, 1979.

Kingery, Robert E. Review of *The Pearl. Library Journal,* vol. 72, 1 Nov. 1947, p. 1540.

Kino, Eusebio Francisco. *Kino's Historical Memoir of Pimería Alta: A Contemporary Account of the Beginnings of California, Sonora, and Arizona.* pp. 1683–1711. Translated by Herbert Eugene Bolton, U of California P, 1948.

Koth, Karl B. "Crisis Politician and Political Counterweight: Teodoro A. Dehesa in Mexican Federal Politics, 1900–1910." *Mexican Studies/ Estudios Mexicanos,* vol. 11, no. 2, 1995, pp. 243–271. *JSTOR,* www.jstor.org/stable/1051922.

Krause, Sidney J. *"The Pearl* and 'Hadleyburg': From Desire to Renunciation." *Steinbeck Quarterly,* 7, no. 1, pp. 3–17. Ball State University. dmr.bsu.edu/digital/collection/steinbeck/id/3460/rec/24.

Langione, Matt. "John Steinbeck and the Child Reader." *The Steinbeck Review,* vol. 2, no. 2, 2005, pp. 9–27. *JSTOR,* www.jstor.org/stable/41581980.

Levant, Howard. *The Novels of John Steinbeck.* U of Missouri P, 1974.

Lieber, Todd M. "Talismanic Patterns in the Novels of John Steinbeck." *American Literature,* vol. 44, no. 2, 1972, pp. 262–275. *JSTOR,* www.jstor.org/stable/2924509.

Lisca, Peter. *John Steinbeck: Nature and Man.* Thomas Crowell, 1978.

_____. *The Wide World of John Steinbeck.* Rutgers U P, 1958.

Martínez, Rogelio. *México en la obra de John Steinbeck [Mexico in the Work of John Steinbeck].* Palibrio, 2017.

McCarthy, Paul. *John Steinbeck.* Frederick Ungar, 1980.

McElrath, Joseph R., Jr., Jesse S. Crisler, and Susan Shillinglaw, editors. *John Steinbeck: The Contemporary Reviews.* Cambridge U P, 1996.

McParland, Robert. *Citizen Steinbeck: Giving Voice to the People.* Rowman & Littlefield, 2016.

Metzger, Charles R. "Steinbeck's *The Pearl* as a Nonteleological Parable of Hope." *Research Studies,* vol. 46, 1978, pp. 98–105.

Meyer, Michael. "Diamond in the Rough: Steinbeck's Multifaceted Pearl." *The Steinbeck Review,* vol. 2, no. 2, 2005, pp. 42–56. *JSTOR,* www.jstor.org/stable/41581982.

_____. "Wavering Shadows: A New Jungian Perspective in Steinbeck's *The Pearl.*" *The Steinbeck Review,* vol. 1, no. 1, 2004, pp. 132–45. *JSTOR,* www.jstor.org/stable/41581954.

Moore, Harry Thornton. *The Novels of John Steinbeck: A First Critical Study.* Normandie House, 1939.

Morris, Harry. "*The Pearl*: Realism and Allegory." *The English Journal,* vol. 52, no. 7, 1963, pp. 487–505. *JSTOR,* www.jstor.org/stable/810771.

"New Novels." Review of *The Pearl. New Statesmen and Nation,* vol. 36, 6 Nov. 1948, 400–1.

Noble, Don, editor. *Critical Insights: John Steinbeck.* U of Alabama P, 2011.

_____. *The Steinbeck Questions: New Essays in Criticism.* Whitston, 1993.

Owens, Louis. *John Steinbeck's Re-Vision of America.* U of Georgia P, 1985.

Parini, Jay. *John Steinbeck: A Biography.* Henry Holt, 1995.

Phillips, Dana. "Ecocriticism's Hard Problems (Its Ironies, Too)." *American Literary History,* vol. 25, no.2, 2013, pp. 455–467. Oxford, *American Literary History.* doi.org/10.1093/alh/ajt017.

Prescott, Orville. Review of *The Pearl,* by John Steinbeck. *The New York Times,* 24 Nov. 1947, p. 21.

Railsback, Brian E. *Parallel Expeditions: Charles Darwin and the Art of John Steinbeck.* U of Idaho P, 1995.

Review of *The Pearl. Booklist,* 15 Dec. 1947, p. 152.

Rice, Rodney. "Circles in the Forest: John Steinbeck and the Deep Ecology of *To a God Unknown. The Steinbeck Review*, vol. 8, no. 2, 2011, pp. 31–52. Wiley. onlinelibrary.wiley.com/doi/abs/10.1111/j.1754-6087.2011.01146.x.

Ricketts, Edward, and Jack Calvin. *Between Pacific Tides*, 3rd ed., Stanford U P, 1962.

Sams, Edward Boyer. "The Haunted Tree: Two Versions of John Steinbeck's *The Pearl." The Steinbeck Review*, vol. 11, no. 2, 2014, pp. 189–96. *JSTOR*, www.jstor.org/stable/10.5325/steinbeckreview.11.2.0189.

Schultz, Jeffrey, and Luchen Li. *A Critical Companion to John Steinbeck: A Literary Reference to His Life and Work.* Facts on File, 2005.

Searway, Robert. "Conflicting Views of Landscape in John Steinbeck's Literary West." *The Steinbeck Review*, vol. 12, no. 2, 2015, pp. 175–89. *JSTOR*, www.jstor.org/stable/10.5325/steinbeckreview.12.2.0175.

Shillinglaw, Susan. *Carol and John Steinbeck: Portrait of a Marriage.* U of Nevada P, 2013.

Shillinglaw, Susan, and Kevin Hearle, eds. *Beyond Boundaries: Rereading John Steinbeck.* U of Alabama P, 2002.

Simmonds, Roy. *John Steinbeck: The War Years, 1939–1945.* Bucknell U P, 1996.

Smith, Stevie. "Short Stories." Review of *The Pearl. Spectator*, vol. 181, 20 Oct. 1948, p. 570.

Steinbeck, Elaine, and Robert Wallsten. *Steinbeck: A Life in Letters.* Penguin, 1989.

Steinbeck, John. "Argument of Phalanx," an unpublished essay in a letter to Richard Albee circa 1936, Letter obtained from the Bancroft Library at The U of California Berkeley, with the assistance of The Martha Heasley Cox Center for Steinbeck Studies, San José State U, San José, CA 95192.

Steinbeck, John, and Edward F. Ricketts. *Sea of Cortez: A Leisurely Journal of Travel and Research, with a Specific Appendix Comprising Materials for a Source Book on the Marine Animals of the Panamic Faunal Province.* Viking, 1941.

Steinbeck, John IV, and Nancy Steinbeck. *The Other Side of Eden: Life with John Steinbeck.* Prometheus, 2001.

Steinbeck Quarterly Journal. Ball State University Digital Media Repository, dmr.bsu.edu/digital/collection/steinbeck.

St. Pierre, Brian. *John Steinbeck: The California Years.* Chronicle, 1983.

Sugrue, Thomas. "Steinbeck's Mexican Folk-Tale." Review of *The Pearl. The New York Herald Tribune Weekly Book Review,* 24 Dec. 1947, p. 4.

Tedlock, E. W., Jr., and C. V. Wicker, eds. *Steinbeck and His Critics: A Record of Twenty-five Years.* U of New Mexico P, 1957.

Timmerman, John H. *The Dramatic Landscape of Steinbeck's Short Stories.* U of Oklahoma P, 1990.

_____. *John Steinbeck's Fiction: The Aesthetics of the Road Taken.* U of Oklahoma P, 1986.

_____. "The Shadow and the Pearl: Jungian Patterns in *The Pearl.*" Benson, *Short Novels,* pp. 143–160.

Valjean, Nelson. *John Steinbeck: The Errant Knight.* Chronicle, 1975.

Wagner-Martin, Linda. *John Steinbeck: A Literary Life.* Palgrave Macmillan, 2017.

Weeks, Edward. Review of *The Pearl,* by John Steinbeck. *Atlantic Monthly,* Dec. 1947, p. 138.

Zirakzadeh, Cyrus Ernesto, and Simon Stow, editors. *A Political Companion to John Steinbeck.* U P of Kentucky, 2013.

About the Editors

Laura Nicosia, PhD, earned her doctorate at New York University and is Professor of English at Montclair State University, New Jersey, where she teaches all things American literature, Young Adult/Children's Literatures, and literary theory. She is a New Jersey Council for the Humanities Public Scholar, serves as the New Jersey State Ambassador to the Assembly on Literature of Adolescents, and is a Past-President of the New Jersey Council of Teachers of English. Nicosia is the author of *Educators Online: Preparing Today's Educators for Tomorrow's Digital Literacies* (Peter Lang, 2013), co-editor of *Through a Distorted Lens: Media as Curricula and Pedagogy in the 21ˢᵗ Century* (Sense, 2017), and co-editor of the soon-to-be-released edited collection, *Dear Secretary DeVos: What We Want You to Know About Education* (Brill, 2019).

Nicosia is currently working on three book-length projects, one of which she is co-editing with her husband, James F. Nicosia: *Examining Images of Urban Life: A Resource for Teachers of Young Adult Literature* (under contract with Meyers Education Press, summer 2020). She is also undertaking archival research on Gloria Naylor, and completing a monograph exploring images of the "monstrous other" in young adult literature.

James F. Nicosia, PhD, fell in love with John Steinbeck's *East of Eden* in his senior year of high school, shortly after being defeated by *The Great Gatsby* (which he later learned to love). He started reading Steinbeck extensively (along with other works) and changed his major from accounting to English. He subsequently earned his doctorate at New York University, where he worked with Harold Bloom in his studies of Poet Laureate Mark Strand. Bloom would later write the introduction to Nicosia's book, *Reading Mark Strand* (Palgrave Macmillan). He teaches Grammars of English, Young Adult Literature, and all periods of American literature at Montclair State University in New Jersey. He is a reviewer for Voice of Youth Advocates; publishes the Boy Book of the Month website for reluctant readers (www.BoyBookoftheMonth.com); and regularly speaks to teachers and young readers about invigorating their reading lives.

Contributors

Elisabeth Bayley, PhD is an Advanced Lecturer in the English Department at Loyola University Chicago. Her focus is on American Literature. She has published articles on Willa Cather and John Steinbeck.

Christopher Bowman is a PhD candidate in the English literature program at the University of Minnesota. He specializes in twentieth- and twenty-first-century American literature and film, with research interests in ecocriticism, environmental humanities, John Steinbeck, and climate-change fiction. He is currently working on his dissertation, entitled: *Climate Change of Mind: Revisiting Dust Bowl Narratives in a Time of Anthropogenic Climate Change.*

Kyler Campbell is an Instructor of English at Charleston Southern University where he teaches Composition and Literature. He earned his BA from North Greenville University and his MFA in Fiction from Converse College where he completed a thesis on ecocriticism in contemporary Southern literature. His creative work has appeared in *Longshot Island, Sheepshead Review, Driftwood, Hawaii Pacific Review,* and elsewhere.

Emily P. Hamburger earned her undergraduate B.A. from Yale University with a major in American Studies and a J.D. from Columbia Law School. She previously worked as an attorney and editor in New York, New York and in Princeton, New Jersey. She is a graduate student in the English Department of Montclair State University and a recipient of the 2019 Lawrence H. Conrad Memorial Scholarship as well as the 2018 Mary Bondon Award for outstanding achievement in literary study.

John J. Han (PhD, University of Nebraska-Lincoln) is Professor of English and Creative Writing and Chair of the Humanities Division at Missouri Baptist University in St. Louis. Han is the author, editor, or translator of twenty-one books, including *The Final Crossing: Death and Dying in Literature* and *Worlds Gone Awry: Essays on Dystopian Fiction.* His articles on Steinbeck appeared in *The Steinbeck Review, Steinbeck*

Studies, and *The Moral Philosophy of John Steinbeck*. Currently, he serves as an editor of *Steinbeck Studies*.

Tammie Jenkins (PhD, Independent Scholar, Alumni of Louisiana State University) holds a Doctorate of Philosophy in Curriculum and Instruction from Louisiana State University in Baton Rouge. Her recent publications include "(Re)Imagining Race, Gender, and Class as Choice in Octavia Butler's *Wild Seed*" (Scripta Humana), "From Harlem to Haiti: A Niggerati Renaissance in Caribbean Negritude" (Rowan & Littlefield Publishers), and "Visualizing Cultural Spaces: (Re) Imagining Southern Gothicism in the Film *Midnight in the Garden of Good and Evil* (1997)" (Königshausen & Neumann).

Dr. Arun Khevariya is an educator and Steinbeck scholar from India. Holding a doctorate in American Fiction, his articles and research papers have been published in journals and magazines of national and international repute. A participant of "Teaching Excellence and Achievement Program 2012" he has shared his educational experiences at Gallaudet University, Washington DC and Montana State University. His efforts in education have earned him recognition and appreciation by The Ministry of HRD, The Government of India and the Department of States. His current affiliation is at Kendriya Vidyalaya Sangathan (India).

Melinda Knight is Professor of English and the founding director of the Center for Writing Excellence at Montclair State University, New Jersey. Her research interests include the intersections of class, gender, identity, and race in American literature, manifestations of aestheticism and decadence, the impact of urbanization on cultural products, and representations of the American West. She earned a PhD in American Civilization at New York University and a BA in Spanish and American Literature at Cornell University.

Kelly MacPhail is an Assistant Professor at the University of Minnesota Duluth, where he teaches in the Departments of Philosophy and of English. His interdisciplinary research focuses on Transatlantic literary modernism, environmental criticism, ethics, and belief studies; and he has published on subjects as diverse as modernist poetry, Puritan sermons, film noir, animal domestication, nautical fiction, and the Western.

James Plath is the R. Forrest Colwell Endowed Chair and Professor of English at Illinois Wesleyan University, where he has taught American literature, film, creative writing, and journalism since 1988. He is the author/editor of *The 100 Greatest Literary Characters, Critical Insights: Raymond Carver, Critical Insights Film: Casablanca, John Updike's Pennsylvania Interviews, Historic Photos of Ernest Hemingway, Remembering Ernest Hemingway,* and *Conversations with John Updike.*

Jericho Williams is a Professor of English at Spartanburg Methodist College who researches American and African American literature. He has published essays in *Ecogothic in Nineteenth-Century American Literature* (Routledge, 2017), *Critical Insights: Inequality* (Salem, 2018), and *Critical Insights: Richard Wright* (Salem, 2019), and he is the author of a forthcoming essay about Nella Larsen's *Passing* (*South Atlantic Review,* 2019).

Lowell Wyse teaches courses in literature, composition, and environmental humanities for Broward College (Florida) at the Center for Global Education in Lima, Peru. He holds a PhD in English from Loyola University Chicago's Modern Literature and Culture program, with a specialization in twentieth-century U.S. literature, geography, and the environment. His article "The World-Brain and the Watershed: The Spatiality of Steinbeck's Environmental Vision" is forthcoming in *Steinbeck Review* (Fall 2019).

Michael Zeitler is Professor of English at Texas Southern University. He is the author of *Representations of Culture: Thomas Hardy's Wessex and Victorian Anthropology,* co-editor of *Race and Identity in Barack Obama's Dreams of My Father: A Collection of Critical Essays,* and a regular contributor to journals on British, American, and African American literature and culture. A transplanted Californian who in his youth read Steinbeck and explored the mountains and tide pools of Central California and the Pacific Coast, his current research focuses on John Steinbeck, American history and the California Dream.

Index

Gladstein, Mimi 21, 83
globalization xv
"Golden Handcuff, The" xxxi
good and evil xvi, xxv, 35, 42,
      108, 125, 135, 138, 143
"Good Lion, The" 49
Good Samaritan, the 121
Gospel of Matthew 122
Grapes of Wrath, The vii, xviii,
      xxi, xxv, xxvii, xxxiii, xxxiv,
      7, 12, 15, 17, 18, 47, 78, 90,
      95, 97, 103, 106, 136, 146,
      147, 161, 164, 175, 176, 177
Gray, James 160
Great Gatsby, The 191
Great Pearl of the World 92
greed viii, xii, xv, xvi, xvii, xxiv,
      xxvii, xxviii, 9, 34, 36, 40,
      62, 72, 73, 74, 93, 102, 105,
      108, 119, 126, 131, 135,
      136, 137, 138, 139, 140,
      156, 157, 158, 160, 182,
      186, 193, 197, 200
Grito de Dolores (Cry of Dolores)
      4

Hagar 200, 201
Hamilton, William 150
harmonization 32
harmony 30, 32, 36, 144, 194,
      199, 200
Hawthorne, Nathaniel 123
Hayashi, Tetsumaro 20, 26, 27,
      105, 135, 161
health care xv, 107, 174, 175
Helmi, Moh Imawan 141
Hemingway, Ernest 21, 45, 57,
      150
Henning, Carol xxxii

Henry, Frederic 48
Hersey, John 46
Hidalgo 3, 4, 6
Historical Memoir of Pimería Alta
      8, 13
Holiday magazine 49
holism 68
Hopkins Marine Station 7
hostility 46, 139, 168
"How a Neglected Novella
      Became a Classic" x
Hughes, Langston 191
humanity xiii, xiv, 39, 40, 41, 42,
      43, 104, 142, 143, 152, 177
humiliation 158
hunger 88, 102, 118, 139, 156,
      163, 175
hybrid xvi, 198
"Hymn of the Soul" 18

Ibsen, Henrik xxvii
ideology 104, 187
Igbo landing 195
Igbo slave revolt 195, 197
ignorance 140, 169, 204
illusion 37, 38, 154
imagery xxviii, 20, 21, 25, 49, 67,
      92, 127
imagination 47
immigration xxviii
imperialism 103, 104, 166, 172
indeterminism 151, 153
Indians (see also Indigenous
      peoples) 9, 11, 13, 21, 24,
      74, 76, 166, 176, 183, 192
Indigenous peoples (see also
      Indians) 3, 4, 6, 7, 8, 9, 10,
      11, 12, 16, 25, 37

individualism xii, xxxv, 6, 142,
181
individuality 110
In Dubious Battle xxxiii, xxxiv,
81, 136, 161
industrialization 5
inequality ix, xiv, xv, 3, 69, 107,
116, 118
infancy 153
injustice 70, 157
innocence 135, 139, 144, 148,
194, 199
instability 156, 174
irony xxviii, 25, 53, 55, 56, 71,
118, 126, 182
isolation 200

James, William 151
Jobes, Katharine T. 56
John Reed Club xxxiii
Johnson, Lyndon B. xxxvi
John Steinbeck Society 20
Jordan, Robert 48
Juana xii, xvi, xxv, 11, 12, 31, 32,
38, 41, 50, 51, 52, 53, 56,
66, 67, 68, 69, 73, 77, 80,
81, 82, 84, 85, 86, 96, 101,
104, 108, 110, 111, 112, 115,
117, 122, 123, 126, 127,
131, 132, 133, 138, 140,
141, 143, 145, 146, 158,
159, 160, 165, 166, 167,
168, 169, 170, 171, 172,
176, 183, 184, 185, 186,
187, 188, 189
Juárez, Benito 4, 5
Jung, Carl 22, 89, 124
justice xiii, 77, 92, 96, 145, 151

Kazan, Elia xxxvi
Kelley, James C. 85, 90
Khaleghi, Mahboobeh 196
King James Bible 123, 134
Kino viii, xi, xii, xiii, xiv, xv, xvi,
xvii, xix, xxiii, xxv, xxvi,
xxvii, 7, 8, 10, 11, 12, 13,
19, 21, 22, 23, 24, 27, 30,
31, 33, 34, 35, 36, 37, 38,
39, 40, 41, 42, 48, 50, 51,
52, 53, 55, 56, 61, 66, 67,
68, 69, 70, 72, 73, 77, 80,
81, 82, 83, 84, 85, 86, 87,
88, 89, 96, 98, 99, 100, 101,
102, 103, 104, 105, 107,
108, 110, 111, 112, 113, 114,
115, 116, 117, 118, 119, 122,
123, 124, 125, 126, 127,
128, 129, 130, 131, 132,
133, 135, 136, 138, 139,
140, 141, 142, 143, 144,
145, 146, 147, 150, 157,
158, 159, 160, 161, 165,
166, 167, 168, 169, 170,
171, 172, 173, 175, 176,
183, 184, 185, 186, 187,
188, 189, 190, 191, 192,
193, 194, 196, 197, 198,
199, 200, 201, 202
Kino, Eusebio Francisco 8
Klages, Mary 103
Krause, Stanley J. 94

land reform 6
landscape xii, 33, 34, 35, 38, 41,
42, 66, 67, 84, 93, 101
La Paz vii, xxi, xxxiv, 9, 22, 24,
30, 35, 36, 38, 40, 65, 70,
71, 73, 75, 78, 80, 81, 82,

oppression xxvii, 12, 116, 144, 157, 187, 188, 189
Origin of Species, The 150
otherness xix, 191, 192, 198, 199, 200, 201, 202
Otis, Elizabeth 10, 136
Owens, Louis 23, 74, 101
ownership xix, 4, 178, 184, 185, 186, 190, 202
oysters 9, 48, 52, 61, 65, 69, 70, 71, 73, 87, 88, 98, 102, 127, 128, 137, 172

Pacific Ocean vii, xxi, 64
Pacific Tides xiii, xxxiv, 7, 13, 95, 96, 103, 106
paisano 173
parable vii, viii, xi, xiii, xiv, xv, xvi, xvii, xxii, xxvi, xxvii, 10, 19, 22, 23, 24, 25, 45, 47, 49, 56, 57, 62, 72, 77, 87, 89, 94, 105, 107, 108, 109, 110, 115, 118, 119, 121, 122, 123, 124, 125, 126, 128, 129, 130, 135, 136, 137, 138, 139, 147
paranoia 40
Parini, Jay 16, 45, 125
Parker, Theodore 151
passion 179, 180, 183, 188
pastoral xi, 33, 34, 35, 36, 38, 39, 42
Pastures of Heaven, The xxxiii
Pearl Buyers 36, 38
Pearl of La Paz, The 124
Pearl of the World, The vii, ix, xxi, xxii, xxxiv, xxxv, 8, 16, 45, 124, 157, 186
pearl parable 72

Pearl Week xxix
Perkins, Max 46
phalanx theory 80, 84, 89, 174, 181
philosophy x, xxxiii, 73, 83, 89, 93, 95, 130, 153, 156, 181
physics 89, 153
Pilate dead 195
Pinctada mazatlanica 62
Pineda, Adela 12
Plan de Ayala 6
poison xiv, xv, 52, 84, 88, 102, 107, 111, 115, 116, 117, 118, 158, 172, 176
Porfiriato 5, 6, 7
possession vii, xv, 52, 144, 158, 159, 160, 167, 176, 184, 187, 189, 200
postcolonial criticism 103
poverty vii, ix, xiv, xv, xvii, xxi, 3, 50, 51, 107, 118, 143, 144, 147, 165, 168, 171, 173, 190
power vii, viii, xxiv, xxvi, xxxiii, 5, 7, 10, 11, 23, 25, 36, 65, 70, 87, 96, 113, 114, 133, 145, 152, 155, 159, 160, 161, 167, 168, 169, 172, 178, 180, 183, 185, 189
powerlessness 118, 143
predator xiv, 40, 41, 98, 117
Prescott, Orville 17
Principles of Geology, The 150
Prodigal Son 121
protection 40, 61, 102, 138, 142
psychology 89, 142
Pteriidae 61
purgatory 61

Sower, the 121
Spanish Civil War 46, 47
Spectator 17, 29
spirituality xxviii, 132, 170
Steinbeck and the Environment 28,
    64, 74, 75, 76, 90, 91, 133,
    190
Steinbeck, Carol 78
Steinbeck Center Foundation, The
    xxviii
Steinbeck, John Ernst, Jr. xxxi
Steinbeck, Olive Hamilton xxxi
Steinbeck Quarterly xxx, 20, 26,
    27, 28, 29, 105
Steinbeck Review, The xxx, 13, 14,
    20, 26, 27, 29, 76, 119, 134,
    190
strength xxiv, 50, 52, 54, 61, 74,
    132, 170, 174, 181, 185
suffering vii, xvi, xxi, 126, 127,
    128, 133, 155, 163, 174,
    175, 176, 185
Sugrue, Thomas 18
suicide 195, 197
Sun Also Rises, The 47, 48
Superman 150
superorganism 7, 81
survival xi, 7, 34, 38, 39, 40, 68,
    69, 72, 96, 97, 99, 100, 101,
    102, 104, 127, 153, 156,
    168, 192, 193
sustainability xii, 72, 103
Sweet Thursday xxxiv, 94
symbolism viii, xi, xxiv, 22, 57,
    121, 126, 129
sympathy xvii, xxiv, xxxii, 147,
    160
syncretism 132

System of Synthetic Philosophy
    150

terror xvi, 35, 113, 141
theodicy xvi, 121, 131, 132
theopoetics xv, 121
theory of evolution 153
Thus Spoke Zarathustra 150
Tiffney, Wesley N., Jr. 83, 90, 91
Time 17, 27, 206
timelessness viii, xviii
Timmerman, John H. 124
Tinker, the 179, 180, 181, 182,
    187, 188
To A God Unknown 164
To Have and Have Not 48
Tomás, Juan 12, 38, 82, 85, 88
Tortilla Flat xviii, xxv, xxxiii,
    xxxiv, 15, 97, 106, 163, 164,
    165, 171, 173, 174, 175,
    176, 177
tradition ix, xiii, xiv, 8, 48, 63,
    96, 108, 110, 111, 194, 196,
    201, 202
tragedy xix, xxvii, 25, 35, 118,
    124
transcendentalism 151, 162
trauma xiv, 108, 115, 123
Travels with Charley xviii, 76
Treaty of Córdoba 4
Treaty of Guadalupe Hidalgo 4
Twain, Mark 21

urbanization 230

victim vii, xvii, 35, 37, 41, 69,
    136, 139, 163, 182
victimhood 145
Vietnam War xxxvi

Villa, Pancho 11
violence xix, 62, 70, 74, 85, 87,
88, 89, 126, 131, 135, 140,
159, 165, 166, 168, 171,
173, 178, 182, 187, 188,
194, 199
Viva Zapata! 3

Wagner, Jack xxiii
Wagner, Max 146
Warfield, Adrienne 22
Wayward Bus, The 45
"Weary Blues" 191
Weeks, Edward 18
Westbrook, Perry D. 150
Western Flyer, The ix, 8
white oppression 144
white racism 145
Whitman, Walt xxxiii

Wide World of Steinbeck, The 18,
28
wisdom 99, 112, 143, 146, 169,
172, 192, 196, 200
Woman's Home Companion vii,
xxi, xxii, xxiii, xxxv, 8, 16,
18, 45, 78, 157
Wordsworth, William 147
Working Days 90
World War I 173
World War II x, 15, 79
Wylder, Delbert E. 49

xenophobia xxvii

Zapata 3, 6, 11, 14, 24
Zapata, Emiliano 3, 11, 14, 24
Zola, Emile 154
zoology 7